The Sultans

Also by Jem Duducu

The Busy Person's Guide to British History
The British Empire in 100 Facts
Deus Vult: A Concise History of the Crusades
The Napoleonic Wars in 100 Facts
The Romans in 100 Facts
Forgotten History: Unbelievable Moments from the Past
The American Presidents in 100 Facts

You can find Jem on Twitter and Facebook as @HistoryGems.

The Sultans

The Rise and Fall of the Ottoman Rulers and Their World

JEM DUDUCU

AMBERLEY

This edition published 2020

Amberley Publishing
The Hill, Stroud
Gloucestershire, GL5 4EP

www.amberley-books.com

British Library Cataloguing in Publication Data.
A catalogue record for this book is available from the British Library.

ISBN 978 1 4456 9914 1 (paperback)
ISBN 978 1 4456 6861 1 (ebook)

Map design by Thomas Bohm, User design.
Typesetting and Origination by Amberley Publishing.
Printed in the UK.

Contents

To my father, the most magnificent Ottoman since Suleiman

To my mother, thank you

And to my sister, now you know

Special thanks to Armağan Doğan, MSc. Architecture,
PhD Candidate: History and Theory of Art & Architecture

.

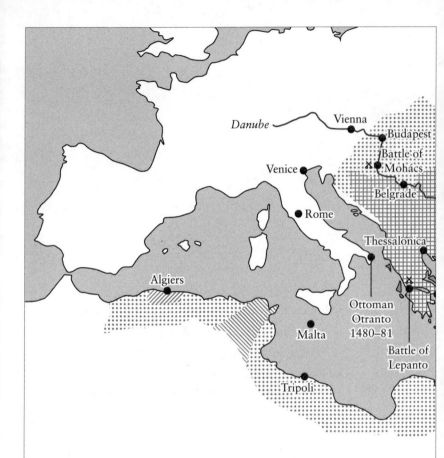

The Ottoman Empire in:

1326 (death of Osman)
1481 (death of Mehmed the Conqueror)
1520 (death of Selim I)
1566 (death of Süleyman I)
1683 (second seige of Vienna)

0   600   N

kilometres   ↑

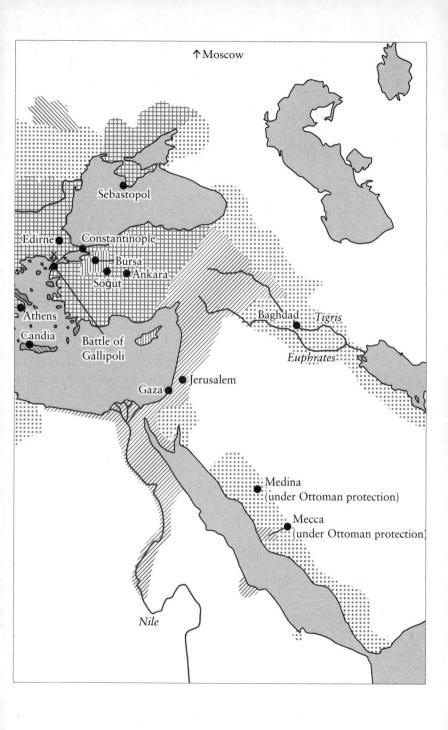

Introduction

The Ottoman Empire existed from roughly 1300 to 1922 (when the empire formally 'ended' will be discussed later). That's more than 600 years. This gives it more staying power than the British, French or Mughal Empires. It stretched from the towns of central Europe to the deserts of Asia. At its peak, the Black Sea and the Red Sea were Ottoman lakes, and virtually the entire North African coast owed allegiance to the sultan. So you would think that, like these other empires, there would be echoes of this civilisation across more than a dozen countries. There are, but these echoes can be hard to find.

Many countries have gone out of their way to pretend that the Ottoman Empire never existed. Greece is a good example of this: although all too aware of their 400 years of occupation (the white pleated skirts, the *fustanella*, worn by Greek soldiers, have 400 creases in them, one crease for each year they were ruled by the sultans), the Greeks are far more concerned with classical Greek civilisation and the Byzantine Empire – periods that had far less bearing on the country as it is today – than they are with the fact that Thessalonica (the second-largest city in Greece) was an Ottoman city from 1430 to 1912. Greek Independence Day, celebrated every year on 25 March, commemorates the humiliation of occupation; the assumption is that everything was worse under Ottoman rule. History, however, rarely unfolds in such absolutes, and this perspective ignores the fact that during this 400-year period the Greek heartlands were at the very epicentre of a vibrant multicultural, multi-religious society.

Looking at the news any time since the First World War, and seeing the regularity of violence in countries such as Syria, Iraq, Israel, Yemen and Lebanon, anyone could be forgiven for thinking that the region had always been like this. But the truth is that these relatively new countries have been built on the corpse of the old Ottoman Empire. For centuries these lands, while hardly nirvana, faced nothing like the levels of conflict they have experienced over the last century – yet the Ottomans receive no credit for having kept the peace in ways that have since stumped America, the UN and Europe.

There is only one country that revels in its Ottoman past and that's the Republic of Turkey, another relatively new nation. It is thanks to centuries of European ignorance and to nation-building in Turkey that the Ottoman sultans have become 'Turkish sultans'. Quite often in European Renaissance literature the sultan was referred to as the 'Great Turk', a title that would have meant nothing to the Ottoman court. So let's clear this up at the very beginning: the Ottoman Empire, for most of its existence, predated nationalism (and much later we'll see how that concept played havoc with the Ottoman system, as it did with most empires of the nineteenth century). The attacking forces at Constantinople in 1453 weren't all 'Turks'; in fact not all the besieging forces were even Muslim. Calling anything Ottoman 'Turkish' is like saying that the Soviet Union was uniquely 'Russian'.

I hope this helps to explain why the phrase 'Turk' or 'Turkish' is never used in this book to describe anything that is Ottoman. Indeed, the idea of a Turk in Turkey signifying an ethnicity rather than a culture does not stand up to scrutiny. The peoples of Anatolia were, genetically speaking, a mixed bag in the fourteenth century, and while everyone in Turkey is proud of Osman's successes with just 300 horsemen, that's not enough of a gene pool to start a new ethnicity. No amount of flag waving can change the fact that the DNA of a passionate Turkish national may indicate a lineage from Arabia or the Balkans (as I found out when a DNA test uncovered my own genetic history). Some of the most famous sultans had to dye their beards dark brown; if their mother was Ukrainian and their grandmother was Russian, and so on and so forth, there isn't much 'Turk' left in the 'Great Turk' DNA.

While the culture of the Ottoman Empire was unique and distinct, its ethnicity was always an illusion. When the system broke down, it should have come as little surprise that allegiance to the old ways evaporated quickly. Since Turkey is the only country harking back to the empire it has been able to recast the past in its own image, and while this may help Turkish nationalism it is downright unhelpful in looking at a polyglot Islamic empire.

There are a scant few books in English about the entire Ottoman dynasty. There tends to be a lot on the fall of Constantinople; Suleiman the Magnificent generates a bit of interest, and there's plenty on the endgame of the empire, particularly linked to the First World War. What this book sets out to do is to deal with these milestone events, but also to fill the gaps and take the reader on a journey through a world that began in the Middle Ages and finished in the era of industry, flight and telecommunications. This book's starting chapter overlaps with the first book I wrote for Amberley Publishing, *Deus Vult: A Concise History of the Crusades*, because understanding the political situation in the Middle East as the 'Eastern Crusades' were winding up is necessary to explain how just one man, with only some 300 mercenary horsemen, founded such an enduring empire.

Looking at most countries through the lens of their rulers in the Middle Ages makes sense for the reason laid down by France's Louis XIV (to quote a slightly later monarch): 'I am the state.' Both Louis and his Ottoman contemporary, Mustafa II, were autocratic rulers. To understand them is to understand the national policies of their day. The Ottomans remained absolute rulers for most of the story of the Ottoman Empire, and a look at each sultan therefore tells us something about the time of his rule.

The Ottomans, as an Islamic power, used the Islamic calendar (which is about 600 years 'behind' the Christian one). An Islamic year is based on the lunar cycle, which means it's about 354 days long, so the dates drift across the Gregorian (modern European) calendar. To stop this turning into a mathematical nightmare, all dates will be Christianised. I have also opted for anglicised spellings wherever possible in order to keep things familiar in what can be, at times, a dizzyingly exotic subject.

While researching this book I was genuinely taken aback by the animosity for the empire held by some people with no direct link to the lands ruled by the Ottomans. One person, with a degree in History, said, 'I hate them. They destroyed the Greek civilisation.' When I tried to say that it wasn't as simple as that, he would have no further conversation on the topic; his mind was made up. When talking about the Ottoman forces in the First World War, someone else said (I am paraphrasing to keep things polite), 'Maybe they would have done better if they hadn't been so busy hanging Armenians.' Later on in the book I do not shy away from the atrocities carried out by Ottoman forces, but to focus on those to the exclusion of everything else that was happening at the end of this era is myopic, to put it, once again, politely. What these two examples reflect is the lingering fear and revulsion some people in the West still have with regard to the Ottoman Empire.

As my name suggests, I have Ottoman (Turkish) ancestry. My father is a proud Turk; however, I was not brought up in Turkey nor can I speak the language. I am aware that a number of topics I will be looking at are controversial for a number of nations and ethnicities, but I have no agenda. I am trying to present the facts as they are, not as some might wish them to be. It is never my intention to offend, only to inform.

While all cultures love a good story, it's my experience that the Turks are particularly fond of a well-told tale, and I have included a number of legends surrounding the sultans. I make it quite clear when we are in the realms of the fantastic rather than the historic, but I think these traditional tales add a sense of the rich culture in which they occur. In addition, there are my own family stories that I will weave into later parts of the book in an attempt to make some events more immediate.

Empires, by their definition, contain many nations and languages, so that is not a unique feature of the Ottoman Empire. What is truly distinctive and remarkable is that the name of the empire comes from just one family. The very first ruler was Osman, and the last, more than 600 years later, was Abdülmecid II; and yet these two men could trace a direct line from one to the other. Over all those centuries, the dynasty never died out, was never deposed or replaced. (Compare that to the English throne – even the Tudors barely made it past a hundred years.) But that is not to say that it was a happy family, because, as we shall see, the story of the Ottoman sultans is tainted with blood, betrayal and madness. It is remarkable to think that, although this feels like a long-dead civilisation, there are still people alive today who were born as Ottoman subjects.

1

A Tree Then Sprouted from His Navel

The 1290s were a time of chaos in the Middle East. In the region around what is now Syria and Iraq there were two rival empires vying for power. To the south, with their capital in Cairo, the Mamelukes, fierce slave warriors who had overthrown the old regime a few decades earlier, held the regional power; to the north and east, the Mongol Empire of the great khans was in charge. At this same time there was a third empire in play, the Byzantine Empire, which looked as if it had been all but wiped out by the Fourth Crusade nearly a century earlier, but the imperial title had been restored once again to the Byzantines. However, what had once been the Eastern Roman Empire was a shadow of its former self and was now more indebted to Italian trading powers than an imperial power in its own right. It certainly could not project its power into central Anatolia.

When, in 1289, the coastal city of Tripoli fell to the Mamelukes, there remained one last crusader city in the Holy Land: Acre, with its mighty walls. That, too, fell to the Mamelukes in 1291. Contrary to popular belief, this was not the end of Christian activity in the Middle East. The Christians still held Cyprus, and used it as a base of operations to attack Muslim shipping. In 1300 they achieved an amphibious landing and captured the small island fort of Ruad, just off the coast of Syria. While the gains were tiny, the Mamelukes were determined to stop a return of Christian forces to the mainland and threw their navy into the fray. Eventually, after several years of fighting, and besieging Ruad, the Mamelukes recaptured it; but at the same time they faced another (and largely successful) invasion of Syria by the Mongols.

What has any of this got to do with the Ottoman Empire? Enter Osman, a Seljuk Turk, the man who is seen as the founder of the empire. (His name is sometimes spelt Ottman or Othman, hence the term 'Ottoman'.) The Seljuks had arrived from the Asiatic steppes to the east but had been in Anatolia for generations. Had Osman tried to establish his power base fifty years earlier or later, the political landscape would likely have been quite stable and any attempt at building his own independent realm would have been quickly extinguished. More than anything else, Osman was the right man in the right place at the right time. Nature abhors a vacuum, and it's the same with power.

Söğüt is a small town in western Anatolia. It wouldn't even be a footnote in history if it wasn't for the fact that it was here that Osman first consolidated his power. Söğüt, then, was the first capital of the Ottoman Empire, but it's quite telling that in roughly the first 150 years of the empire it had four different capitals. As the empire grew and controlled ever larger and more impressive cities, the old capital was easily forgotten; Söğüt was dropped as the capital as quickly as possible.

The patriarchs of Osman's family were a succession of men who made no mark on history. Ertuğrul, his father, is known only because he is cited on the coins that Osman minted. No other contemporary power thought he was worth a mention. Osman's grandfather, Suleiman Shah, managed to drown in the Euphrates in 1227 – and that's virtually all we know about him. (The tomb of Suleiman Shah became global news in 2015. After the breakup of the Ottoman Empire his tomb ended up a few kilometres inside Syria, but there was an internationally recognised agreement that the tomb was technically Turkish territory. In 1974, when the area was due to be flooded, Suleiman's tomb was carefully moved to a new location that came under ISIS control in 2014/15. ISIS had shown nothing but complete contempt for history, and the Turks were not going to risk Osman's grandfather's tomb falling to fanatics. So, in February 2015, a Turkish military convoy technically invaded Syria – hence the news coverage – and removed the casket of Suleiman Shah. There are plans to rebury him, but at the time of writing this hasn't yet happened.)

While Osman's family had been in Anatolia for decades, he had yet to get the blessing of more powerful Seljuk rulers to formally take over the family and become a *bey* (chieftain). From

1280, when he became a *bey*, until he died in 1323/24, he greatly expanded the lands under his control, almost exclusively to the detriment of the ever-weakening Byzantine Empire. Osman must have calculated that he wasn't yet powerful enough to challenge the larger powers to the east, so he nibbled away at the Byzantine hinterland – and there wasn't much the Byzantine rulers could do about it. They did try. In 1302, the Byzantines sent a small army in an attempt to curb Osman's advances. The two sides met at the Battle of Bapheus, near the Byzantine city of Nicomedia. Osman's cavalry made short work of the smaller Byzantine force (which was bolstered by Alan mercenaries, who knew a lost cause when they saw one and didn't join in the battle). Osman was very much a warrior in the mould of other great cavalry officers of the Middle Ages, such as Genghis Khan before he won an empire, and for the next 300 years sultans would regularly be seen in battle; but as the empire matured and began to wane, so the sultans began to shirk their duties on the battlefield.

It was with the coronation of Osman's successor that the tradition of wearing Osman's sword, girded by his belt, began. This was the Ottoman equivalent of being anointed and crowned in the West and was a reminder to all of the thirty-six sultans who followed that their power and status came from this legendary warrior and that they were martial rulers. This certainly rang true in the first half of the empire's history. Osman's lavishly decorated sword and belt are the Ottoman equivalent of the crown jewels, but it's doubtful that what is seen today (on display in the Topkapı Palace Museum in Istanbul) is what Osman held in his hand. Putting it simply, Osman was unlikely ever to have had such an impractical sword, but it could be that the original blade was later plated and embellished.

Osman was definitely real, but in some ways he's like King Arthur in the West, a founder of an idea and a near-mythical figure. During his lifetime Osman was so unimportant that we have absolutely no contemporary sources about him. We don't know what he looked like; we have no proclamations extant from his reign. This was the Ottoman Dark Ages. Because there is such a dearth of information from this early period, many books about the Ottoman Empire spend most of their time exploring the empire in its heyday, from roughly the mid-1400s to the mid-1600s. While it is true that this was an era of remarkable achievements, to focus on this period gives a distorted view of the evolution of the empire. The rulers and events in the first 150 years of the story quite often get summarised in the first chapter of books on the empire, and things really only get going with the siege of Constantinople in 1453, as if everything prior to that doesn't count. But to gloss over this early period does it a complete injustice as there were some significant events that fundamentally shaped the empire prior to that key moment. You will find the account of the siege of Constantinople about a quarter of the way through this book because it happened about a quarter of the way through the timeline of the Ottoman Empire. This is my attempt to redress the balance and to tell the story of the empire without overemphasising any particular era.

So, while the early 1300s were the Dark Ages of the Ottomans, a little over a century later the empire was in rude good health, and with this came the desire to revisit the founder and give Osman a legacy. As a consequence, gleaning the real Osman from all the myth-making becomes virtually impossible. Foundation myths tell something about the times in which they were created, like Rome with Romulus and Remus, and so it is that we come to the legend of Osman's dream. Osman had an ally in a local religious leader called Sheikh Edebali. They were obviously close because Osman ended up marrying one of Edebali's daughters. According to the legend, Osman went to Edebali for guidance and had a dream when he spent the night at the sheikh's house. The imagery varies, but the key part is that Osman allegedly remembered that 'a tree then sprouted from his navel and its shade encompassed the world'. On top of this rivers began to flow and mountains formed, and we are clearly now in metaphorical territory suspiciously similar to the florid prose of a later Ottoman literary style that a thirteenth-century cavalry *bey* wouldn't use.

When Osman asked Edebali what all this meant, his response echoes the Biblical account of Joseph and his dreams, a story that would certainly have been known to Islamic scholars. Edebali was apparently delighted with Osman's dream, declaring that it meant that Osman would be the founder of an extraordinary dynasty which, like the canopy of the tree, would encompass many lands. It was also, allegedly, this revelation that sealed the marriage to Edebali's daughter. So the story of the dream marks out Osman as a man with a great destiny. He was only a local warlord at the time, but the concept was clear: as his family moved from generation to generation and grew, so would his realm. The earliest reference to this dream is from around a century after the event is said to have taken place and is clearly a case of descendants adding lustre to an obscure ancestor. It is, however, a story that is still taught in Turkish schools and can be seen as similar to other apocryphal stories, such as the young George Washington being unable to lie about the cherry tree or King Alfred burning the cakes.

Osman's powers during his own time were, in reality, very limited. He chose not to fight stronger Seljuk warlords in Anatolia and went for the easier pickings of the terminally ill Byzantine Empire. An example of his limitations is seen in his attack and capture of the city of Ephesus. This once great and ancient city was well past its prime by the time Osman arrived in the early 1300s, but it was important as one of the last major Byzantine settlements left in Anatolia. It seems Osman captured the city with relative ease, which was surprising in itself (as will be seen with the long siege of Bursa), but what was even stranger is that it did not become part of Ottoman lands; instead it became part of the Emir of Aydin's fiefdom. In other words, it is likely that Osman was only part of the attacking army and that he didn't at this time have enough power to challenge the emir of a now obscure realm.

Another early legend about Osman is interesting because it has been largely forgotten. The tale centres on a disagreement between Osman and an uncle called Dündar, who wished to keep peace with a neighbouring Christian lord when Osman didn't. The argument turned deadly, and Osman shot Dündar with an arrow. While the story alludes to the growing power of Osman's forces, indicating an ability to take on a neighbour who previously had been thought best to deal with peacefully, it portrays Osman as a man ruthless enough to kill close family members to get what he wanted. Again, this story is not contemporary to Osman and could be just as contrived as the tale of his dream. This part of the Osman legend was dropped from later accounts of his life because it didn't portray him in a good light and may have been deemed bad PR. No one knew then that the killing of an uncle would be mild compared to the blood that would be spilt in the halls of power in the generations to come.

Osman was married to two women (under Islamic law, a man could have up to four wives). This modest setup shows the Ottoman court had yet to create its famous harem, but as these already existed in other Islamic seats of power it underlines the limited resources of the Ottomans at this time. Osman's first wife was Malhun Hatun and his second was with Rabia Bala Hatun, who was the daughter of Sheikh Edebali. He had eight children with these women (seven boys and one girl; the ratio, while not impossible, could be biased as the births of daughters were not always as carefully recorded as those of sons).

As Osman aged, his mind would naturally have turned to his succession. His eldest son, Alaeddin (son of Rabia), would have been the logical choice as the new *bey* of the embryonic Ottoman Empire, but the actual successor was his second son, Orhan (son of Malhun). Later on you will see how, over the centuries, the scramble for the throne led to bloodshed among the feuding siblings and sometimes resulted in civil war, but this was one of the most harmonious transitions of power not only in Ottoman history but in fourteenth-century history in general. This story is roughly contemporary with Edward III's rise to power in England. By contrast, even though Edward was the rightful heir to the throne, his father (Edward II) was (possibly) murdered, he had to be rescued from a Nottingham prison in a daring raid, and he had to order the execution of his mother's lover before securing the crown that everybody agreed was his to begin with.

Back in Anatolia, it seems Alaeddin recognised that Orhan was the natural-born warrior, whereas he was more a man of learning who didn't fit the mould of the great warlord. He was, by all accounts, a pious man who was admired and respected by everyone. He personally paid for the construction of a mosque which, while small in size compared to the later great mosques of the sultans, is one of the earliest surviving examples of Ottoman architecture. So, while Orhan got on with conquering, Alaeddin became what is considered to be the first grand vizier of the Ottoman Empire. In modern parlance, this means he was the sultan's chief advisor and oversaw the day-to-day administration of the empire. In particularly modern vernacular he was Orhan's prime minister, but in many instances he was also a warrior and a pasha (general) who led campaigns. The title Grand Vizier of the Ottoman Empire was to last until 1908.

Before talking more about the reign of Orhan I, the first Ottoman ruler of enough land to be considered an empire (although at this point it was a very small empire), we should pause to recognise Alaeddin's achievements. One of the main reasons why there are no legal codices or any discernible legal framework from the era of Osman is that he didn't create any. Osman was very much like his contemporary Anatolian warlords, more worried about fighting and booty than about building a state. Orhan and Alaeddin, however, recognised that their territory was evolving into something new and different.

Osman and Orhan are not known as Osman I and Orhan I, but by the title *ghazi*. This is a specific Arabic/Islamic term that was originally linked to anyone who had military experience but had morphed into a title with a more religious connotation under the wars of the Prophet and the expansion of the original caliphate (the Islamic community); by the Middle Ages, it was generally linked to any Muslim warrior who had shown prowess in battle. It was still a title of respect but had more of a religious implication than was usually justified by events. One of the most famous *ghazis* in the Middle Ages was Saladin, and, while he did famously fight against the Christians in Syria, he actually spent more of his career fighting Muslim powers than Christian ones. While Orhan was busy being both ruler and *ghazi*, Alaeddin was seeing to the affairs of government, and it was under his management that the conquered territories around Söğüt started to form a more coherent realm. His impact was huge, long-lasting, sensible and a little dull.

While Osman had minted coins (one of the few contemporary pieces of evidence that he existed), they were little more than local copies of other coinage in circulation at the time. Alaeddin went substantially further. The monetary system was simplified and standardised, which helped trade because any realm with stable, reliable and high-quality coinage had the upper hand in trade negotiations. In addition to the monetary system, Alaeddin overhauled the military by creating and funding a standing army of regular troops. Anatolian warlords tended to run a completely martial realm, but as the Ottoman lands expanded that traditional system was found wanting. Many of the new subjects weren't born horse archers, and it was recognised that in order to make use of the manpower available, greater use of infantry and archers would have to be made and these roles integrated into the army. While it was true that this army couldn't be as mobile and couldn't use the classic 'attack and feint' of the legendary horse archers of the era, it was larger and more flexible than before. The most famous warriors of the Ottoman Empire were the Janissaries, and, while they were not formed until a generation later, it's worth noting that they were not cavalry but infantry, a marked departure from the traditional Turkic form of warfare.

In addition to revamping the monetary system and the army, Alaeddin's third reform – perhaps the most important of all – involved, of all things, clothing. This probably sounds odd, but right from the start of the empire there was a multitude of different ethnicities under the sultan's authority and Alaeddin understood that this was something to be encouraged and enhanced by the regulation of dress. Western travellers to the empire would later marvel at the kaleidoscope of colours and fashions worn by the empire's peoples, the different attires identifying the wearer as a Jew, an Albanian, a Greek and so forth. This was not to single out any group for discrimination but to provide a visual reminder that it didn't matter who your god was or what language you spoke, everyone in the empire lived under the authority and protection of the sultan.

Clothing

A typical Muslim Ottoman male wore a *mintan* (a cross between a waistcoat and short jacket), with *şalvar* (loose, baggy trousers) held up with a *kuşak* (sash). A brimless cap (usually white) or turban was worn on the head. The poor wore simple collarless shirts with a *cepken* (waistcoat). A typical Muslim woman wore *şalvar* (trousers) and a *gömlek* (blouse), with a scarf to cover her hair and, on some occasions, a veil. Later in the empire it was common for a kind of uniform to be worn according to the nature of the work carried out. These, too, tended to be colourful and distinctive.

It's in this very early time in the empire (1320s and 30s) that it is possible to see the inherent problem of 'empire' in general. As an empire grows, assets are regularly acquired and loyal subjects can be rewarded with new lands and possessions. There is every reason to keep pushing forwards, and the prospect of rewards creates a momentum of its own. And yet all empires reach a limit, at which point assets remain static, and loyal subjects can only defend what is already theirs. New court favourites have to wait for another great family to lose favour or forcibly take someone else's lands. The rulers go from being conquerors to jugglers as they try to keep the powerful happy, and the status quo leads to ever more discontent. Alaeddin's rational reforms acknowledged the problems to come, and thanks to his actions the empire would continue to grow and flourish for centuries.

According to Sharia (Islamic) law, all non-Muslims had to pay a tax. In Arabic this was called the *jizya*; in Ottoman Turkish it was called *cizye* (there is no 'j' in the Turkish alphabet, but the letter 'c' is pronounced like an English 'j'). The *cizye* was a payment made to cover the protection of non-Muslims in an Islamic state and was, as might be imagined, enormously popular among Muslim rulers. In the early Middle Ages, when Sicily was under Islamic rule, the rulers stopped non-Muslims from converting to Islam because the amount of *cizya* being collected was reducing as the proportion of Muslims in the population was increasing. It was a similar story in the Ottoman Empire, where *cizye* was collected from Christian and Jewish communities and, at its peak, was one of the Ottoman treasury's main sources of income. The system meant that there was a very real monetary incentive to be an inclusive empire, and attempts to convert communities to Islam were discouraged for practical financial reasons. Compare this to the religious wars and inquisitions going on in Europe at the same time, and the Ottomans look far more reasonable. The tax on non-Muslims was not abolished until 1856, some 500 years later. By the time of Alaeddin's death the Ottoman lands were already a polyglot realm of different ethnicities. The capture of previously held Byzantine lands (particularly on the Aegean coast of Anatolia) meant that a significant minority of Ottomans were, in fact, ethnically Greek Christians and would be an integral part of the empire until it ended in the twentieth century.

All these changes took place in just one generation and show a remarkable increase in the confidence of Ottoman power, so it is not surprising that Orhan no longer saw his position as subordinate to the Seljuk rulers to the east. No longer were coins minted with the names of an overlord. Orhan's lands were now, emphatically, his 'Ottoman' territory, and he owed allegiance to no one.

Orhan, while a great conqueror, also knew when diplomacy was called for. The nascent empire he inherited trebled in size over nearly four decades under his leadership. Almost all these conquests (like his father's) were at the expense of the Byzantine Empire, simply because they were the equivalent of picking low-hanging fruit. The Byzantine Empire was on its last legs; it had greatly diminished resources, and the Byzantine court was fractious, with regular coups and counter-purges. In the 1320s there was a civil war, followed by another in the 1340s. All this instability and division helped the fledgling Ottoman lands grow in a zero-sum game with Byzantium. It was a soft target for a growing power that was not yet ready to pick a fight with a larger and stronger opponent.

This relationship to Byzantium meant that two myths have grown up around the Ottoman Empire. The first is that it was a zealous Islamic empire, hell-bent on the destruction of Christianity. It was no such thing. The choices of targets were eminently practical rather than religiously motivated. The second myth is that this was an 'eastern' empire. Again, it was no such thing. From the very beginning the empire put much of its focus on expanding west, not east. By the end of Orhan's reign parts of modern-day Greece were now part of the empire, and parts of Europe were integral to the empire until the day it was dissolved. Two out of four of its capitals were in Europe, and, looking at it from a practical point of view, it is roughly 1,500 kilometres from Istanbul to Vienna – and yet it's nearly 2,200 kilometres from Istanbul to Baghdad. For later sultans it was simply easier and quicker to wage war in Europe than in Asia.

At the start of Orhan's reign, the Ottoman lands were of minor importance to both the Byzantines and the Anatolian warlords; Orhan was merely one of many princelings of no notable significance. However, by the time of his death in 1362, Orhan's lands certainly rivalled what remained of the Byzantine Empire. The starting point of this achievement was the successful siege of Bursa, a siege that had been started by Osman and took nine years to resolve. Bursa, while fortified with city walls, was by no means one of the great fortress cities of the East; Antioch, Constantinople and Acre were all far better defended. While later in history the Ottomans became much feared for their siege craft and cannons, in the fourteenth century they were still, at heart, horse archers who could win a pitched battle but found that their arrows and cavalry were all but useless against a walled city.

Sieges
When faced with a siege, there are three main ways to resolve it: a negotiated settlement, a direct assault or starvation (of the defenders). The negotiated settlement happened more often than you might think. Garrisons rarely wanted to die for the cause, although if they could hold out for relief there was every reason

---

to sit behind their thick walls and wait. The rules of sieges may sound barbaric now, but they served a purpose in their day. If the defenders gave up their fortifications, they could expect to leave with their honour and pretty much anything they could carry. However, if they resisted and the attackers finally breached the walls, they could expect no mercy. There is a brutal logic in this because it encouraged defenders to come to the negotiating table to avoid unnecessary bloodshed.

Starvation was a long, slow process. If any supplies were to get behind the walls, the siege would simply go on for much longer. Basic hygiene, as it was understood at the time, had to be observed both inside the fortifications and outside by the besiegers. An outbreak of diseases such as cholera could annihilate the attacking forces far more efficiently than any attack from inside the walls. However, if the besiegers could surround a city, and if they had time on their side, this was a low-risk strategy and a guaranteed way to win. Starvation worked better with cities because there were more mouths to feed, and no amount of bravery offers protection from hunger. This kind of tactic (used for thousands of years by most civilisations) is now considered to be a war crime due to the disproportionate suffering of civilians.

Direct assault was always the least preferred option. Defences are never impenetrable, and it was the job of defensive architects to work out how many men it would take to kill one member of the garrison. These multipliers meant that some sieges saw barely more than a hundred men successfully see off tens of thousands of the enemy. To get past these defences, an entire martial art form evolved. Tunnelling under the walls of a city was a technical and dangerous business, but once the passages were collapsed the walls would usually come down with them. Then there were the highly sought-after giant siege engines, designed to rain down projectiles – anything from rocks to pots of Greek fire to diseased animals (to spread pestilence within). Later, cannons were used to batter the stone walls of these citadels. There were also giant siege towers, designed to roll up to the walls and allow easy access for attackers. Siege ladders, battering rams – the list of siege machines and weapons goes on and on. All of these were extremely expensive in terms of materials, resources and lives.

The siege of Bursa was a long, slow slog in which the Ottomans tried to starve the population and drain the city of its resources. Byzantium was in the grip of civil war at the time, so the chance of any relief force coming to the aid of the besieged city was remote. When the siege was over, it ended neither with a dramatic assault nor with a pile of dead Byzantine warriors being trampled over by triumphant Ottoman forces. The tactic of waiting out the forces of Bursa paid off when, in 1326, Byzantine governor Evronos paid Orhan what was, in essence, a ransom that allowed him to escape to Constantinople with the great and good of the city. So the nine-year siege ended with a rather ignominious bribe and the Byzantine elite slinking off across the Marmara Sea. Hardly the stuff of legends. But that didn't matter to the Ottomans, who, for the very first time, had besieged a city with significant defences and captured it. Bursa was a far bigger deal than Söğüt, so Bursa almost immediately became the new capital of the Ottoman Empire. (Despite never having lived there, Osman is buried in Bursa, not Söğüt.) The fall of Bursa was hardly a high point for either the Ottomans or Byzantium. The long-drawn-out siege showed the severe limitations of a power in its infancy, one unused to siege warfare, but a win is a win. Now the Ottomans had a capital worth boasting about.

However, shortly after Orhan's successful capture of Bursa, the Byzantine civil war came to an end, and the new emperor, Andronikos III Palaiologos (Andronicus), raised an army to push back Orhan's territorial gains. It was a sign of the political realities of the time that Andronicus's army numbered a few thousand, many of whom were mercenaries, an unreliable bunch in the face of a superior force. Orhan's army was approximately twice the size of the Byzantine force when the two sides met at Pelekanon (in Anatolia) in June of 1329. Orhan had chosen his base of operations wisely when he took the high ground and sent out some horse archers to pepper the Byzantine front lines with arrows, only to beat a hasty retreat, the classic attack-and-feint manoeuvre of horse archers. It had worked many times before, but Andronicus was wise to the lure of the retreating horsemen. Instead, the two sides clashed sporadically over the day, the Byzantine forces failing to make any headway and the Ottomans unable to flank and penetrate the ranks of Andronicus's men. As dusk settled, the two sides were still probing each other, and it was then that Andronicus was wounded. It was not a serious wound, but as the sun set rumours began to swirl around the Byzantine force, and a minor wound became a mortal one – and a mortal wound of course meant that Andronicus was now gone. The alarm was unnecessary; Andronicus was fine. He recognised that the rigid formation of his forces was melting away and that this was the pivotal moment of the battle. He tried to stop his army from retreating, but his efforts were futile. As panic set in, the retreat turned into a rout, and this meant that the former cohesion of the Byzantine force completely broke down, giving Orhan the opportunity he had been waiting for. The Byzantine force that had acquitted itself so well throughout the day was annihilated. It had been undone by rumour and panic.

Andronicus escaped the rout and managed to get back to Constantinople, where he would continue to rule for more than a decade, but his defeat at the Battle of Pelekanon would cast a long shadow over his reign. If things had gone Andronicus's way, that battle would have opened the door to recapture all the territories that Osman and Orhan had conquered. Now, after such an emphatic defeat, no Byzantine emperor would ever again send an army into Anatolia. Although the scale of the strategic victory was not apparent to Orhan at that time, it had been his first victory in pitched battle against the Byzantines and was celebrated throughout the Ottoman territories. What Orhan did know was that he could now turn his attention to an even bigger prize.

One reason why Andronicus had fought in the area of Pelekanon was because he knew that Orhan had begun a siege of Nicaea (now called Iznik, of pottery fame), a crucial Byzantine city where the Council of Nicaea, in the fourth century, had confirmed the books of the Bible (among other things). While it had been briefly lost to the Seljuks, it had been recaptured for Byzantium in 1097 during the First Crusade. When Constantinople fell to the Fourth Crusade, Nicaea became the seat of power in exile from 1204 to 1261. By the 1300s it was the second-largest city in the Byzantine Empire, second only to Constantinople. Losing it would represent a further crushing defeat for Andronicus. Now he could only hope and pray that the defenders would hold out more effectively than those in Bursa.

Because Nicaea bordered on a lake, it had always been a tough city to besiege. Again the Ottomans did not have the siege equipment to carry out a direct assault, but the lands around the city were now under Orhan's control. This meant that while a direct siege was difficult, his mobile cavalry could easily intercept convoys and caravans heading to resupply the city. Orhan prepared to play the waiting game, but this siege resolved itself in a third of the time it had taken for Bursa. In 1331, about three years after Nicaea had been surrounded, it surrendered. Had Nicaea fallen before Bursa, it is likely that this would have become the Ottoman capital as it was bigger and had significant authority and prestige. As it was captured just five years after Bursa, however, there was no impetus to move the capital again. The success of the siege cemented Orhan's power in the region, which meant it was almost inevitable that he would control all of north-west Anatolia.

For the next decade or so, Orhan continued to push back Byzantine influence in the region. Nicaea had been the toughest nut to crack, so after that victory villages were swallowed up in his advance. The last major city left in the region was Nicomedia (now Izmit), and that fell to Orhan in 1337. The only thing Andronicus could do was to look on in horror. For Orhan the issue was no longer the Byzantines, but the Turkish *bey* of Karesi.

Karesi (the present-day north-western Turkish city of Balıkesir and its surrounds) had been the fiefdom of the most westerly of the patchwork of Seljuk principalities in Anatolia. There had been times when the Karesi chieftains had supplied the Byzantines with mercenary forces and other times when they had happily plundered the local Byzantine territory. The Republic of Turkey likes to assert that there have been a myriad of 'Turkish Empires', and in one sense this is correct. As a warlord of mobile horse archers, Osman shared a cultural outlook that would have been familiar to Attila the Hun, Kilic Arslan and Genghis Khan. The assumption is that because they were culturally similar, they would have been the best of friends. To dispel this notion one need only look at the histories of France and England, where for centuries the aristocracy of one was intermarried to the other, where their courts even spoke the same language and where, in terms of religion, architecture and even societal structures, they were very similar – these things in common did nothing to prevent the two nations from trying to tear each other apart for centuries.

What happened next between the Ottoman *bey* and the Karesi *bey* proves this point. Of course the two leaders had many things in common, both culturally and ethnically. They even agreed that Karesi was a territory worth fighting for. It's just that Orhan wanted to conquer it, and by now he had the resources to do it; he just needed a pretext. Fortunately for him, this occurred when the old *bey* died and his two sons went to war over who would rule next. This gave Orhan the excuse he needed to invade under the pretext of acting as a peacemaker. He wanted it to appear as if he was doing everyone a favour by calming tempers and ending a civil war. By 1345 one of the brothers had been killed and the other had been captured by Orhan's forces. The civil war had been a veneer to cover what was a naked grab for power, but it had worked like a dream. Orhan now controlled all of north-western Anatolia, which meant that, for the first time, he now ruled the coast that was one side of the Sea of Marmara. On the other side of this treacherous stretch of water stood Constantinople.

But there was even more to it than that. In Europe, the Ottoman Empire has always been seen as the alien 'other' empire, bringing the East to the West whether it wanted it or not. This first century of Ottoman expansion led to the last gasps of the crusading movement, the largely violent Christian response to Islam (there is much more about this in my book *Deus Vult: A Concise History of the Crusades*). However, a look at a map of the Ottoman Empire at its peak shows that it covered far more Muslim territory than Christian. This was not handed over willingly but captured through conquest. While the Ottoman Empire never did conquer Persia, these two Islamic powers clashed for centuries, Muslim killing Muslim. For such allegedly noble *ghazis* of Islam, the Ottoman sultans spent a surprisingly large amount of time fighting other Muslim rulers and principalities. And all of this started with the capture of Karesi. Not only did this victory solidify the fledgling Ottoman state, but it also gave the empire a taste for expansion against all types of neighbours. This led to a zero-sum game against not only the Byzantine Empire, but all Muslim rulers across the Middle East and beyond.

Just before these events, the Byzantine Emperor Andronicus died, leaving his nine-year-old son as the new emperor. That was never going to satisfy the Byzantine court, and a new civil war erupted. Orhan had been careful to keep cordial relations with Andronicus after their initial clash; the Byzantines weren't going to stop him in Anatolia, but it seemed best not to needlessly antagonise them. However, once this civil war broke out, Orhan carefully weighed up the two sides before coming down in favour of the usurper, John VI Kantakouzenos. It was a shrewd move. The new emperor now owed his victory, in part, to his most menacing enemy, putting John VI in a tough political situation – not least because he had also allied with the Serbians, who took a large part of Byzantium's remaining territory in the Balkans as payment. The Byzantine Empire's lands were reduced even further. By 1347, what had once been a weak and ageing empire was now in its death throes. John VI was emperor of Constantinople and the lands immediately surrounding the city – and not much else. He had allied himself with avaricious men, for which he paid a heavy price.

To make matters worse, the Black Death swept through the region in the middle of this conflict. It had travelled from the Crimean peninsula to Constantinople and, from there, on into Europe. Obviously the pestilence affected all sides, but Byzantium saw an eye-watering death toll. The Ottoman territories, however, largely avoided the devastation of plague. At worst Orhan's lands were on the fringes of the pandemic and, compared to countries like France or England, got off very lightly, which allowed the Ottomans to bounce back faster than almost all the powers in the West.

Orhan married six times, and two of his wives were the daughters of Byzantine emperors. One of them was Theodora, daughter of John VI Kantakouzenos, Orhan's ally in the civil war. They married in 1346, when she was just fourteen and he was sixty-five, indicating a politically motivated union; however, they did have at least one son. John VI Kantakouzenos' motivation for marrying his daughter off to the infidel was to tie Orhan to his cause, which would give him access to Ottoman support against his (many) enemies. For a time it worked, but the Byzantines couldn't help themselves. The court dissolved into deadly intrigue, and civil war broke out yet again between the vying factions in Constantinople. A messy situation was further aggravated by the interests of the courts of the Balkan kings and the trading powers of Venice and Genoa. Orhan helped out when it suited him and when circumstances coincided with his own interests.

Once the deadly pathogen of the Black Death had passed, Orhan and Alaeddin got on with moulding their recent conquests into a new and vibrant society. For the most part, the rest of Orhan's reign was less about conquest and more about consolidation. By now the Ottoman lands were noticeably different from the old Seljuk fiefdoms of the past. The Ottoman Empire had arrived.

2

The Moonlight Attack
on Europe

By the 1350s Orhan was getting on in years, and it was about this time that some of his sons began to shine through. Murad (sometimes spelled Murat) was the son of one of Orhan's Turkish wives; so, too, was his brother Suleiman. There were other sons as well in Orhan's (modest) harem, and the Ottoman line looked to be in good health for at least another generation. Murad was like his uncle Alaeddin; he went to the *madrassa* (Muslim religious school) in Bursa, where he lived not with soldiers or members of the aristocracy but with scientists, theologians and artists. He was bright and eminently capable. But it was Suleiman who was the apple of his father's eye and, clearly, the chosen one. He was a hunter and a warrior, Orhan's dynamic, brave and energetic son.

The tale is still told of how Suleiman Pasha came to be the first Ottoman leader to capture territory in Europe when he led a small band of men to the Byzantine fortress of Tzympe on the Gallipoli peninsula in 1356. He successfully infiltrated the fort in the dead of night and planted an Ottoman banner on European lands for the very first time – except, like Osman and his dream, this is a later bit of myth-making. It is a wonderfully evocative legend disguising the more mundane reality that, after suffering the devastation brought on by the Black Death, the fort (as well as the surrounding area) was rocked by a massive earthquake. It was wretched land, deserted by the Byzantine authorities, and as such was an easy gift from the Byzantine Emperor John Kantakouzenos to Orhan.

Suleiman Pasha was every bit as dashing as the legend suggests, but he died in an unfortunate hunting accident in 1357. This put Murad in pole position to become Orhan's heir. While it is tempting to think how things might have been different if Suleiman had ruled the empire, it turned out that Murad was no slouch in his desire to expand Ottoman realms through conquest. Tzympe Castle became Çimpe Castle, and now the Ottomans had territory across the Bosphorus Strait as well as on the Gallipoli peninsula. The fort was an immensely important site, commanding the narrowest stretch of this busy waterway. The Byzantine Empire may not have had the resources to revitalise the fortification and the surrounding area, but the Ottomans certainly did, and the gift would come back in later years to haunt the Byzantines.

Now Orhan had lands that could only be accessed by ship, but the resources of the Ottoman Empire still had limitations. Navies are expensive, and Orhan was not in a position to justify the costly construction of an entire Ottoman fleet. At the time the dominant naval powers in the eastern Mediterranean and the Black Sea were the city states of Venice and Genoa. So, for a while, the fledgling empire was mainly reliant on trade and transport deals with these Italian Christian powers. This further muddied the waters with Constantinople and the West as the Ottoman lands reached ever westward, invariably to the detriment of the Christian Byzantine emperors.

Constantinople was still a vitally important trading hub for both Venice and Genoa, but at the same time these rival nations were not going to ignore the rising new star in the area. The papacy was growing increasingly uneasy over the deals with the infidel being brokered by the Italian traders and the spread of Muslim influence into Europe for the first time. A small Genoese fleet was carrying out pirate raids along the Anatolian coast, and in 1356 it got lucky and kidnapped Orhan's son Khalil (by Theodora). So now a prince of both the Ottoman and the Byzantine courts was being carried off over the horizon, although the Genoese insisted that the fleet was acting independently of anything officially sanctioned by the Genoese Doge. Orhan, in an unusual admission of weakness, went to emperor John Kantakouzenos to ask for assistance to get Khalil back. In a unique moment in history, the Byzantine fleet set sail to help the Ottomans. Khalil was recovered after an enormous ransom was paid, and the alliance between the Ottoman and Byzantine rulers had paid off. Tensions, however, were rising; the status quo could not last. Nevertheless, during Orhan's lifetime it just about held together.

Tzympe was not the most exotic prize Orhan was to win during his reign. Ankara, in central Anatolia (and now the capital of the Republic of Turkey), was captured by Orhan. The town itself was not significant then, and it wasn't ruled by a fearsome Turkish *bey*; it was a trading town run by a guild called the Ahis. They were semi-independent but technically under the authority of one of the great Mongol hordes. Orhan calculated that the town was too far away from the Mongolian power base to be very hostile to a fearsome (and better-resourced) power, and he was right. Nonetheless, this was a move that would have been too bold even for Orhan at the very start of his reign. Ankara would soon leave the Ottoman sphere of influence for a time (more on that later), but the capture of this far-flung location showed once again how far the empire had come in the space of just one generation. The lands ruled by Orhan were still comparatively small, but the Ottoman rulers were both ambitious and capable, and their lands were growing rapidly.

By the late 1350s Murad had taken the reins of power. Orhan was semi-retired, which allowed him time to mourn the death of Suleiman and to enjoy the fruits of his labours. He died in 1362 in his early eighties and was buried alongside his brother Alaeddin (who had pre-deceased him in 1331/32, sources are vague on the date) in the family tomb in Bursa, the brothers immortalised as a highly effective team in their final resting place.

Murad was now the official leader, and it was during his reign that a number of features of Ottoman rule became standard. For example, he was the first ruler to take the title 'sultan'. This wasn't immediate, but came more than twenty years later in 1383, when there was no doubt that the Ottomans had become the pre-eminent power in western Anatolia, and in part of Greece and the Balkans too. By then even the Byzantine emperors were paying tribute to him. It was clear he was no mere *bey* or pasha, and so the new title of sultan was created. Like his father, Murad was able to use the existing Ottoman lands as a jumping-off point for further expansion, something that would not have been possible without a strong army. And it was under Murad that, within the Ottoman army, the elite core of Janissaries was formed. The name Janissary is the anglicised version of *yeniçeri*, which in Turkish means 'new soldier'.

Janissaries

We will return to the Janissaries many times throughout this book because their story is irrevocably entwined with that of the sultans. Although they evolved over the centuries, the original Janissaries were the elite infantry of the Ottoman army. They were a symbol not only of the power of the Ottoman sultans, but also of the Ottomans' move away from their roots as cavalrymen. It is quite telling that the greatest victories under the sultans were not cavalry engagements but pitched battles or sieges, and these could only have been achieved with an army very different to the one that Osman led.

In their very early days, the Janissaries were simply one-fifth of the men captured in battle by the Ottomans. They could expect to either become slaves to the aristocracy or soldiers fighting for their enemy. This may sound odd, but the Janissaries are an example of one of the first standing armies. In the Middle Ages and later, most countries had an aristocracy that would train for war, and the vast bulk of the forces were men who owed a certain number of days of military service in return for land. This was the core of the feudal system. There were some notable exceptions, such as the Mongols and the Mamelukes, but the armies Murad was fighting were largely made up of men who probably didn't want to be fighting at all. Under the Ottomans these captured men were paid, given proper equipment, housed and fed. It was likely to be a better situation than the one they had been born into.

This method of recruitment very quickly evolved into the *devşirme* (collection) system, when boys (sometimes as young as six) were forcibly taken from their Christian homes to live with Muslim families. As well as learning to fight, they were taught Ottoman Turkish, absorbed Ottoman culture and converted to Islam (including being circumcised) before being formally inducted into the Janissaries, where they lived celibate lives in barracks. Known as the 'blood tax' by Christians, this was a barbaric practice in which the administrators of the *devşirme* would tour the Christian regions of the empire to seek out the toughest, strongest and bravest boys. The reason the Muslim Ottomans picked on the Christian communities is a quirk of Islamic law, which states that no Muslim can be a slave. This is why some Muslim groups have decried other Muslims as 'fallen' or 'false', which then allows them to enslave the population. The Ottomans followed the letter of Sharia law and chose exclusively non-Muslims to fill what would have been slave roles. Of course, after conversion, they were now Muslim slaves – a contradiction that no one dared to point out.

Enslaving children and forcing them to fight is cruel and abhorrent, but things weren't quite as black and white as they might appear. The great Muslim empire of the Mamelukes was made up of a warrior class with exactly the same origins as that of the Janissaries – before their uprising in the mid-thirteenth century, the Mamelukes had been Christian slave boys who had converted to Islam and were brought up to be fierce fighters. How good were they? Well, they were the first army to defeat the Mongols in battle. So the idea of a Muslim convert slave army as the backbone of an empire was not original to Murad. After that there is the question of what other options these boys had, and the answer is 'not many'. Left in their communities, they were likely to become peasant farmers, scratching out a living on the land, paying their taxes and dying as forgotten nobodies. The collection system gave strong boys the chance to bring glory to their families, so a poor boy from Bulgaria might grow up to lead thousands of troops into battle. When too old to fight, Janissaries often became government administrators or viziers (ministers), and a few even became grand viziers to the sultan. With prospects like this, boys were not always hidden from the collectors of the *devşirme* because many families saw this as an opportunity for their sons.

When I read about the Janissaries I wonder why they didn't rise up and rebel as the Mamelukes had done. While this did happen much later, those rebellions were based on threats to the power they held in the Ottoman court and not on any perceived unfairness regarding their lot in life. If the early Janissaries had resisted the system, it wouldn't have lasted for centuries – but it did. That tells us something about the successful inculcation of knowledge and values in these boys and the *esprit de corps* of the men in the Janissary ranks, who fought hard and were much feared across Europe and the Middle East. The irony is that the European chronicles invariably consider the Janissaries as 'Turks', whereas in terms of first language, DNA and place of birth, they often had more in common with the men they were fighting than the Europeans realised.

In a way, the Janissaries can be seen as the precursors of the modern 'Turks'. As mentioned briefly in the introduction, the current population of the Republic of Turkey is not, ethnically speaking, one people. The republic is a melting pot of all kinds of long-forgotten groups. Genuinely ethnic Turks come from central Asia and look very different to the occupants of Anatolia. However, the Turkish and Ottoman cultures run deep in the Republic of Turkey. The Janissaries were, likewise, outsiders who became integrated into the new society.

I am aware that many Turks might have an adverse reaction to any suggestion that they are not blood-pure Turks – even if they acknowledge that, logically, the suggestion may be true. My father was devastated to find out he has no ethnically Turkish blood and is largely (in terms of DNA) Bulgarian with a splash of Arab, a completely logical Ottoman mix. In a way, this was hardly surprising news because the Duducu family had been living in Shumen, Bulgaria, for as long as anyone can remember (until my grandfather migrated to Istanbul in the 1930s). So, at some point, the family stopped identifying as 'Bulgarian' and instead identified as 'Ottoman'. The facts have not deterred my father, who remains proud to be a Turk. 'Turkishness' then is less about blood and more about an idea. Any modern Turk (a citizen of the Republic of Turkey, founded in 1923) would happily lay down his life for his country, a country that isn't even a century old and never existed prior to the Ottoman Empire, and the Janissaries were the same. They would have known of their origins and they certainly would have looked different to each other and to some of the Ottoman aristocracy around them, but these men were willing to die for the cause and were immensely proud of their position in Ottoman society.

The Janissaries are a physical reminder of two hard truths: that the Ottoman Empire relied on slaves (the women in the later harem in Topkapı Palace were all Christian slave girls), but also that slavery is sometimes more complicated than the European/African crime familiar in our culture. In the Ottoman Empire, a slave's life wasn't always automatically worse than life as a free man or woman.

The second truth is that Ottoman society was principally a martial one. For centuries the sultans were rulers, but they were also warriors. The Janissary system was elaborate and costly, but for a society that placed martial prowess above most other things, it was a price worth paying.

Here again we have a section of Ottoman society readily identifiable by their clothes. The Janissaries wore vivid colours – deep greens, vibrant blues and rich reds. Colour was expensive before artificial dyes, and the richer the colour the more times it had to be dyed. Colour, therefore, was a symbol of status, and these ex-Christian slaves were dressed as wealthy men. Great plumes of (usually white) feathers sprouted from the tops of their hats, known as the *börk*, the whole ensemble making them one of the most colourful armies in history (as was noted numerous times by Western sources). Until the mid-fifteenth century, the Janissaries were archers as well as melee (close-quarter) troops. Then, in the fifteenth and sixteenth centuries, as the bow began to be phased out on the battlefield, they became elite musketeers. Their main disadvantage was their lack of armour. Compared to their Western contemporaries on the battlefield (and this was during the Hundred Years War), the European knights often wore full plate armour. The Janissaries by contrast were woefully under-protected, but without armour they were agile, and their training, group cohesion and loyalty meant that they were never to be underestimated on the battlefield.

The Janissaries marched and fought to music because it was thought that music made them march faster and fight harder. Additionally, some of the chronicles from the West attest to the disquieting effect the music had on the enemy, giving a psychological advantage to the Janissaries, who are often credited with having the first official military band. An advancing host of Janissaries would have been terrifying both to see and to hear.

The Janissaries were, a little strangely, fixated on food. You would think that an elite corps of warriors might use as their symbol a sword or a lance, but no. The *börk* had a place in front to hold a spoon, denoting the 'brotherhood of the spoon', which symbolised that the Janissaries ate, slept, fought and died together in a kind of enclosed order similar to that

---

of the Christian military orders, like the Knights Hospitaller. The names of their ranks within the corps are generally food related, such as 'First Maker of Soup', and the most valued item of any Janissary regiment was its stew pot. While these great cauldrons produced meals for the troops, they were also the place where the men gathered at the end of the day, a symbol of the comradeship of the corps.

Meanwhile, back in the Ottoman court, Murad turned out to be the very best of both his father and his uncle. He was a great warrior, but he was also an innovative administrator. Like his uncle before him, Murad revolutionised the army and the Ottoman relationship with its Christian subjects when he created the Janissaries. However, the main component to any economy is its currency, and Murad made this more relevant too. The *akçe* had been the standard coinage of the Ottomans from the time of Osman. Some in circulation were gold, but the silver ones became more common during the times of Osman and Orhan. Murad added a copper version, and this new coin replaced the more expensive (and therefore more regularly debased) silver coin. Throughout this era the Ottoman money had to compete with more established currencies, most notably the widespread and highly regarded currencies of Venice and Genoa. However, the Ottoman currency was beginning to develop a positive reputation, which helped with trade negotiations because a strong currency indicated a healthy state. Murad didn't just have an eye on the army.

This sultan was the first Ottoman ruler to grow up with an established state around him. Bursa would have always felt like an Ottoman city to Murad. His ideas could be grander in scope than those of Osman simply because he had far more in the way of resources. So it was that Murad was the first Ottoman ruler to push into Europe and is, therefore, the first Ottoman ruler to generate worry among Christian rulers other than the Byzantines. He also recognised that his lands were too extensive to be directly ruled by him, so he split the empire into two provinces: the Anadolu (Anatolia) province, encompassing all the lands east of the Bosphorus, and the Rumeli (the Balkans) province, which encompassed everything on the other side – Europe, in other words.

Christian concerns about the growing power of Murad turned into war in the 1360s. Ever since the 1090s, the popes had called for holy wars, crusades, against the infidel in the East. The story of the crusades is a long one, but they had morphed from straight journeys to Jerusalem into all kinds of Christian military activity. By the 1360s, crusaders were fighting Orthodox Christians in what is now modern-day Ukraine, expanding Aragon in the Iberian peninsula and conducting high seas piracy against Muslim shipping in the eastern Mediterranean. It was a far cry from those earlier days when the goal had been to capture Jerusalem. However, Pope Urban V managed to whip up enough enthusiasm in Europe to create a crusade against the Ottoman capture of Byzantine land in Europe around Gallipoli. This was the so-called Savoyard Crusade, led by Amadeus VI, Count of Savoy. It was a coalition force uniting the kingdoms of Bulgaria and Hungary with knights from Western Europe, with support from the Byzantines; its purpose was to oust the Ottomans. (Interesting aside: In order to gain Western support, the then current Byzantine Emperor, John V Palaiologos, had to bring the Greek Orthodox Church back into alignment with the Roman Catholic Church after the schism in 1054, something that had been the goal of popes for centuries. The powerful Byzantine Church had always resisted, but in 1354 the Byzantines, now on their last legs, reluctantly and regretfully agreed to reunify the Church in return for military assistance.) In August 1366, Western crusaders, along with an alliance of Bulgarians and Byzantines, arrived by ship in the Dardanelles and surrounded the town of Gallipoli. On the very first night, the governor and all the high-ranking residents of the town escaped and were nowhere to be seen when the people threw open the gates to the crusaders the next day. It had been a surprisingly easy victory for the Christians and is considered one of the last effective offensive attacks ever achieved in a crusade – although it was unlikely ever to be the stuff of legend.

Amadeus spent roughly the next year roaming around the edges of Constantinople, attacking various Ottoman forts and outposts. They were small change, and because the crusade was meant to be self-financing through plunder Amadeus urgently needed any goods he could lay his hands on to pay for the ships that had brought him to the Dardanelles. That he found it difficult to raise funds from the plunder strongly implies that these lands were poor. Also, had Amadeus attacked a key territory such as Bursa it is certain that Murad would have brought the full might of his forces to counter the modestly sized crusade. Instead, he waited. Rather than attempt to reclaim Gallipoli as part of some great campaign, Murad put his military might to one side and used his canny political mind instead. Once again, the Byzantine court eventually descended into internecine conflict, followed by naked aggression. The resulting three-year civil war between John V and his son Andronicus IV meant one of them was going to ask for Ottoman assistance. It was Andronicus who made the best deal, and the entire area that had been captured by the crusade was returned to Murad in 1376–7. The crusade's achievements had been fleeting and were undone by the self-destructive tendencies of the Byzantine court (which had reneged on the unification of the two churches as well).

Murad had recaptured an area of land without having to go to war, but another prize taken from the Byzantines was gained through force as Byzantium's third city of Adrianople was attacked by the Ottomans around this time. The exact date is contested, but what isn't contested is that, although it was extremely important to the Byzantines and had stout walls, Adrianople was feebly defended. The main defending force was annihilated during a night battle called the Battle of Sırp Sındığı, in English the 'battle of the destruction of the Serbs'. You can tell from the title it was a decisive Ottoman victory. The defenders were a mixture of Bulgarians and Serbs and their army was of considerable size. The Ottomans may have had the smaller force, but they had the element of surprise when they slipped into the Christian camp under the cover of darkness and decimated the allied army. Those not killed or wounded fled into the night, leaving Adrianople vulnerable. It seems that the actual siege wasn't conducted by Murad's forces but by Turkish allies. The reason for this theory is that, although there can be little doubt that Adrianople fell in the 1360s, Murad did not take full control of the city until 1376.

Coffee

Coffee drinking comes from fifteenth-century Yemen. It is thought to have originated with Islamic holy men who wished to drink something that wasn't alcohol but still had a kick to it. It was not a feature of the empire at this early stage, but over the years the Ottomans developed a reputation for being extremely effective night fighters. While it could have been just

---

luck that some of their more daring night raids paid off, there is speculation that this night-time effectiveness might have been due to the caffeine in coffee. As Muslims, Ottoman soldiers would not have indulged in alcohol, whereas Western soldiers would have drunk beer or wine at the end of the day, and the alcohol would have made them lethargic and clumsy. 'Turkish coffee' is espresso with hair on its chest. In a midnight battle where these two drinks were facing each other, it's hardly surprising that later Ottoman armies did well in night-time raids.

Another puzzling thing about the capture of Adrianople is that it was renamed Edirne and turned into the third Ottoman capital – but ten years after it was captured. (Bursa was captured and immediately made the new capital.) The reason for the gap is unknown but, as previously speculated, it could have been due to its capture by allied forces rather than by Murad himself. Regardless, in 1371 the Serbs were back for revenge, fully intent on recapturing Adrianople. The numbers of the forces are contested, but it seems the Serbian army could have numbered in the tens of thousands, while the Ottomans had a basic garrison of fewer than a thousand. Better yet, the governor of the city, Lala Şâhin Pasha, had been the leader of the Ottoman forces in the earlier battle.

This seemed to be the perfect opportunity for some delicious revenge. However, Lala Pasha decided to use the tactic that had worked before and took the high-risk strategy of sallying out from behind the walls of the city to attack the Serbian camp at night. It was his only option. At the time Murad was campaigning in Anatolia (where he captured Antalya, a town on the south coast, which enabled the Ottomans to open up maritime trade with the Middle East and beyond for the first time), so it would be months before a relief force could come to Lala Pasha's aid, and in the meantime he was seriously outnumbered. Lala Pasha therefore used the same tactic with exactly the same outcome, and a significantly smaller Ottoman army shattered a much larger Serbian one. It was a terrible humiliation and ensured that Adrianople would remain Edirne and beyond Byzantine Greek control (it is now the most westerly city in the Republic of Turkey).

Once the Ottomans had secured Edirne, the door to the Balkans opened. In the same year the towns of Chernomen, Sozopol, Drama, Kavála and Serrai were all captured. With two major defeats in a decade, the forces of the Balkan princes were diminished, while the status of the 'Turks' as fearsome warriors now bordering Christian lands only added to the growing reputation of Ottoman power. By the late 1370s, the Byzantine capital of Constantinople was completely surrounded by the Ottomans. In every way that mattered, it had become an Ottoman vassal state and paid Murad an annual stipend. Its only contact with the outside world came from the still functioning, still profitable trade routes with Venice and Genoa. It seemed time was about to run out for the once-great emperors of the Eastern Roman Empire. It was a similar story for the *beys* of Aydin. These were the Turkmen rulers who, in the time of Osman, had taken Ephesus. They had once been the premier power in south-western Anatolia, but now all the lands adjacent to them were held by Murad, whose eldest son Bayezid was fighting against the Karamanids, another Turkish group, in central and south-eastern Anatolia. It was Bayezid's rapid (some would say impetuous) deployments and tactics that would give him the nickname *Yildirim* (lightning bolt). Bayezid was a long way from the heartlands of Ottoman territory and did well to fight the Karamanids to the negotiating table, further spreading Ottoman influence while enhancing his reputation.

Apart from a temporary loss of territory at the start of the Savoyard Crusade, Murad's only serious military setback came in the mid-1380s when Lala Şâhin Pasha was pushing into Serbia with around 20,000 light cavalry horse archers. The fact that this was not the main Ottoman army but a scouting/raiding mission is yet another indication of how far the Ottomans had come in the space of just one generation. (By comparison, an English army of the time would struggle to reach 10,000 men, although English archers would make up for their lack of numbers.) Pločnik was a small Serbian town that Lala Pasha knew was defended by a large Serbian army. Despite putting out scouts, he could not find the Serbian host. However, the Serbs were very much in the area and they struck when Lala Pasha's men were out of formation, busy plundering the town and the surrounding area. The Serb heavy cavalry managed to box in the more agile but lightly armoured Ottoman cavalry and annihilated it. The Serbs themselves had their own horse archers and used them on their flanks to harass and further spread chaos in the ranks of Lala Pasha's cavalry. Having lost a significant portion of his troops, Lala Pasha had no choice but to retreat. This victory for the Serbs meant that their heartlands were safe, and the Battle of Pločnik is celebrated as a time when the Serbs held their Muslim enemies at bay.

However, this is not to say that it was a serious defeat for Murad. Methodical and patient as ever, he carefully built up his main forces and invaded Serbia in 1389. While a number of battles have already been mentioned, we now come to one of the epic clashes that have echoed down the centuries. The Battle of Kosovo is keenly remembered in a number of countries, and, indeed, the area of Kosovo is still in a state of unease today because of what happened there more than six centuries earlier. Kosovo itself is tiny, but it was a network hub. In an area of dense forests and jagged mountains, it was an important crossroads. Whoever held Kosovo held the key to the Balkans. If it fell, the Ottomans would have multiple directions in which to advance.

As always with medieval clashes, exact numbers of troops are hard to determine, but it seems that Murad had a force of roughly 30,000 against a smaller Serbian force (numbers quite often gravitate to the 20,000 mark – particularly impressive considering their defeat, just a few years earlier, at Adrianople). The Serbs were led by Prince Lazar, and while Murad was in charge this time he also had several sons at the battle, notably his second-oldest, Yakub Çelebi, and his oldest, Bayezid, who had already proved to be a natural at the art of war. Most of Murad's forces were cavalry, and although the Janissaries were also there they only numbered around 2,000. The Battle of Kosovo illustrates the classic differences between the Eastern and Western tactics of the day. Murad needed space to position his horse archers, who could charge, feint and harry from afar. The Serbs, with their heavy European armour, were slower but their steel armour made them harder to hurt.

It was the Serbian heavy cavalry that struck the first blow of the day. Charging in their classic wedge formation, they smashed into Murad's left flank like a freight train into a pen of livestock. However, after the initial shock, the Serbs got bogged down in hand-to-hand fighting and the heavy cavalry made no further impact; they had to be content with pinning down just one of Murad's flanks. The rest of the Serbian army attacked, and Murad's centre was pushed back but held. This would have been where the Janissaries were fighting, and it was only the right wing, led by Bayezid, which didn't falter under the initial assaults by the Serbs.

The fighting was brutal. Both sides record that their losses were high, so it was like a meat grinder on the day. The Ottomans began a counter-attack led by Bayezid's flank. He managed to start pushing the Serbian forces back, creating some much-needed momentum for the Ottoman attacks. By the end of that bloody day it was Bayezid's troops who had effectively routed the Serbian infantry. As the butchery continued something pivotal happened, but unfortunately the only accounts come from poems and much later versions. So, let's try to unpick the most likely sequence of events based on what can be discerned. A contemporary account states that twelve Christian noblemen, 'having penetrated the enemy lines and the circle of chained camels, heroically reached the tent of Murat [*sic*] ... (and killed him) by stabbing him with a sword in the throat and belly'.

While this contemporary account claims to describe how Murad died, it doesn't quite ring true. The idea that a dozen Serbs were able to break through the entire central force of the Ottoman army, which we know held for the whole battle, doesn't make sense. Instead, there is a later report that as the Serb lines crumbled a Serbian aristocrat (often named as Miloš Obilić) pretended to defect and was brought before the sultan. Murad, sensing that any change to the battle would finally break the deadlock, met Miloš in his private tent, where the Serb lunged forward and stabbed Murad before the guards reacted and hacked Miloš to death. This would make more sense against the overall events of the day. Either way, after twenty-seven years of rule, Murad lay dead in a pool of his own blood, the first (and only) Ottoman ruler to die not so much 'in' battle as 'during' battle. Of course, had the contemporary version of the raid been true, the entire Ottoman army would have been alerted to the fate of Murad and most likely would have dispersed when the news broke of the death of their sultan. As it was, a lone assassin would have meant that his death could be kept secret until after the battle.

The Serbian leader Lazar also fell in battle (again there are conflicting accounts of exactly what happened). It is rare to have both sides admit to heavy losses, and it is even rarer to have the leaders of both sides die in the same battle. It was an epically bloody clash in which it is almost impossible to overemphasise the scale of the carnage, and as such it remains an integral part of Serbian history. Both armies retreated from the field of battle. To historians this means it was an inconclusive clash, but according to Serbian history this is the time when Serbia held back the Muslims. However, the Ottomans could absorb the heavy losses far better than the Serbs, who had thrown all they had into the fight. Furthermore, in Bayezid the Ottomans were lucky enough to have one of the most fearsome warriors in Ottoman history at the scene and ready to take over his father's throne, whereas the Serbs had Lazar's son, Stefan Lazarevic, who was still a child. What seemed initially to be a deadlock was actually a long-term strategic victory for the Ottomans as the Serbs never truly recovered from their losses at the Battle of Kosovo. For the time being, however, the mighty Ottomans had been halted by the brave sacrifices of the Christian Serbs.

Kosovo was defended by Serbian blood, and this is still very much remembered in Serbia. Because of this, Serbians still consider Kosovo to be 'theirs' even though the ethnic and religious makeup of the area no longer reflects this. Today Kosovo and its surrounding area is a Muslim enclave, which rankles Serbian sensibilities – and before someone says they should get over it, let's look at an apt analogy for the British reader. How would a Brit feel if the area around the Battle of Hastings was called 'Little France' and was a place where everything British was rejected? What if it was an area that served only French food, where the locals spoke only French and played accordion music under the Tricolour (apologies for the French clichés, but you get the idea)? An analogy closer to home makes the Serbian position more understandable.

Murad is that rarest of people, someone who has two tombs. Islamic law requires that the dead be buried almost immediately, but Kosovo would have been the wrong place to bury Murad. After all this time, it was not yet under Ottoman control. Instead, a compromise was made: Murad's internal organs were deposited in a tomb that still stands today in Kosovo. The mausoleum was ordered and paid for by Bayezid and is the first example of Ottoman architecture in the territory of Kosovo. You can see how potentially inflammatory that is to the Serbian community, and yet any attempt to remove the tomb or the remains would be equally offensive to the local Muslim population – and of course to the Republic of Turkey. Murad's body was transported not to Edirne, the newer and closer capital of the empire, but to Bursa, where he was laid to rest with the early Ottoman rulers. In fact, Bursa would continue to be the city of the tombs of the sultans until the conquest of Constantinople in 1453.

As if the previously mentioned deaths were not enough, there was another high-profile death at the time of the Battle of Kosovo. Bayezid, on hearing of the death of his father, found his younger brother Yakub Çelebi and strangled him. Whereas the previous rulers had had good relationships with their brothers, in this instance there appeared to be little or no hesitation on Bayezid's part, and it is with Bayezid that we start to see the deadly game siblings played as they jockeyed to become the next sultan. Bayezid did such a good job of wiping Yakub Çelebi from history that very little is known about him. Bayezid wanted the focus to be on him, and that's exactly what he got.

Prior to Bayezid, the early Ottoman rulers were multi-layered, able to balance governing with martial prowess, spirituality with diplomacy. Bayezid, by comparison, was far less nuanced; he was a warrior first and foremost and he was a very good one. His ruthless act of fratricide was to be the first death in a reign that, at times, seems to have been one long military campaign and little else. This does, however, make Bayezid's an unusually good story.

3

A Storm from the East

Bayezid was an intelligent man who carried out some remarkably thoughtful strategies. For example, after the slaughter at the Battle of Kosovo, he married Lazar's daughter, Princess Olivera Despina, a union that placed a veil of legitimacy over Serbia's new status as a vassal to the Ottomans. Despite the marriage and the fact that she was now living in the growing imperial harem, the princess (unusually) did not convert to Islam, but she did have quite a hold on her husband, even going out on campaign with him. This put her in considerable danger, as we shall see later.

Bayezid was also clever in his clashes with the Muslim rulers of Anatolia, where he would often try to create a legal precedent for an attack (similar to the way Orhan interceded in a Muslim civil war in his role as a 'peacemaker'). This was another deceit to cover the reality of Bayezid's expansionist imperial policy. The Turkmen of Anatolia had regularly supplied Bayezid with cavalry and soldiers to fight in Europe, so to avoid any conflict of interest or betrayal, a large proportion of the troops he used in Anatolia against these erstwhile allies were Serbs and Byzantine soldiers (as well the loyal Janissaries). This is a reminder that an 'Ottoman' army was not the same thing as a 'Turkish' or, indeed, 'Muslim' army.

As we know from earlier mentions, the Seljuk realms of south-western Anatolia were now surrounded by Ottoman lands. In 1390, just a year into his reign, Bayezid pounced. Three independent states ruled by local *beys* were captured in one campaigning season, including Aydin, the state which had demanded Ephesus from Osman nearly a century earlier. But Bayezid didn't stop there. On through the winter of 1390 and into 1391, he travelled as far as the Mediterranean shores of south-central Anatolia and then turned his army north, conquering all before him until he reached the northern coastline and could look out on the Black Sea. Every Turkish alliance raised against Bayezid fell under his sword as he led his triumphant army across Anatolia, mopping up the areas his ancestors either didn't have the time or the power to overcome. The speed of his conquests made his epithet of 'lightning bolt' seem ominously accurate. Now the whole of western and central Anatolia, including both sides of the Bosphorus Strait, were under Ottoman rule. Bayezid's lands stretched unbroken into the Balkans – except for the fortress city of Constantinople. Surely it was only a matter of time before it fell to him.

Hadith

Non-Muslims are aware that the Muslim holy book is the Qur'an. What is less well known is that there is additional information about the Prophet Mohammed's life in a collection of attributed sayings called the Hadiths. The Hadiths are problematic. They are of unknown origins and vary throughout the Islamic world, and if all of the Hadiths attributed to him truly had been said by the Prophet he would have had little time to do anything other than make memorable declarations. The Hadiths have been the subject of debate among Islamic scholars for more than a thousand years. Some are contradictory, while others are clearly variations of an original, and it is the content of some of these that has been used to justify terrible crimes committed by Islamic zealots. But there is one Hadith in particular that is pertinent to the story of the Ottomans and occurs when the Prophet was being complimented as the greatest general ever. His response was that this could not be true because whoever was able to capture Constantinople would be the greatest ever general. Whether this was ever genuinely uttered by the Prophet Mohammed is, in a way, irrelevant. Belief in the Hadith painted a target for Muslims on Constantinople's walls. The city became an obsession for many Islamic leaders because the whole world, both Christian and Muslim, would remember the name of the man who conquered Constantinople. If, in fact, the Prophet did make this declaration, he chose his target well.

The walls of Constantinople were some of the best ever built, and from the time of Constantine to the time of Bayezid there had been eleven attempted sieges by Bulgarians, Slavs and a number of early Muslim attackers. You can add a further three during Byzantine civil wars. Only one force had got into the city – during the Fourth Crusade of 1204 – but that was more through duplicity than siege craft, so, as far as the whole world was concerned, the walls of Constantinople remained unbreached for more than a thousand years.

Bayezid was naturally cautious about directly assaulting a city that had resisted everyone before him. In the early 1390s, he surrounded Constantinople's land side even though he knew it could still be resupplied by sea. He sought to push away from the city any potential land-based allies so that the isolation from friendly forces would make the emperor, Manuel II Palaeologus (son of John V Palaeologus), accept the inevitable. But Manuel was an emperor who had been taken hostage by Bayezid, and had been forced to join him on his campaign against the Byzantines and allied peoples. He would rather have been the last man standing in the smouldering ruins of Constantinople than do anything Bayezid wanted.

News of the desperate situation in Constantinople, and the fact that Bayezid was further expanding his territory to the detriment of Christian princes, reached Rome. Boniface IX was pope at the time, but he had his own problems as the papacy was currently in the middle of a Western schism. There was a second pope in Avignon, and the two popes weren't exactly exchanging Christmas cards. Boniface called for a crusade, but nobody paid any attention. However, Eastern powers used this as a rallying cry to help justify an uneasy but necessary alliance against Bayezid. So a new 'crusade' marched into Bulgaria. (I put crusade in inverted commas because it had no official support, either from a papal bull of indulgence or from a crusading tax to help finance it.) Troops came from as far afield as the Holy Roman Empire, France, Hungary, Venice and Genoa, and were bolstered by the local forces of Bulgaria and Wallachia (Romania) as well as that essential addition to any crusader army, the Knights Hospitaller. What is telling, however, is that most of these foreign forces only sent small contingents. France was in the midst of fighting England in the Hundred Years War, although this campaign did come during a lull in hostilities. The entire army as a result seems to have been only 14,000–15,000 strong, against an Ottoman army of around 20,000. The leader of this Christian coalition was Sigismund of Luxemburg, who was notoriously hard to pin down with regards to his exact title. At this time he was Prince-elector of Brandenburg, but he would go on to be King of Hungary, King of Germany, King of Bohemia, King of Italy and then, to tidy up most of those titles, Holy Roman Emperor until his death in 1437. Sigismund, like Bayezid, shows how fluid identity was in the pre-industrial era. The idea of nationalism didn't exist at this point in history. This was a time when men ruled territories that were a mishmash of languages, ethnicities and religions, and no one felt the need to do anything about it.

The two sides met near the fortress of Nicopolis, where the crusaders were already laying siege. Nicopolis may have been small, but it was positioned on the junction of a major road and the Danube River, and was, therefore, on a key communications route. Perhaps most shockingly, seeing that much of crusading and Middle Ages history is about sieges, this particular crusading army hadn't thought to bring any siege weapons with them, and they had no siege engineers to build the trebuchets and other siege equipment for a direct assault. Instead, the crusade surrounded Nicopolis and tried to starve out its Ottoman defenders. Discipline in the crusaders' camp was lax, with many treating this more as a hunting party than a military campaign. There were stories of feasting and general revelry, which may have been a psychological ploy to taunt those behind the fortress walls (although after just two weeks the defenders' own stores would hardly have been low). Regardless, the crusaders' carelessness had lethal consequences.

It seems Sigismund was unaware of Bayezid's reputation for moving like a lightning bolt, so when the news arrived that Bayezid's relief force was just miles away it surprised the Christian camp and everyone stopped partying. The French cavalry were sent out and clashed with some of Bayezid's scouts, but the French feigned a retreat, which fooled the Ottomans, who were cut down. When the French knights returned and reported how easy their victory had been, the men in the camp relaxed. It seemed that Christian knights were vastly superior to the Muslim infidel. Nevertheless, the arrival of the Ottoman main army, seemingly from out of nowhere, sent panic through the camp. In the resulting chaos, someone ordered the execution of the thousands of Ottoman captives so far rounded up, and it was back to the bad old days of Richard the Lionheart, who killed his captives during the Third Crusade. Even Western sources say this was a murderous and unnecessary act – and anyway it didn't stop Bayezid from bearing down on the crusaders. When the two sides met on 25 September 1396, the crusader army stood between Bayezid and Nicopolis. This was the ultimate aggressive move, as it meant there was a possibility of being attacked from the rear by the garrison of the fort, and any retreat would have been blocked by the Danube. It was a bold statement of intent, and spirits were high among the Christians after the initial clash between the French and the Ottoman scouts.

Bayezid had chosen a rally point on top of a hill, with his Janissaries in the centre behind a wall of sharpened logs. These massive stakes were designed to break up the European heavy cavalry that was likely to be used to batter either his flanks or centre. Bayezid hid these behind a screen of light infantry, the perfect target for heavy cavalry. On his flanks he had his Serbian infantry and Anatolian horse archers. The heavy cavalry of the French and the Knights Hospitaller took the initiative – and the bait – and charged at Bayezid's centre. The European heavy cavalry, in full plate armour with their lances pointed at the infantry below them, cut through the poorly equipped soldiers like a hot knife through butter – and then they ploughed into the stakes. This anti-cavalry wall of spikes is mentioned by most sources. The European knights may have been clad in steel armour, but their horses were not. There is about ten times the amount of blood in a horse as there is in a man. The stallions would have impaled themselves on the sharp wooden points at charging speed. The riders would have been thrown off with great force, and some would have broken bones on landing. The horses would not have died instantly. Instead the front line would have become a frothing, writhing mess of screaming horses trying to remove their traumatised bodies from the impaling spikes, while gallons of blood poured from their wounds. The front line would have quickly been churned into a gory mess of mud and blood, both human and horse.

All of this was happening under the withering fire of the Janissary bowmen. And yet, even in this Hades of horror, some of the knights were able to break through (and break down) the wall of stakes and continue to push into the centre, where the Anatolian cavalry came in close and the real fight began. Many of the knights were now on foot but believed that their initial shock charge, while halted, had destroyed most of Bayezid's force. They were wrong. Bayezid had sacrificed his lowly conscripts to draw the cream of the crusader forces into a hard fight. Their heavy armour, the fight up the hill and the sheer weight of Ottoman numbers all played against the knights. Bayezid tried to close the trap by sending his Turkish horsemen to surround the crusader flanks, but Sigismund saw what was happening and pushed both his and the Serbian troops forwards to stop the envelopment. In the chaos a number of (mainly French) crusader groups thought all was lost and abandoned the fight. Their departure, while premature, helped ensure victory for Bayezid as the Ottoman force rolled down the hill, causing the crusader ranks to break their formations. Sigismund barely had time to get on a fishing boat to flee to the safety of the Venetian ships waiting in the Danube before the remaining Christian force was overwhelmed. He later said, 'We lost the day by the pride and vanity of these French. If they believed my advice, we had enough men to fight our enemies.' While blame can be heaped on the French, Bayezid held the advantage throughout the battle, and Sigismund was simply outclassed by a superior general.

After the battle, Bayezid, a man who had not hesitated to murder his own brother, was horrified to find the massacred Ottoman prisoners in the crusader camp. He picked out the Christian nobles worth ransoming and ordered that the rest of the troops be massacred in retaliation. The men were stripped naked and bound together in groups of three or four, with their hands tied. Then they were paraded in front of Bayezid, where they were either decapitated or had their limbs hacked off, while the captives who were to be ransomed were made to watch. By the afternoon Bayezid either got bored or felt the point had been made and stopped the macabre procession. Thousands lay dead, a number similar to the number the Christians had murdered. But far more lay dead in the field behind him. The Battle of Nicopolis was a bloody but emphatic victory for Bayezid. It highlights his ruthless efficiency and how, after nearly a decade of campaigning, he had yet to face defeat. He had fought against many different enemies in many terrains and on many occasions. He was truly one of the great generals.

Now Bayezid turned his attention to the one prize that had so far eluded him: Constantinople. Since all his battles and conquests had been land-based he had had no need for a navy, and he lacked the siege craft and equipment to capture the city. Even if he could hastily construct a navy, he would have been unable to match the quality of ships produced by the established Italian fleets – so Bayezid stuck to what he was good at. He sat it out at the walls of Constantinople and kept pressure on the city. The major relief force the Byzantines had been desperately awaiting had been destroyed at Nicopolis. It was only a matter of time until Constantinople surrendered, and, as Bursa and Nicaea had demonstrated, the Ottomans were more than willing to wait years for a major walled city to capitulate.

Then a storm arrived, a most unexpected twist of fate. As fearsome and proficient a warlord as Bayezid was, he wasn't the only one. Far to the east, in modern Uzbekistan, there was another general who was to lead the last great wave of conquests on horseback. He was the 'Sword of Islam', the mighty and terrible Emir Timur, known in the West as Tamerlane (and referred to by the latter hereafter).

Bayezid was born into the leadership of a growing empire. He was taught by the best scholars, lived in a palace and expected to inherit the Ottoman realm. Tamerlane's start in life could not have been more different, born as he was into poverty. In his twenties he was reduced to livestock theft, and it was while attempting to steal some sheep that he was shot by two arrows, one in his right leg and another in his right hand, where he lost two fingers. These injuries paralysed him down the right side of his body and gave him his name, 'Timur the lame' – Tamerlane. Despite his lowly start in life, Tamerlane, from an early age, had shown every bit as much ability to lead as had Bayezid. Both were men of war, fearsome in their conduct and lightning fast in their attacks. But Tamerlane took things to another level. While the massacre of Christian knights after the Battle of Nicopolis was condemned in Europe (although it was the Christians who had carried out the first massacre), we are talking about 2,000 to 3,000 men. Think instead of Isfahan, a city in Persia (modern Iran). When it capitulated without a fight, Tamerlane allowed its residents to continue as normal. But when Isfahan rose up against Tamerlane's tax inspectors and killed them, the people of the city could not have known what a catastrophic mistake they had made. Tamerlane arrived with an army and massacred the entire population. He was emulating the terror tactics of the Mongols under Genghis Khan – except that Tamerlane was cunning. He left after the massacre, only to return one week later, when he knew he would find some survivors, those who had been hiding under bodies or successfully concealed in the ruins. When he came back, he killed everyone who had survived the first massacre. Outside the city, Tamerlane left a grim warning. An eye-witness counted more than twenty-eight towers constructed of about 1,500 heads each – that's at least 42,000 people, although the actual death toll is put at 100,000 to 200,000. And this wasn't the only massacre he carried out.

It is a gross understatement to say that Tamerlane was not a man to avoid a fight. He was once an ally of Tokhtamysh, Khan of the Golden Horde, a Mongol ruler who had crushed other Mongol rulers and had re-imposed Mongol rule on the Russians. It was almost inevitable the two would fall out, and they fought across great swathes of central Asia for a decade. Tamerlane eventually beat the Mongol khan; however, it is the battle for Delhi in 1398 which best shows both his ingenuity and his calm under pressure. Tamerlane's army was made up largely of light cavalry horse archers, much like the Mongol armies of a century earlier. At Delhi he faced a vast Indian army, supported by armour-plated elephants. Tamerlane knew that horses refuse to charge elephants, which was a major problem under the circumstances, but he came up with a cunning plan because he also knew that all animals are terrified of fire. He took the pack camels from his supply corps and loaded their backs with hay and sticks. Then he ordered these bundles to be set alight and the camels prodded forwards. As this wall of stampeding and screaming camels charged towards the elephants, they panicked and began trampling the Indian army. Tamerlane won and captured Delhi.

Putting all these stories together (and there are many more), it is obvious Tamerlane was a military commander of great talent. Even though he was now in his mid-sixties, he set his sights on the Ottoman Empire. During the few years between Delhi and his eventual clash with Bayezid in 1402, Tamerlane fought as far afield as Georgia, Baghdad and Damascus. He was heading inexorably west, and that meant Bayezid's lands were the obvious next target.

Bayezid was still besieging Constantinople when he heard the news that Tamerlane was moving into Anatolia with an entire army. He reluctantly left the Byzantine capital, allowing it to catch its breath until he returned. When Bayezid heard that the local Turkish chieftains in central Anatolia were switching their allegiances to Tamerlane, he could almost hear the hooves of Tamerlane's troops. Bayezid did not underestimate the force he was up against. It was said by multiple sources that he gathered together the largest army the West had ever seen. While it may not actually have been as big as the entire might of Rome's legions, it is still estimated to have been around 85,000 strong. Compare that to the Battle of Agincourt in 1415, when the French and the English between them could muster only around a quarter of that number. The size of Tamerlane's army is unknown but was even bigger, perhaps even twice the size of Bayezid's. The Ottoman sultan marched his army across Anatolia in the searing summer sun until the two sides met in the field of Çubuk, just outside the town of Ankara, in an epic clash between the generation's greatest military leaders (I have a soft spot for Henry V, but he wouldn't have stood a chance against these men and their resources). Neither Tamerlane nor Bayezid had ever before lost a battle, but one of these men was about to taste defeat for the first time.

It is fair to say that the Battle of Ankara was a pivotal historic clash, and this is because the impact of the events of 20 July 1402 would be felt for many years to come by people in many different lands. It was far more important than the Battle of Agincourt – then again, Shakespeare never wrote a play about Bayezid (although Marlow wrote one about Tamerlane) – and yet this pivotal conflict is obscure in the West because nobody from the West fought in it. To be fair, Bayezid would have brought together forces from all over his empire, so Greeks, Serbs and Bulgarians would have been fighting on that day, but they were Ottoman subjects who never got to tell their story to the chroniclers in Italy or France. I mentioned earlier that Bayezid's Serbian wife, Olivera Despina, sometimes rode out with him, and she was with him on this campaign.

A Storm from the East

The days leading up to the battle were a deadly game of cat and mouse. Bayezid knew Tamerlane's force was almost entirely cavalry, and as such was fast and mobile. He spent days scouring the area trying to find Tamerlane and his vast army. Tamerlane, however, was always one step ahead of Bayezid, at one point resting his troops in one of Bayezid's abandoned encampments after he had moved on with his Ottoman army. So, when more than 200,000 soldiers faced each other in central Anatolia, it was Tamerlane who had chosen the site of the battle, and even though Bayezid had the home advantage his troops were tired from the constant marching. Tamerlane brought not only cavalry but also war elephants from his victories in India. Some say he had managed to equip the elephants with rudimentary flame throwers. However, after Tamerlane had seen what happened when elephants encountered fire, this seems implausible. It is more likely (in the author's opinion) that he opted for the traditional arrangement of a small platform with protective wooden walls and a couple of archers on the backs of the elephants. In any case, not only did Tamerlane have the advantage of numbers but he also had armour-plated war elephants, something that Bayezid did not have and had probably never seen. Consequently, his cavalry were all but useless because, as we now know, horses won't charge elephants.

The accounts of the battle are fairly sketchy and often contradictory regarding events when the two armies finally collided. What is clear is that a pivotal point in the battle took place when some of Bayezid's Anatolian vassals switched sides or melted away, meaning that he was at an even greater numerical imbalance against Tamerlane. However, the core of the Ottoman forces (including the Serbs and the Janissaries, two groups who might not have been expected to fight hard in such an historic confrontation) fought bravely. The battle was vicious and the resulting carnage was enormous. By the end of the day it was said that about 50,000 Ottoman troops lay dead; the same was said of Tamerlane's force. If these numbers are true (and there's no way of knowing for sure), it was one of the bloodiest battles in world history prior to the twentieth century. Bayezid might have been up against a man who was his equal in leadership, but Tamerlane simply had more of everything – plus some elephants. Bayezid had thrown all of his empire's resources into the battle, but he couldn't overcome the fact that Tamerlane's empire was bigger. By the end of that violent and sweltering July day, Bayezid's army was in tatters, and he and his wife Olivera Despina had been captured, showing that Bayezid had personally fought to the bitter end. Tamerlane was now the undisputed leader of the Muslim world.

The Ottomans had two very unlucky rulers in quick succession: Murad was the first and only sultan to die in battle, and Bayezid, his son, was the only sultan ever to be captured in battle. There was a story that Bayezid was taken east in a golden cage, but, in a way, what likely happened was even more unusual. Tamerlane always respected a formidable foe, and it was likely that, even as a captive, Bayezid would have continued to enjoy all the luxuries befitting a sultan – except, of course, his freedom. Bayezid was escorted across the vast interior of Asia, through Persia and on towards Tamerlane's capital of Samarkand in modern-day Uzbekistan. But Bayezid never reached the capital. He fell ill and died on the journey east, and his body was returned to the Ottomans. Along with the other Ottoman rulers, he is buried in the family mausoleum in Bursa.

What of Bayezid's wife? Olivera Despina returned with her husband's body and moved back to Serbia, where she split her time between the courts of her brother and her sister. She died peacefully in 1444. As for Tamerlane, his conquests proved to be ephemeral, much like those of Alexander the Great, and his deeds aren't well remembered anywhere other than in Uzbekistan.

The consequences of the Battle of Ankara are significant for several reasons. First and foremost, the battle threw the political landscape of the Ottoman Empire into turmoil. Bayezid had four sons old enough to take power (a fifth joined in later), and, rather than talk things through (or strangle each other), they fought a civil war that was to last for more than a decade. A century earlier, the Ottoman Empire had barely existed; now it threatened to shatter into mere memory.

When reading about Constantinople and the fact that Bayezid had already started to besiege the city, readers might be thinking it really should have fallen by now – and yet most people know that this only happened due to the final siege of 1453. How could it possibly have hung on for another fifty years? The answer is the Battle of Ankara. It left a power vacuum in the Ottoman state and made the Byzantine emperors sigh with relief as the princes fought for the throne. So a second impact of the battle was a reprieve for Constantinople, and the city's fall was again delayed.

Finally, the battle was to be Tamerlane's last great victory. After subjugating the Ottoman state, he turned his attentions to the Far East and began preparing for war against the Ming Dynasty in China. He began his campaign in the winter of 1404, but died on the campaign trail in 1405. After seeing everything that Tamerlane had done prior to this, it's hard to imagine how a weakened and divided China would have withstood his onslaught, but both China and the Ottoman Empire were saved when his empire split into warring factions (although his descendants would later invade India and set up the Mughal Empire). Some people like to claim that Alexander the Great was the mightiest general in history because he fought for eight years across Asia and was never defeated; Tamerlane captured much of the same area but did most of it paralysed down one side of his body, and he went undefeated for more than thirty years. Somehow, Tamerlane is never mentioned in the same breath as Alexander.

The immediate future of the Ottoman Empire after 1403 seemed most uncertain thanks to the period of civil war fought among the princes, namely Mehmed Çelebi, Isa Çelebi, Süleiman Çelebi, Musa Çelebi and, later, Mustafa Çelebi. The title *çelebi* has no satisfactory English translation but means 'wise', 'of noble birth', 'clever' and 'conscientious', all in one word. These men may have had the title, but they really weren't all that *çelebi*. Mehmed Çelebi was chosen by Tamerlane to be the new sultan, but, as he was the youngest son of Bayezid, his brothers were unlikely to allow him to achieve such an easy rise to power. Bayezid's oldest son, Süleiman, held the capital (Edirne) and ruled all the European lands of the empire. The second son, Isa Çelebi, established himself as ruler of Bursa, the old capital, where the tombs of all the Ottoman rulers were located. Mehmed Çelebi ruled the lands to the east (which were also closest to Tamerlane's conquests). Musa Çelebi came late to the game because he, like Bayezid, had been captured at the Battle of Ankara. This decade-long period was known as the Ottoman Interregnum, when no one was in charge and it wasn't clear to anyone who should be the new sultan.

Mehmed and Isa clashed first when they fought a pitched battle against each other. Isa lost and escaped, but Mehmed sent assassins after him, and he was murdered in the *hammam* (Turkish bath).

Meanwhile, in an attempt to garner popular support, Süleiman began making favourable deals in the Christian lands he ruled. The Serbs, Bulgarians and even the Byzantines felt the burden of Ottoman rule lift, but this freedom soon led to revolts against any kind of Ottoman authority. The populations of these lands could sense weakness; now was the time to shrug off the yoke of Muslim rule. By 1410 Süleiman was not only putting down rebellions, but also fighting his brother Musa. Musa won the battles, and in the process Süleiman saw his army's loyalty drift towards his bother. There are two conflicting reports about how he died. One says Musa ordered his death; the other says that Süleiman was surrounded and killed by disgruntled villagers after fleeing yet another defeat on the battlefield. Either way, Süleiman died and Musa's power rose. It seemed survival of the fittest was starting to hold true for the Ottoman bloodline. Musa put down the Christian revolts, and in 1411 besieged Constantinople for good measure. However, he lacked the resources of his father, and in the meantime Mehmed did a deal with the Byzantine emperor. While Musa was pinned down besieging Constantinople, Mehmed arrived on the scene and, ironically, wound up fighting another Ottoman, even as the siege of the city continued.

The two sides met at the Battle of Çamurlu in July 1413, but this battle started very unusually. Before a shot had been fired, Hassan, the leader of Mehmed's Janissaries, walked alone towards Musa's army, where he spoke out to the assembled men, asking that they change sides. When they agreed, it seemed that the bloody civil war had come to a peaceful end. Musa, however, was far from happy and charged at Hassan, cutting him down. Musa, in turn, was struck by an arrow fired by another Janissary officer on Mehmed's side, so battle commenced. Mehmed won and Musa died as he tried to retreat. The irony of this situation was that Mehmed, the man Tamerlane had declared to be the next sultan, became the next sultan anyway – but only after his brothers lay dead.

Mehmed faced a shattered realm, with many of the states that had been conquered by Murad and Bayezid now semi-autonomous in defiance of his rule. His victory over Musa also meant he had inadvertently lifted another Ottoman siege on Constantinople. He needed to consolidate his power or risk losing everything.

Mehmed had only just settled into his new role as undisputed sultan when the fifth brother, Mustafa Çelebi, captured at the

Battle of Ankara, suddenly arrived on the scene. Quite why he was released so late is unknown. If the plan was to cause further trouble in the Ottoman Empire, it worked. When Mustafa arrived at his brother's court, he asked if they could split the empire between them. While asking is the polite thing to do, Mustafa was never going to be taken seriously and certainly not after Mehmed had had to fight so hard, for so long, to become sultan and rule both Edirne and Bursa. Mustafa didn't take the rejection well and raised an army. But by now Mehmed was very experienced at fighting rebellious brothers, and Mustafa was quickly defeated and (a little unusually) exiled to the island of Lemnos. The fact of the matter was Mustafa had been an annoyance rather than any kind of existential threat to the empire; that time had passed. For long years no one had been in charge, but Mehmed soon got to grips with the situation and brought to heel the Bulgarian and Serb princes who had once had the audacity to think they could resist Ottoman rule.

The Byzantine emperor had recognised that the Ottoman state was weak and vulnerable when it had so many claimants to the throne. For centuries they had been masters of diplomacy and guile. This was in part through necessity because as their resources dwindled the solution of sending an army to deal with the problem became less and less of an option. Instead, by fostering alliances, brokering deals and even arranging advantageous marriages the emperors had managed to resolve difficulties that brute force never could (it's from here that we get the term 'Byzantine plot', meaning complex, convoluted, intricate and murky). So the Byzantines were experts of cunning, and a ploy to introduce another pretender to the throne was a typical Byzantine plot. It seems that the emperor had managed to do a deal with Orhan, a son of one of Mehmed's brothers and therefore a man who would want revenge, not to mention his direct bloodline to the title of sultan. Again, like Mustafa, Orhan was up against a man who had vast experience of dealing with deadly family feuds. As such, Orhan was quickly isolated and, again, Mehmed chose not to kill his challenger (it's conjecture, but perhaps Mehmed had had his fill of fratricide and other family murders) but to have him blinded instead (an old Byzantine method to ensure an opponent was unfit for imperial office).

After all this you would think that Mehmed could finally get on with ruling unopposed, but you'd be wrong. Musa left a poisoned chalice for Mehmed. He had elevated a religious fanatic by the name of Sheikh Bedreddin to the position of his personal religious adviser. The sheikh was charismatic and a great public speaker. He had helped Musa keep his army together, and now he was preaching against Mehmed's rule. Sheikh Bedreddin's version of Islam borrowed bits from all the cultures and religions of the Ottoman Empire. He was a populist and his message was anti-wealth, which was a problem for the landed gentry and for a hereditary ruler. A popular religious leader is harder to neutralise than a military enemy: attack his followers and you look like a tyrant; kill the messenger and you risk making him a martyr or something even greater (just ask the Romans about the problem posed by Jesus). After years of discord between the sheikh and the state, it wasn't Mehmed but his grand vizier, Bayezid Pasha, who caught up with the rebellious cleric and hanged him outside the northern Greek city of Serres. Fortunately, there was no backlash; it seemed the sheikh had held the movement together with his own personality and there was nobody who could take his place. The religious rebellion thus ended with his hanging.

Having dealt with so much instability and uncertainty Mehmed is sometimes referred to as the second founder of the Ottoman Empire, and it is a valid point. A lesser man would have seen his lands fragment and accept that the empire had been reduced to a rump of lands in western Anatolia; from there the empire might well have dissolved completely. It was under Mehmed that the Ottoman Empire faced its most serious threat until the twentieth century, but through brute force, guile and a little luck he managed to repair the damage wrought by the civil war. By the early 1420s, he even had enough stability to go back to expanding the empire. Mehmed died in May 1421, aged just forty. It's not clear how he died, but there was no foul play. Perhaps, after the previous nineteen years of capture, war and rebellion, he was just worn out. However, after the long period of volatility and all the hard work to rebuild the empire, it was understandable that his court officials felt uneasy about the passing of power to the new sultan, Mehmed's son, who would be Murad II.

Even in death, Mehmed had one last vital duty to carry out. Since time was needed to ensure the smooth transition of power to his son Murad, Mehmed's death was not initially reported. The lack of sightings of the sultan led to the Janissaries becoming suspicious, so to stop the gossip an important Islamic law was broken: Mehmed was not buried immediately. Instead, Mehmed's close circle of advisors came up with a macabre plan and had the body of the dead sultan placed in a litter. An official would hide underneath the sultan and (presumably using wires) manipulate his arms so that it appeared Mehmed was stroking his beard. Unbelievably, this worked and bought the time the courtiers so badly needed to have Murad ready to be installed on the throne and to avoid another period of uncertainty. (That was to come anyway, but you have to admire the effort.)

4

Ghosts of the Past Return

Murad II, just sixteen years old, was successfully installed as the new sultan in 1421, and we now have the first Ottoman ruler with a Roman numeral as part of his name.

Murad II was a very young sultan overseeing a realm that had suffered decades of instability. He very much needed to be a capable ruler. His namesake had been killed at the Battle of Kosovo, his grandfather had died a captive of Tamerlane, his father had been forced to fight a bloody civil war against his brothers, and, while Mehmed had done an excellent job of calming the waters after such a tempestuous period, Murad II was in a position to watch everything implode again. Therefore, while Murad II is sandwiched between two more famous periods of Ottoman history, he is vital to the story. Without him, the Ottoman Empire would have had a shelf life of just over a century – and this would be a much shorter book.

Murad II's first problem was another claimant to the throne. At the start of his reign he was hardly more than a boy, succeeding to a throne won through violence and bathed in blood. Enter the Byzantine court, which again played the only card it had by sowing uncertainty.

Although this is not a common term applied to this era, I call it the 'Mustafa Rebellions' for reasons that will become obvious. Mustafa Çelebi, the exiled brother of Mehmed, was back again. When he landed (supported not so subtly by Byzantine ships and troops), he defeated an army sent by Murad II and set himself up as sultan in Edirne.

Names

In general, particularly in Europe, dynasties loved using the same name. For 500 years in Britain, Henry was the name of choice. Edward lasted even longer, from the Anglo-Saxon era to the twentieth century. However, the award for the least originality in monarchs' names has to go to France. Not only did they have eighteen kings called Louis, but ten were called Charles as well. Sometimes rulers changed their names when they ascended the throne so as to have the same name as previous rulers of the dynasty. This makes sense; in the modern world of brand recognition, we understand the idea that a brand name is associated with certain qualities. Monarchs also understood this, and often used the same name as, say, a famous warrior king or one whose name is associated with significant social progress. This connection also explains why some names are never used again. In the case of England, there was only ever one King Stephen because he usurped the throne, his son wasn't king and he ruled during what was, essentially, a twenty-year civil war. Who would want to be associated with that? Considering that the Ottoman story is all about one dynasty, it's interesting that sultans were often willing to have different names. While some names crop up more often than others, it seems the sultans were willing to be their own men rather than relying on name recognition to enhance expectations.

It seemed as if the Ottoman lands would be divided and a bloody civil war would tear it to pieces yet again. The only thing that could save the situation was a quick victory for one party or the other, but things were looking bleak for the Ottoman dream.

Mustafa gathered all the troops he could and landed his army in Anatolia. Murad II was looking dangerously vulnerable, but the teenage sultan pulled together his own army and met Mustafa in battle. Quite unexpectedly, Murad II was able to outmanoeuvre his uncle, and the sheer raw skill of the young sultan led to a number of Mustafa's troops switching sides. What had looked like an easy victory for Mustafa turned into a chaotic rout. He fled back across the Bosphorus while Murad II stopped to negotiate naval support from the Genoese. After some brief haggling, Murad II marched on Gallipoli, his uncle's new base of operations. The Ottoman and Genoese armies besieged the town, eventually storming it and capturing Mustafa, who was brought before Murad II and executed. The threat to the stability of Murad II's reign had been permanently neutralised. All this happened within months of Murad II's accession to the throne, and he had shown remarkable martial and organisational ability for a sixteen-year-old. It was clear that the new sultan had enormous potential and was not to be underestimated.

Murad II knew that this rebellion had been backed by Constantinople, and he vowed to seek revenge. Enough was enough – it was time to wipe out the one remaining stronghold of Byzantium. Murad amassed a great army and laid siege to the city. The army Murad brought to the walls of Constantinople was large, and his troops were battle-hardened. He also brought a new weapon – for the first time, cannons were used in an attempt to breach the city's seemingly impregnable walls. In those early days the gunpowder was mixed on the field of battle, greatly reducing its effectiveness. Not only that, but any moisture also reduced the efficacy of the charge. This meant that while the cannons were making plenty of noise and their stone ammunition was striking the walls, it was probably with less force than would be generated by a traditional trebuchet. The use of cannons does, however, show that a very young sultan was willing to try new techniques to crack an old problem.

While the cannons weren't as effective as had been hoped, all the Byzantine emperor could do was cower behind his thick walls and pray for a miracle. Murad II's forces dwarfed the resources of the emperor, so even though he could not force a direct assault, the young sultan could always pick up where his father and grandfather had left off and surround the land side of the city to wait.

But Murad had another problem. While he was busy trying to conquer Constantinople, his brother (also called Mustafa), with the backing of various Anatolian nobles, was encouraged to rebel. This Mustafa, often called 'Baby Mustafa' because he was just thirteen at the time, was clearly being manipulated by the nobles. While he may have been just a figurehead, he was the excuse the Anatolian chieftains needed to secure more autonomy. The threat to Murad II and the cohesion of the empire was very real. All of this was happening a long way from the walls of Constantinople, but despite the distance and the logistics Murad reacted quickly. He lifted the siege on the city (where, yet again, the emperors of Byzantium were given a reprieve) and headed east. Meanwhile his brother, who had been thwarted in an attempted siege of Bursa, had captured Nicaea, showing that he was a genuine threat and not to be taken lightly. Meanwhile, Murad, even while heading towards war with his younger brother, approached some of the duplicitous Anatolian *beys* and made them an offer they couldn't refuse. As a result, they betrayed Baby Mustafa. Murad then ordered the execution of his second blood relation called Mustafa within a year, ending the rebellion. While Baby Mustafa was obviously not the first to die in the Ottoman succession disputes, he was the youngest. Sadly, this was to set a precedent. Bayezid had strangled his adult brother, and that was shocking, but now children were being murdered to secure power. However, unlike Bayezid, Murad II had no other option if he wanted to retain power.

Within the first eighteen months of his reign, Murad II had had to fight two rebellions and had besieged Constantinople – and he wasn't yet eighteen years old. All this shows a young man possessed of considerable natural talents. It can't even be argued that he was lucky. He had confronted serious threats to his rule and had handled them with speed and skill. A lesser ruler might well have continued the siege of Constantinople, which, if carried out successfully, would have given him much glory. However, Murad II took the pragmatic approach and did something he probably didn't want to do but which was the right course of action to secure his throne. Everything about his start as sultan showed a great deal of maturity for one so young. After coming close to catastrophe, the next few years of Murad's reign were devoted to stamping his authority on all the erstwhile subject and vassal states. Byzantium began to pay tribute again, the Anatolian warlords were subjugated and Murad II felt secure enough to look at expanding the Ottoman realms once more. In 1422, Murad II arrived at the largest city under Byzantine control other than Constantinople – Thessalonica – which he surrounded with a naval blockade (the first one by the Ottomans) and land forces.

The Byzantines were, at first, the main source of resistance, but mid-siege they handed the city over to the Venetians. This sounds odd, but it actually matched the political assumption of the time that it was better for Byzantium to lose their only other major city to Venice than to the Ottomans; the Venetians were at least nominal allies. Also, given what we know about Byzantine politics and intrigue, they might well have been able to negotiate the return of the city at some later point. At the time, then, it was seen as a wise strategic move to hand Thessalonica over to the Venetians, with their far greater resources, rather than to suffer its inevitable loss to Murad II. If handing over the city seems bizarre, it seems just as surprising that the Venetians would accept Thessalonica as their responsibility in the midst of a siege. What must be remembered is that, by the fifteenth century, Venice was nearing its zenith of power. What it lacked in land it more than made up for in trading power, with an extensive trade network along the Silk Road and offices across Europe and the Mediterranean, backed by one of the world's largest navies of merchant galleys and cogs (larger sailing ships). Its resources were greater than those of some kingdoms. For Venice to obtain a major Eastern trade city in return for the expense of a successfully defended siege seemed a low-risk strategy, particularly compared to the costly war Venice was currently waging with Milan. Furthermore, Venice was used to dealing with the fledgling Ottoman Empire; it had always had more resources and was better funded than the Ottoman Empire, so the Venetians had reason to believe this would be an easy victory. However, they were wrong.

The siege dragged on until 1430, greatly draining the resources of the Venetians, who realised too late just how costly the defence of the city would be. Eventually, after years of encirclement and with the inhabitants on the brink of starvation, Murad II thought the right time had come to carry out an assault, and the city finally fell to him. He had made the correct calculations; the resistance was minimal, and Murad II's losses in what could have been a bloody assault were light. After such long resistance, he allowed his troops to carry out a three-day sacking of the city, and the Janissaries and other troops were able to leave laden with all kinds of loot. Thessalonica would remain an Ottoman possession into the twentieth century and its fall was an ominous sign of how powerful the Ottoman Empire had become – and how Genoa and Venice were now at a tipping point when they were no longer the automatic masters of the area. It was by no means the end of an era, but it was a sign of how far the Ottoman state had come. As a footnote to this changing balance of power, it was under Murad II that the Ottoman navy evolved and grew to notable size, as the siege of Thessalonica shows. While they could not yet threaten the Italian trading nations, the Anatolian horsemen had now become sailors too.

While conducting this siege, Murad II also spent time in south-eastern Anatolia bringing the Karamanid rulers to heel. This was another Turkish domain which had been semi-autonomous for centuries but was now under Ottoman rule. Strictly speaking, it was not yet part of the Ottoman Empire but a vassal state, required to deliver regular tribute and soldiers when ordered to do so. Murad II had altered the face of the empire. From teetering on the edge of implosion it was now confident and expanding, and his struggle with the Karamanids demonstrated again that not all Ottoman expansion was to the detriment of Christian European powers. The Karamanid lands were much further away from Edirne than Bulgaria and Serbia, which showed that Murad II expanded wherever he could rather than automatically picking on nearby Christian princes simply because of their religion. Having said that, after the Karamanids and Thessalonica fell, the Balkans were, again, a target for expansion. Sigismund of Luxemburg (he of the Battle of Nicopolis) had created a new chivalric order in the style of the Order of the Garter, which had been formed a few generations earlier by Edward III of England. These knightly orders were fashionable and popular in the high Middle Ages because they gave access to rulers on an unofficial basis and upheld the core moral principles of the age. Sigismund created the *Societas Draconistarum*, the Order of the Dragon, an association that dedicated itself to the fight against Christendom's enemies – in essence, fighting against Ottoman expansion. One such leader and member of this prestigious order was Vlad II of Wallachia, known as Vlad Dracul (Vlad the Dragon, after he received the title). You might well think that this was Vlad the Impaler, but that was his son, Vlad III Dracula (or 'son of the dragon', which makes the name sound a little more legitimate and a little less terrifying once it has been put in context).

Vlad II spent his time in the eastern courts of Europe, including the Byzantine court, while he waited for his half-brother Alexander I Aldea, Prince of Wallachia, to die or make a mistake. Alexander had become a vassal to the Ottomans, so in 1436, when Alexander died, two things happened: Vlad swiftly made a successful move on the throne, and then he refused to ratify the vassal status of Wallachia, provoking Murad II into war. However, before anyone could react to this newly antagonistic situation, in 1437, Sigismund died; this meant that Vlad couldn't count on support from neighbouring Hungary, where there was a local peasant uprising. Vlad knew how vulnerable this made him, and it must have been through gritted teeth that he went to Murad II's court in Edirne and swore an oath of loyalty. Murad II tested that loyalty just a year later when he invaded Hungary and ordered Vlad to supply troops, which he did. The Ottoman army made good progress, capturing a number of towns along the Sebeş River. When they got to the town of Sebeş itself, it was Vlad who carried out the negotiations – which allowed a peaceful resolution to what otherwise could have been a costly siege. It seemed as though Vlad was playing his role as loyal Ottoman vassal well. A few weeks later and the Ottomans were at the important trade centre of Sibiu, where they laid siege for just over a week while forces not engaged in the siege scoured the local lands, getting as far as Braşov, more than 100 miles to the east. It was at this point that Murad II decided to lift the siege and head for home. It had been a successful campaigning season, with virtually no losses; his army had taken many captives and was now laden with booty – and Vlad had become the obedient vassal.

Vlad II is a symbol of the complexities of being a Balkan Christian prince in the early era of the Ottoman Empire. He desperately wanted to resist but simply didn't have the resources to do so. Murad II (and other sultans) would have preferred to have more allies whose allegiance was based on loyalty rather than on coercion, but they didn't yet have the administrative framework to support that. Instead, there was always an uneasy peace that could be shattered at any time – which is exactly what happened in 1442, when the Voivode (Prince) of Transylvania, John Hunyadi, ambushed an Ottoman army and routed them. Unsurprisingly, Ottoman nobles accused Vlad II of treachery, and he was ordered to Edirne, leaving his son Mircea in charge.

Murad II sent another army to teach the Transylvanians a lesson in the meantime, but that, too, was crushed by Hunyadi. Transylvania was perfect ambush country, with mountainous terrain, thick forests and only a few poorly maintained highways. Nobody is quite sure why Vlad II was released, but he was, and things settled down. His freedom came at a high price, however, as he had to agree to an annual tribute of 500 Wallachian boys to become Janissaries, and his sons Vlad (who will later become 'the Impaler') and Radu became hostages of the Ottoman court. Vlad II was back as a loyal Ottoman subject at exactly the moment the papacy decided to throw one last crusade against the Ottomans into the mix.

Pope Eugene IV was a Venetian who had been forced to flee Rome after he had backed Venice against Milan in the aforementioned war between the two states. This shows a bias towards Venice, and the idea of rallying Europe behind a crusade against the infidel was good PR, which also helped Venice. Furthermore, it allowed the Catholic Church to attempt to again talk to Byzantium about the unification of the Orthodox and Catholic Churches. This was a big deal. The reunification had been ratified at the Council of Florence (that city was a Venetian ally) in 1439. The Byzantine Emperor, John VIII Palaiologos, attended the council with 700 luminaries from the Byzantine court and church. However, the attempt at reconciliation between the churches failed on the streets of Constantinople when the fiercely independent residents refused to agree its legitimacy. Putting this to one side, a papal bull was created that allowed funds to be raised for a crusading army to head east. But this crusade wasn't like the crusades of old. They were about aggressive attacks pushing into new territories and fighting for God by reclaiming holy territory. This crusade was to be a defensive war to bring Christian states in the Balkans back from the brink of permanent absorption into a Eurasian empire; it was also an exclusively eastern European endeavour. England and France were in the final throes of the Hundred Years War, Spain and Portugal were busy pushing back Islamic power on the Iberian peninsula, the Italian states were fighting each other (again) and the Holy Roman Empire was busy with other things. This crusade was drawn largely from Hungary and Poland (both ruled by the young King Vladislav III), Croatia and Wallachia, with some Bulgarian rebels working with a small detachment of Teutonic Knights. Predictably, John Hunyadi was among the leaders eager to fight Murad II.

Things got off to a good start for this crusade. The assembled force was larger than might have been expected for a later crusade, consisting as it did of around 30,000 knights and soldiers who headed into Serbia in the winter of 1443. Its first challenge was the successful capture of the fort at Nish, after which it defeated three different Ottoman relief forces just before the snows of winter blocked the mountain passes. These were not huge setbacks for Murad II, who could always come back to fight again, but by now he had been sultan for more than twenty years and had been vigorous in his duties, so he signed a peace treaty with Vladislav III, guaranteeing an end to hostilities for the next ten years. With peace secured, and in the knowledge that he left the empire in a far better state than when he had inherited it, Murad II retired. This meant that the new sultan was the youngest so far. Mehmed II was just twelve years old, but with his father never too far away and with peace agreed on the European borders, this was the perfect time for the young boy to start learning the ropes. However, the Christians had been negotiating in bad faith, and in the summer of 1444 the crusade was on the move again. Murad II, realising that his twelve-year-old son was in no way equipped to fight a lightning campaign across the Balkans, came out of his self-imposed retirement and rallied his troops to counter the duplicitous crusaders.

Murad II faced the crusader army near the Black Sea fortress of Varna in November 1444. Murad II had more troops, but the sides seemed to have been relatively evenly matched, and the initial clashes were tentative. The Ottoman cavalry probed for weaknesses on the flanks, but they were stoutly resisted. John Hunyadi recognised that some heavy cavalry might be used to break one of the Ottoman flanks and told King Vladislav III to wait until he could organise such an assault. Meanwhile, Murad II's personal tent could clearly be seen by the Christian commanders, and this seems to have beguiled the young king. He ignored the sage words of the more experienced commander and ordered his personal retinue to charge at the Ottoman centre and capture Murad II in his tent.

This moment of bold attack and ultimate failure was, in a way, something like the clash between Richard III and Henry Tudor at the Battle of Bosworth Field about forty years later. Had Vladislav III (or Richard III) broken through the personal guard of the enemy general, he would have cut off the head of the snake and resistance would have melted away. It was a risky strategy, and in both cases the annals agree they got very close to success. Men will fight hard by the side of their king, but if the king is in a high-risk situation in the thick of battle and something goes wrong, it goes wrong quickly and spectacularly. Again, in both cases, the attacking kings paid for their gambles with their lives. Vladislav III's horse either fell into a slit-trench defence around Murad II's tent or was stabbed. In any case, the horse fell and the king was killed by an Ottoman mercenary called Kodja Hazar, who decapitated Vladislav III and presented his head to Murad II.

John Hunyadi returned to see that he could do nothing to assist the failing attack on the Ottoman centre, but he tried to push forwards to reclaim the body of the fallen king. However, with the death of its leader, the crusading army faltered and began to retreat. Murad II was in no mood for mercy. The Christians were chased down and thousands were killed as they tried to flee the battlefield. The ones who were spared were rounded up and sold into slavery (the growing Ottoman navy needed rowers for its galleys). It was a shattering defeat after the high of the Battle of Nish. As for the few men who avoided death or enslavement, winter set in and many died of exposure. John Hunyadi made it back to Hungary with tales of annihilation and a vengeful sultan.

Four years later, in October 1448, there was a final throw of the dice as Hungary and Wallachia met Murad II at the Second Battle of Kosovo. In the intervening time, John Hunyadi had managed to depose Vlad II and showed himself to be a zealous defender against the rising Ottoman tide. This time Hunyadi had about 25,000 troops versus an Ottoman army double that size, and this time both sides brought cannons. Murad II also brought his son Mehmed to be in charge of one of the flanks. Mehmed was then sixteen, about the same age as Murad II had been when he ascended to the throne. This epic clash lasted three days and can be divided into three phases. First of all, the Ottoman flanks were attacked and then reinforced with cavalry. Secondly, John Hunyadi sent in the heavy cavalry to break Murad II's centre, which nearly worked but, when the Hungarian cavalry got bogged down, his infantry was vulnerable to the Ottoman cavalry, so what had started as a potential breakthrough ended up breaking the main force of his army. The last and final phase took place when Hunyadi's encampment was being defended with cannons. The Janissaries overran the camp, killing or capturing most of the remaining force. Hunyadi evaded capture by the Ottomans, only to be imprisoned by a local lord who first toyed with the idea of handing him over to Murad II but, after receiving 100,000 gold florins, thought it would be a better idea to allow him to return to the Hungarian court. It was another overwhelming victory for the Ottomans, which made it two in four years. This humiliation would be remembered in the West when, in less than ten years' time, Byzantium would be desperately calling for help.

After more than twenty years in power, Murad was still protecting his western borders from invasion and was still unable to fully control areas that were vassal states. An example of this occurred in at least in one such state, where hostages were still taken to assure allegiance, and the practice was by no means unique to the Ottomans. Throughout history, if two powers made an uneasy alliance, members of the family of one side were passed over to the other as a gesture of goodwill, trust and, of course, leverage.

Hostages

The hostage-taking scenario had an exotic twist with the Ottomans because the sons of Byzantine emperors and certain Balkan princes spent their youths in the Ottoman court, which gave them access to the science and learning that a pre-Renaissance Europe didn't have. This was the era of the great Islamic astrologer Ala al-Dīn Ali ibn Muhammed, an Uzbek scholar who spent his early career in Persia but later settled in the Ottoman Empire. Ali Kuşçu, as the Ottomans called him, had the intellectual and empirical confidence to challenge the classical Aristotelian model of astronomy, and, for the first time, separated natural philosophy from Islamic astronomy. This allowed astronomy to become a purely empirical and mathematical science. Compare this to Galileo, who, 150 years later, was put under house arrest by the Inquisition for having the empirical data to show that the earth orbited the sun rather than the other way around.

The Ottoman court would have been an alien world to these young princes. Arabic was the *lingua franca,* not Latin. They would hear the Islamic call to prayer in places where churches were the exception, not the rule. While the young Europeans were strangers in a strange land, these exchanges offered intellectually stimulating ideas and showed the benefits of Ottoman rule. So, rather than being 'hostages' in the usual sense of the word, they were treated as honoured guests. They often rubbed shoulders with the sultan's sons and sometimes went on campaign as well. To be blunt, some of the hostages had more luxurious lives, with better schooling, in the Ottoman court than anything they would

---

have had in their own lands. However, time and again, and not just in Ottoman history, there are examples of these hostage outsiders, who had been accepted in the ruler's court, rebelling against it at the first opportunity. It's baffling to think that even though this strategy so often failed, the practice continued. After years of living a privileged life, the main lesson that Vlad II's son, Vlad III ('the Impaler'), seemed to have brought back to Wallachia with him was that he must do everything in his power to fight against the Ottoman peril. He was neither the first nor the last to return home seething with resentment over the easy life he had had in nominal captivity.

Another means of shoring up an uneasy alliance was through marriage. Murad II had four wives; three of them were women from the Anatolian dynasties to the east, but his fourth wife was Mara Branković, known in Ottoman history as Sultana Marija. They were married in 1435 when she joined Murad's harem. This union was an attempt to keep Serbia nominally independent, but the above battles put an end to that. What is especially interesting about Sultana Marija is that after her husband's death, she stayed on as an advisor to Mehmed II. Later in her life she even acted as an intermediary between the Ottomans and the Venetians when they finally went to war. While a pawn in the game of diplomacy, she is also a reminder that many queens (or in this case a sultana) were not from the dynasty or the lands they married into, and yet these women, unlike the political hostages, were, by and large, loyal to their new homes.

Meanwhile, Murad II had had a busy reign dealing with political near-chaos at the start and then serious invasion threats later. He had already tried to abdicate once, but by early 1451 he was worn out. Even though he had ruled for nearly thirty years, he was still relatively young when he died at the age of forty-six, but he had been able to look back with pride at all he had accomplished. The empire had been on the brink of collapse when he became sultan in his teens, but by the time of his death it had grown and had overcome all the immediate threats. And, perhaps most importantly, in his son Mehmed II, Murad knew he was passing the torch to a capable young man. Murad II was buried with the other early sultans in Bursa, but he was the last one to rest there. Mehmed II was to be buried somewhere far more famous.

5

The Animal Hide and the Emperor

Mehmed II was not the first son of Murad II, nor was he the son of one of his wives. Mehmed II was the son of one of the many concubines in the royal harem. Little is known about her or her family, but many legends have grown up around her because of her very famous son. Quite how Mehmed got to the top of the heap is a bit of mystery, but we know Murad II had already selected him as his successor about a decade earlier (he had become Sultan Mehmed II when his father briefly retired).

Harems

As soon as Westerners hear the word 'harem', the mind instantly fills with images of beautiful women in silk veils, lounging in lavish surroundings, gold trays piled high with exotic fruits. That's a Western fantasy. 'Harem' is specifically a Turkish word from the Arabic *haram*, which means 'forbidden' or 'sacrosanct'. It was an area of the royal residence set aside for the exclusive use of the women (wealthy men of high position might also have had a 'harem' in their homes). The royal harem, the most famous perhaps being the one in Topkapı Palace, typically housed dozens of women; at its peak in the sixteenth and seventeen centuries, there were about 300. The population dramatically increased as the princes and their own harems were brought in from the regions and absorbed into the Seraglio (Topkapı Palace).

The harem was the home of the sultan's mother, wives, daughters and other female relatives as well as the concubines

---

(who were there purely for the sultan's pleasure). The power of the Ottoman court was based on a strict hierarchy, with the sultan at the top; the Ottoman harem was also a hierarchy, with the sultan's mother, the *valide* sultan, the supreme ruler. Wives were next in rank and others followed according to how well they played the power politics of this all-female domain. The women were guarded by black eunuchs (their emasculation guaranteed all children were the sultan's and simultaneously ensured that no man except the sultan had access to the women) and were served by other, lowly, harem girls. My favourite fact told during a tour of the Topkapı harem is that even the cucumbers were mashed so the women only 'knew' the sultan – which is thorough planning.

These women were not 'Turkish', nor were they born Muslim. In Islam it is forbidden to be a slave, so, as with the Janissaries, the girls in the harem were Ottoman captives or Christians (often Greeks) brought in from the regions. A new arrival might not see the sultan for years, if ever. In the meantime she worked as a servant and became well versed in harem etiquette, learning to dance, play a musical instrument or recite poetry. If she caught the sultan's eye and became a favourite, a *gözde*, she would learn how to please the sultan in the bedroom. This was an opportunity, which might mean that she could bear a son and become the mother of the next sultan – and with that role came considerable power. As a result the competition was fierce and the intrigue was intense, but the reality for most of the women was at best harem work, or at worst seeing your son murdered as another woman schemed to get her son on the throne. While harem life meant a life of luxury and ease for some, it was a gilded cage from which few ever escaped, one that had a dark side and showed that women were just as ruthless as men in the pursuit of power, position and wealth.

Let's consider the implications of every sultan's mother being a European. It meant that after a few generations, the sultans simply didn't look very 'Turkish'. There are records of some sultans dying their fair beards to look more 'Turkish' (the hair on their heads was covered by their turbans), and it appears that some even had blue eyes. At the empire's pinnacle under Suleiman the Magnificent in the 1500s, the sultan (sometimes referred to as the 'Grand Turk') was ethnically about as 'Turkish' as the King of England.

For generations, when the new sultan was proclaimed, all the other male children in the harem were strangled (in other words, all of the new sultan's brothers and half-brothers) to ensure the line of succession was pure and unchallenged. Did the justification begin when Bayezid strangled his own full brother on his accession? Did the civil war between brothers in the early fifteenth century give further impetus? The answers are unclear, but it is safe to say that the Ottomans took 'survival of the fittest' to a whole new level. During the later periods of the empire, the sons of the sultan lived in the harem until they were sixteen years old, when it was considered appropriate for them to appear in the public and administrative areas of the palace. The Topkapı harem in Istanbul, which was where the harem was based for most of the empire, was, in essence, the private living quarters of the sultan and his family rather than just a pleasure palace.

When Mehmed II became sultan, technically for a second time, he was in possession of a very large empire. Belgrade (yet to be conquered) marked its western frontier, with about two-thirds of Anatolia under his direct rule. However, in the very centre of his empire was a prize anomaly, one that was still in the hands of the old enemy Byzantium. Many, including Ottoman sultans (as we have seen), had besieged Constantinople, and all had failed. Mehmed II intended to change this.

Mehmed spent more than a year preparing to conquer the city, and no expense was spared. Of all the military costs a ruler will incur, armies are actually the cheapest. It is telling that the requirements for this army were the last item on Mehmed's list. Instead, while he was constructing a new fort a short distance from Constantinople, he was investing in the navy and the newest, biggest siege guns to breach the walls, which had stood for longer than a thousand years. All of this was eye-wateringly expensive, and shows that his was a carefully crafted plan to remove this thorn in the side of the Ottomans and to defeat the Byzantine Empire once and for all. Mehmed knew that even with these preparations success was in no way guaranteed, but he intended to leave nothing to chance, showing he had a remarkably mature head for a nineteen-year-old.

Mehmed's fort, Rumelihisarı (Rumeli Castle), was built on the European side of the Bosphorus, directly across from Anadoluhisarı (Anatolia Castle, built earlier by Sultan Bayezid I) on the Asian side at the strait's narrowest point. It seems that on some level the Ottomans had long understood that Constantinople could not be defeated unless they had control of the waterway. But Mehmed's fort also had a more sinister name, Boğazkesen, which is a pun in Turkish. As mentioned, the fort was built on the shores of the Bosphorus Strait, which was known as the Boğaz or 'throat' in Turkish. 'Kesen' means 'cutter' – so the castle was called the 'throat cutter' because it could fire its cannons across the Bosphorus, in effect 'cutting' the strait.

Legends

According to legend, Mehmed II asked the Byzantine Emperor for some land on which to build his castle. The emperor responded by throwing him an animal hide, saying, 'You can have as much land as this covers', and the Byzantine courtiers had a good laugh at Mehmed II's expense. The sultan thanked the emperor for such a generous gift and left. When he arrived at the site he had in mind, he ordered the hide to be cut into fine leather string and, using this, he marked out the boundaries of the space needed for his new fort. This never happened. Mehmed II did not seek permission from the terminally ill and terminally shrinking Byzantine Empire for anything. He built his fort precisely where he planned and nobody had the power to stop him. The Byzantine Emperor Constantine XI knew exactly what Mehmed intended and the threat this posed to his city, but all he could do was protest vociferously, to no avail. The reason for mentioning the legend is that it tells us something about the attitudes around Mehmed II. While he was later seen as a conqueror, he was seen first and foremost as intelligent. This characteristic is often overlooked in Western literature when writing about the Ottomans, many of whom were regarded by their contemporaries as both smart and shrewd.

A thirteenth-century wise man from Persia called Nasreddin Hodja has survived the test of time and is still a popular folk figure in modern Turkey. He is portrayed as a comical character whose jokes are sometimes silly and sometimes philosophical,

---

> but always with a common-sense point. He is based on a real man who clearly had a quick wit and whose stories have been preserved and, no doubt, exaggerated over the centuries. Nasreddin Hodja is instantly recognisable because he is always portrayed riding his donkey backwards. The reason for this is evident in one of his tales. A man asked the *hodja* (teacher) why he always sat the wrong way around on the donkey and he replied, 'I am sitting the right way on this donkey; it is the donkey that is the wrong way around.' Boom, boom!

The tales of Nasreddin Hodja would have been known to all the sultans, and a clever solution was admired and commended by Ottoman sources. This philosophy can also be seen in the attitudes of one of Mehmed II's tutors. Ak Şemsettin was a Syrian polymath who, while steeped in Islamic Sufi religious thinking, was also an astronomer and scientist (before the concept had a word). He recognised that disease was not spontaneous or caused by sinful deeds, but by tiny 'seeds' that infected the body. This was a description of microbes and bacteria centuries before any similar theory in Europe and before the invention of the microscope. Ak Şemsettin combined devout faith with scientific exploration, where the only truth (in science) was through observation. Mehmed II was a mischievous youth who needed to be beaten to get him to pay attention, but over the years he soaked up both the science and the faith that Ak Şemsettin taught. Mehmed II was deeply influenced by his teacher's outlook on life and he, too, became a genuinely religious man, but never at the expense of rejecting new scientific theories. Indeed, it was Ak Şemsettin's influence, in part, that brought Murad II out of retirement when the young sultan was in power and out of his depth. But putting aside the politics of the court, this is another example of the practical and clever thinking that is often overlooked when Westerners describe Islamic empires and by modern Islamic fanatics who think that science and Islam aren't compatible.

Meanwhile, back on the Bosphorus, a young Mehmed II continued the dynastic (and Islamic) tradition of being smart and fully preparing for the campaign ahead. After the site for Rumelihisarı was chosen to control the narrowest point on the Bosphorus, the fortress was erected quickly, in about a year, and did exactly what it was designed to do. In conjunction with its partner on the opposite shore, Anadoluhisarı, it was able to control the flow of trade for the benefit of the Ottomans and Mehmed II rather than for the Byzantines, Venetians and Genoese. It was garrisoned with 400 Janissaries and equipped not with catapults and crossbows but with the very latest technology in cannons. The Ottomans meant business. A Venetian ship coming from the Black Sea ignored the order to halt and, without warning or ceremony, was bombarded and sunk. The surviving Venetian crewmen were beheaded as a warning of the consequences for anyone failing to heed orders from Rumelihisarı. This proved the efficacy of Mehmed's plan and got the immediate attention of everyone who used the Bosphorus.

Ak Şemsettin had one last part to play in Ottoman history when Mehmed II was finally ready to tighten the noose on Constantinople. The tutor was with the young sultan when he claimed to have found the resting place of Abu Ayyub al-Ansari, and Ak Şemsettin readily verified this. The enormity of such a discovery cannot be overstated. Abu Ayyub was one of the Prophet Muhammad's companions. Not only that, but Abu Ayyub had been the Prophet's standard-bearer and was one of the very first *ghazis*. Further, he had led the first Islamic attempt to conquer Constantinople. Finding his tomb (a little conveniently) was akin to the miraculous discovery of the Holy Lance (the spear that pierced Christ's body on the cross) at a time when all hope was lost on the First Crusade (this also seemed a little convenient, something that some of the crusaders at the time commented on). The comparison isn't perfect, but it's not hard to imagine how electrifying such a discovery would be to this campaign. It was the best of all possible omens for the forthcoming siege. The site of the find was turned into a mosque in 1458, and the Eyüp Sultan Mosque stands to this day.

The Byzantine Emperor, Constantine XI, is an example of how complex the situation had become for any Christian lands in the vicinity of the Ottoman Empire. The Isthmus of Corinth is the narrow stretch of land which connects the Peloponnese peninsula with the rest of mainland Greece. It was here that a young Prince Constantine built a wall across the isthmus, which gave him a strategic advantage when he launched an attack on the Duchy of Athens in 1444. At the time the duchy was ruled by Florence, not Greece, and rather than being a Byzantine ally, the duchy was an Ottoman vassal state. So there were Greeks fighting Italians in Greece. With me so far? Constantine won, but this provoked

Murad II. Constantine tried to use diplomacy to diffuse the situation, but, after stopping the immediate threat of an invasion from the West, Murad II wanted to show everyone who was really boss and attacked Constantine in 1446. He broke down the wall across the isthmus that Constantine had so carefully constructed and 60,000 Ottoman troops poured through. Constantine barely made it out alive. Things became even more counter-intuitive in 1448. The Byzantine Emperor John VIII Palaiologos died without an heir. Several men, including Constantine (John VIII Palaiologos' younger brother), asked Murad II for help to claim the Byzantine throne. Despite what had happened a few years earlier, Murad II backed Constantine, and in January 1449 he became the new Byzantine Emperor Constantine XI. After the death of Murad II he threatened to release one of Mehmed II's brothers (Orhan), a threat which, if carried out, could trigger another Ottoman civil war. It was the only threat with any bite the Byzantines had left, but it was made from too weak a position and served as the pretext Mehmed II needed to mobilise. It's true that he was going to attack anyway, but he was a man of faith and wouldn't have broken a truce arbitrarily. Instead, Constantine XI played into his hands.

With the sounds of war literally in the air, Constantine XI looked to the West and raised the same prize as many emperors had done before: the reunification of the Christian churches and a chance for the Pope to claim victory by doing so. Nicholas V was pope at the time, and he genuinely wanted to help Constantinople. However, Europe was in its usual divided state, and with two recent devastating defeats at the hands of the Ottomans there was little appetite to assist. On 12 December 1452 the Catholic and Orthodox churches were reunited, but it didn't even last twelve months. Nevertheless, given the previous 400 years of acrimony, it was a remarkable achievement even if the preaching of a crusade ultimately came to nothing. Pope Nicholas V ended up sending a small fleet to aid Constantinople, but it was never going to be enough to tip the balance of power. Interestingly, Mehmed II wanted the city but not the bloodshed. This can be seen by the fact that his ambassadors approached Constantine with a generous offer: in exchange for the surrender of Constantinople, the emperor's life would be spared, and he could continue to rule in Mistra (southern Greece) as a vassal. His reply has been preserved by Sphrantzes: 'To surrender the city to you is beyond my authority or anyone else's who lives in it, for all of us, after taking the mutual decision, shall die out of free will without sparing our lives.'

The two sides had now fixed their positions. Constantine XI wisely spent what little he had stockpiling food and repairing the mighty walls, which were more than 12 miles long, with many layers. They were a wonder of the age but expensive to maintain. He depended on Venetian and Genoese assistance, with the city guard, to defend the walls, but his meagre revenues couldn't possibly stretch to an entire mercenary army. Surprisingly, a few of his soldiers were ethnic Turks who stayed loyal to the end. While Constantine XI did everything he could, the situation was a painful reminder of just how much the power of the Byzantines had shrunk. In total it's estimated that Constantine XI had 5,000 to 7,000 fighting men in this final siege.

Meanwhile, Mehmed II had managed to amass an army and a navy of around 100,000. He had seventy ships at his disposal (some were war galleys, others were transports) and the magnificent new siege guns (which came with their charges already mixed by munition experts, meaning that their firepower was far greater than anything at the disposal of Murad II). The mightiest cannon, named 'Basilica', was 27 feet long and able to fire a 600lb stone ball over a mile. It must be remembered here that an Ottoman force was not the same thing as a 'Turkish' force, an example of which is a Hungarian named Orban, the cannon expert who built the Basilica. The Janissaries were, by now, around 10,000 strong, and none of them were ethnically Turkish. Also, spare a thought for the Serbian Prince Đurađ Branković. He had been one of the Christian leaders at the Battle of Varna, fighting against Murad II, and had been one of those who paid to repair the walls of Constantinople. Now he was on Mehmed II's side as a vassal subject. It was 1453, and time had run out for the Byzantines.

Constantinople, like its emperors, wasn't what it used to be. At its peak, under the sixth century AD Emperor Justinian, it had a population of half a million people; by the mid-fifteenth century that number had dropped by around 90 per cent to approximately 50,000. Contemporary chroniclers reported that there was now farmland inside the walls of this once-great city, but none of that took away its lustre as a prize. Ever since a Hadith had targeted Constantinople, the Islamic world had obsessed over it; it had been a goal for centuries. But they were not the only ones. Bulgaria,

Serbia, Rome, Venice and Genoa would all have loved to have taken the city, but by 1453 the only power with any real chance of cracking its impregnable defences was the Ottoman Empire.

Very few moments from history are well remembered across continents. The Battle of Hastings is legendary in Britain, but most Italians have never heard of it. A number of key initiatives, critical battles and pivotal moments have been mentioned in this book, and yet, unless they are part of your country's history (or you have a special interest in that part of history), most are obscure in the wider world. The 1453 Siege of Constantinople, however, is so famous that almost everyone has heard of it. 'It's when the Turks beat the Greeks and kick-started the Renaissance' would be a fairly standard description of what happened, and while almost everything in that sentence is wrong, it's a testament to the impact of this siege that it is widely remembered even today.

And so we come to the siege itself. Accompanied by his bodyguard, Mehmed II arrived in sight of the walls on 5 April; his army and navy had been arriving for days. The siege is generally agreed to have started the following day, on the 6th, when the first thing Mehmed II did was make certain that all outlying fortifications were his. They were easy enough to mop up, and this ensured that there would be no flanking attacks or unexpected raids from these strongholds. It was an eminently sensible tactic from a sultan who had turned twenty-one just a few days earlier.

Islands

Among the outlying areas captured by the navy in this initial sweep were the Princes' Islands, tiny outcrops of rock in the Sea of Marmara, where a small compound had been built to keep wayward Byzantine princes. It was an achingly beautiful Imperial prison and the Ottomans were to use it for the same purpose. Later, the Ottoman aristocracy, followed by wealthy Turks, built lavish summer houses on the main island. Several have fallen into ruin but many are still in use, although no private cars are permitted and most transport, even today, is by horse and buggy. Although, for the most part, the islands are a snapshot of another time, restaurants and bars have sprung up to provide a welcome escape from the city life on the nearby shores.

Meanwhile, back at the siege, while his army was carefully manoeuvring and taking control of the outposts, Sultan Mehmed ordered his siege cannons to start the laborious work of grinding down Constantinople's defences. The Basilica, while fearsome, did have two drawbacks: it took three hours to load, and 600lb stone balls aren't exactly easy to find. As such, the defenders had sufficient time to patch up the damage and used barrels of earth to plug the gaps. These acted as shock absorbers, reducing the impact of the cannon balls and greatly decreasing their effectiveness. As the siege wore on, people came to see the awesome sight of the Ottoman army, in all its glory, attacking the most famous city in Christendom. It was the Italians who pointed out to the Ottoman gunners that to keep firing at points of the wall which had already been damaged was folly. Instead, it was better to fire at different points, grouping every three shots into a triangular formation so as to ensure maximum impact and better chances for breaches. Thanks to this advice from the Christians, the siege cannons were able to work more effectively. Constantinople itself had cannons on its walls, but they were smaller than the Ottoman guns and, as the walls had never been designed to be used as gun emplacements, they often broke free from their positions or even damaged the walls as a result of their force.

Mehmed II wanted to encircle the city as tightly as possible. Constantinople was a triangle, with one side facing land and the other two flanked by water. The Genoese area of Pera (also known as Galata), on the other side of the northern body of water known as the Golden Horn (an inlet running off the Bosphorus where it meets the Sea of Marmara), contained the landmark Galata Tower in an area that had grown up alongside Constantinople over the centuries. During the siege, the Genoese were nominally neutral – but there was a problem with that position. The standard defence to protect Constantinople from being surrounded (and which had been deployed by the time the Ottomans arrived) was to run a great iron chain from the walls of the city, across the Golden Horn, over to Pera. This closed off the channel, which then became a safe haven.

On the day that a few Venetian ships came into view, they were not low-profile galleys but high-sided cogs, large medieval merchant vessels. The cogs had been lashed together and not only carried much-needed supplies but also bristled with crossbowmen.

Mehmed II ordered an intercept. Despite the fact that the Ottoman sailors had to clamber up the high sides of the Venetian vessels under withering fire from the crossbows, they carried out their orders with bravery. The battle lasted most of the day, with one side and then the other gaining the advantage. Onlookers cheered as everyone watched the drama unfold. Mehmed II was so engrossed that he waded into the water and called out to his men to keep fighting. However, after a long and desperate clash, the Venetians managed to get to the great chain and were admitted into the Golden Horn. It is said that Mehmed II pulled out parts of his beard in sheer frustration. After such a humiliation, the sultan demanded that the Genoese lower the chain as it was clearly showing favouritism to the Byzantines. The Genoese very politely refused.

What happened next sounds like the stuff of legend, but all the chronicles agree that these events actually took place. Mehmed II ordered a shallow ditch to be dug through Pera to the Golden Horn. The ditch was lined with greased planks and some eighty (yes, eighty) of Mehmed II's warships were hauled across land and launched into the Golden Horn. In the history of the dozens of sieges carried out against Constantinople, no one had ever considered – let alone successfully executed – such an audacious piece of engineering. The defenders were horrified when they saw Ottoman ships in the Golden Horn. They barely had enough troops to man the landward walls, so to stretch their forces even thinner in order to garrison the (longer) seaward wall was a terrible blow. Constantine XI and the Venetians agreed a plan to immolate the Ottoman navy with fire ships, but the news got back to the Ottomans, who were waiting for them. The counter-attack failed completely. As a sign of his immense displeasure Mehmed II ordered that the forty Venetian survivors be impaled on spikes opposite the walls so the defenders would have to confront the meaning of their defeat. Constantine XI showed equal cruelty by taking his 260 Ottoman prisoners on to the battlements, where he had each one beheaded in full view of the opposing army.

A point about this siege, commented on by all of the contemporary accounts, was its sheer noise. Cries and shouts were nothing new, but the sounds of the largest arsenal of cannons ever yet fired caused a persistent cacophony, accompanied by the Janissary band. Drummers, horn blowers and great cymbals all added to the sound of the siege. Despite all the activity going on at the walls and on the water, Mehmed II had yet another tactic up his sleeve. Tunnelling had been used in many sieges to undermine the walls and cause a breach when the foundations failed. The multiple tunnels Mehmed had ordered were dug by Serbian mining specialists, but among the volunteer defenders of Constantinople was a man by the name of Johannes Grant. There's some debate over whether he was German or Scottish, but he wasn't Greek or Italian, and he was very good at counter-mining. Some half-dozen Ottoman tunnels were broken into and, after intense and claustrophobic underground fighting, destroyed by Greek fire.

For about a week in mid-to-late May, Mehmed II was frustrated again and again as his supposedly 'secret' plans to breach the walls were continually thwarted. It was during this period that Mehmed II again sent an ambassador to meet with Constantine XI, an event that tends to be ignored by both Turks and Greeks. It is better in the storytelling to have one side obsessed with capturing the city at any cost and the other fighting bravely to the last man (rather than seeking a possible escape from martyrdom). The fact of the matter was that both Mehmed II and Constantine XI were men with a genuine understanding of the situation. From Mehmed II's point of view, the siege was eye-wateringly expensive, and, although he now had his ships in the Golden Horn, the walls still had not been breached. The siege could still fail.

Fortifications are sometimes referred to as 'defensive multipliers'. For instance, a well-constructed tower might mean that ten men could fight off 100, so each defender would have a multiplier of ten. Considering the numbers at this siege and the fact that Mehmed II had brought cannons into play, a new technology the walls of Constantinople had never been designed to withstand, it was a testament to the strength of the walls and the courage of its defenders that it took such Herculean efforts to overwhelm a comparatively tiny garrison. As a result of this round of talks, Mehmed's ambassador reported that Constantine was prepared to offer everything the sultan could want: all the outlying fortifications would be recognised as Ottoman and the amount of tribute would be increased (leaving Byzantium forever broke), but the one thing he could not relinquish was the great city itself. He could not be – would not be – the emperor who lost the city without a fight. The talks showed that even after the torture and execution of captives, even after all the gold and blood so far expended in the siege, both sides were still willing to try to find a diplomatic solution. It was reported that even some of the Ottoman generals wanted a peaceful solution and urged their sultan to take the deal. There was no bloodlust or religious zeal in the strategy to capture Constantinople, but everything *except the city* was a deal that fell crucially short for Mehmed. For him the whole point of the siege was to end the anachronism that was Byzantium's existence in the middle of the Ottoman Empire. The talks came to nothing.

By 26 May, Mehmed and his war council began planning what they hoped would be the final assault, which began around midnight on 29 May 1453. The first troops sent in were the Christian contingents, composed of the Serbs and Bulgarians. They were supported by the Azaps, poorly equipped Turkish soldiers. In essence, Mehmed II was sending in the cannon fodder to soak up the initial resistance from the garrison on the walls. These attacks were carried out to the sounds of the Janissary bands playing their intimidating war music, again adding to the noise of battle. The attacks centred on the city gates and the few breaches in the walls that the cannons had made. In the ensuing hours, some of the attackers made it past the walls but were pushed back. As was only to be expected, the fighting was fierce and vicious. Among the attackers was Ulubatlı Hasan. He was one of many Anatolian (Turkish) chieftains who, instead of paying tribute, brought soldiers to the fight, similar to the knights in feudal Europe. Hasan was lightly armoured and armed with a scimitar and circular shield, but, most importantly, he carried a standard and was the first man to plant Mehmed II's flag on the city's walls. His bravery and daring showed that the walls of Constantinople were not unassailable and inspired his men to follow. Hasan, however, was hit by multiple arrows and crossbow bolts. He fell, but his actions and sacrifice added fresh resolve to the attackers, while also demoralising the defenders.

The trickle of Ottoman forces pushing through the breach turned into a flood. The walls fell; the siege had ended in success for the Ottomans, but the final assault was staggeringly brutal. Eye-witness accounts talk of blood flowing in the streets and bodies (of both attackers and defenders) bobbing 'like melons' in the waters around the city. Mehmed II had promised his men three days of plunder, a standard practice of the age after a city had been defeated and was designed to encourage the residents to surrender without the fight. Unfortunately, on this occasion, treasure was not enough, and the conquering Ottoman soldiers massacred thousands; many more were captured and later sold into slavery. It is alleged that when Mehmed II saw the scale of the carnage and destruction he said, 'What a city we have given over to plunder and destruction.'

In the last hours, Constantine XI was seen fighting on the walls. He was a brave man who had almost nothing and faced a united enemy with almost infinite resources. Had he handed over the city without a fight, he would have become a pariah. Instead, he is now an unofficial saint in the Greek Orthodox Church, and many legends have sprung up about him. It was said there was a prophecy that Constantinople would be founded by one Constantine and lost by another (which is true, but the 'legend' seems to have post-dated 1453). Another legend says that an angel rescued Constantine XI by turning him into a marble statue and placing him in a cave near the Golden Gate, where he waits patiently to be brought to life to win back the city for Christendom. This is why he is sometimes called 'the marble emperor'. Finally, the name of Constantine was used as a rallying cry for Greeks during their war for independence with the Ottoman Empire, and he is, unsurprisingly, a national hero in Greece. He was a courageous man who died a martyr but, ultimately, lost. Constantine XI is both the end point of the thousand-year history of the Byzantine Empire and also (arguably) the full stop to the Roman Empire.

The siege took about eight weeks, a remarkably short amount of time considering that this was one of the most famous sieges in history. It is also a salient reminder of how things had changed. Early in this book the Ottomans besieged their first major city, Bursa. They had no siege equipment and could only wait it out. It took nine years before they eventually captured that city. Now the descendants of those warriors had the most technologically advanced siege weapons in the world and had captured a most prized city in less than nine weeks. The empire had come a long way from the time of Osman.

Because its impact was felt in so many different ways, the importance of this siege cannot be overstated. The Byzantine emperors were considered to be 'Greek' by the rest of Europe, but (somewhat unexpectedly) the Byzantines were proud of their Roman heritage, and even though they had been using Greek as their *lingua franca* for about 900 years, the emperors still called themselves 'Roman' emperors and also 'Caesar'. When this Christian 'Greek' Orthodox capital fell, the other great centres of Orthodox Christianity, Kiev and Moscow, picked up the baton. In fact, about eighty years later, the grand princes of Moscow changed their title to the more exalted Tsar, the Russian for Caesar. There was no way that they could have taken such a title had the Byzantine Empire still existed. The Ottoman sultans also added 'Caesar' to their list of titles after 1453, but Mehmed II earned another title on that historic day: 'Fatih'. This simply means 'conqueror', and, like William in England, he was to be the only ruler of his dynasty ever to earn the title.

The repercussions did not end with changes to the Orthodox Church and the transference of titles. While gunpowder had been around for centuries, cannons had never been used in either the size or numbers that they were during this siege. Mehmed II's victory was the first time in history when gunpowder was seen to have played a key factor in victory. Indeed, because of the widespread deployment of cannons, the idea of the high stone wall to stop an enemy attack became obsolete in that year. Mehmed II had shown that cannons had overtaken traditional siege weapons and that a stone wall, however well built, could be broken down quicker than ever before. From now on designs such as star forts (so called because they looked as if they had star-like points) and low, earth-filled walls were used to absorb the shock of siege cannons as the new weapons rendered obsolete those more medieval forms of attack.

As the city's conqueror, Mehmed II now owned all the great buildings inside it, and none was greater than Saint Sophia, known as Hagia Sophia. In the early sixth century AD, Byzantine Emperor Justinian (the last of the Eastern Roman Emperors to speak Latin as his first language) had wanted to build a new church on the ruins of an older, smaller structure. What rose out of the ground was the largest ancient dome ever built and a structure that wasn't to be matched for more than a millennium. For nearly a thousand years this was the world's largest church, a record that remains unbroken. Hagia Sophia is also the pinnacle of Late Antiquity architecture and a reminder that the early Byzantine Empire was every bit the match of the fallen Western Roman one.

Churches

The reason Russia is Orthodox Christian, rather than Catholic Christian, is that when envoys from the Rus capital of Kiev visited Constantinople and walked into Hagia Sophia, they said it was as if they were walking into heaven itself. Had Hagia Sophia been smaller, Rome may have swayed this potential eastern ally. In 1054, in this very church, papal legates excommunicated the entire Eastern Orthodox Church, thereby creating the 'Great Schism', which divided the world's two largest church groups, a fracture that remains today.

To the modern eye, Hagia Sophia looks like a mosque. Prior to 1453, there had been some mosques with domes, but most had open courtyards; there is no need for a roof to keep out the rain in places like Saudi Arabia. But after 1453, this magnificent church became a magnificent mosque, one that heavily influenced Islamic architecture, so that subsequent mosques were made to look like an ancient church, not the other way around. Hagia Sophia was already 500 years old by the time the Ottoman architect Sinan (more on him later) recognised that the structure needed additional support and added buttresses, which is why it still stands today. So, after serving Christians for nearly a millennium, Saint Sophia became one of the Islamic world's largest and most venerable mosques for the next 450 years. After Turkey became a republic, Mustafa Kemal Atatürk, the first President of Turkey, converted the building to a museum in 1935.

A number of legends have already been woven into this book, and here's another about Hagia Sophia and Mehmed II. In one of the great pillars of this church there is a small hole. The legend says that, after conquering the city, Mehmed II strode into the church, pushed his mighty finger into the column and rotated the entire building so that it would face Mecca and become a mosque. Pretty impressive stuff from a mere mortal! The truth, alas, is a little more mundane and a little less colourful. Hagia Sophia was built so that the nave faces Jerusalem (the greatest church on earth should surely point to the most holy city in Christendom; at the time both were Byzantine property). Mosques are always constructed so that the *mihrab* (the point in the wall of a mosque closest to Mecca) faces Islam's holiest city. It just so happens that from Constantinople, Mecca and Jerusalem are in roughly the same direction. This explanation makes more sense than Mehmed II suddenly becoming Superman.

A further impact of the conquest is a little more subtle. When you think of a symbol associated with Christianity, you will instantly think of the cross. If you think of the equivalent symbol in Islam, it would be the crescent moon and star. But why? The reason for the cross is obvious, but the moon and star have nothing to do with the Prophet Mohammed's life. The answer is that while the crescent moon was occasionally seen on Islamic banners prior to 1453, it really became prominent after 1453. In the early era of the caliphate (the Islamic community headed by a caliph), Arab Muslims fought under banners that were solid blocks of colour, quite often green or black. Occasionally they would be embroidered with the elaborate calligraphy of a verse from the Qur'an. However, Turks aren't Arabs and only later converted to Islam (but before the start of this book). Consequently they had a more eastern type of banner called a tug, which was a staff with either yak or horse hair in a circular arrangement hanging from it, rather in the style of the Mongols. This was a very different battle standard, underlining the very different origins of the two groups. Despite the Ottomans having lived for centuries in Anatolia, in the early era of the empire, the tug was still the main battle standard.

The connection with the crescent and star came from atop the spires of the Hagia Sophia, where this symbol could be seen from around the city and came to be associated with Constantinople. While it would be many centuries before the Ottomans would make it the symbol of their empire (the tug was a remarkably long-lasting war banner), it originated from what had been a church in their new capital city. As the Ottoman Empire grew, so did its influence among Muslim societies. Travellers came from the Middle East and the Mughal Empire of India (the descendants of Tamerlane) and took the symbol home with them, spreading it ever eastwards. Today it is on the flag of the Republic of Turkey as well as on the flags of other Muslim-populated countries, notably Malaysia and Pakistan. It is strange to think the image from a Roman church has been used so widely for something so very different from what was originally intended. One structure, two religions, multiple cultures: Hagia Sophia is an iconic building that has influenced the architecture of countless countries and is, in my humble opinion, the most important structure in history.

Meanwhile, the impact of the conquest didn't end with the influences of Hagia Sophia. Earlier I mentioned how many people think the siege was the spark that lit the artistic and scientific flame of the Renaissance in Europe – except there's a problem with that. Donatello is considered to be a Renaissance artist, and yet he was an old man in 1453, with his masterpieces already created. Bracciolini was a Renaissance scholar and humanist, and although he was alive in 1453 he was in his twilight years, his work already completed. Petrarch is seen by many as the instigator of the Renaissance in Italy, and yet he died in 1374. It's also worth noting that in 1204 Constantinople was sacked and then ruled for decades by the crusaders. They would have had access to the same learning then, but nothing came of it. Knowledge-wise, it was still very much the Middle Ages. In fact, late Byzantine art and philosophy fall well short of what Italy itself was creating in the late fifteenth century. History is rarely as simple as X + Y = Z. The fall of Constantinople caused some scholars to flee westwards, which would have stimulated the European rediscovery of ancient art and philosophy, but the fall of Constantinople definitely did not *start* the Renaissance. It is more easily argued that, as the Ottoman Empire headed west, its scholars and libraries, steeped in Islamic scientific knowledge, would have prompted a mixing of local ideas with those coming from Constantinople.

Finally, there's the name of the city. Contrary to assumptions in the West, Mehmed II did not change the name of Constantinople to Istanbul. He was very proud of having conquered this ancient city, so why change the name to something unrecognisable? The Ottoman documentation for many generations after the siege refers to the city as Constantinople. The name 'Istanbul' seems to come from the Greek *stim boli*, meaning 'in the city'. Turkish words don't start with 'st', and foreign words were often softened with the letter 'i', so it was probably from locals saying something along the lines of *istim boli*, meaning 'going to the city', that the name changed. This is conjecture, but it's the best explanation around. What is important is that Mehmed II himself had no desire to call the ancient Eastern Roman Empire capital by any name other than the one it already had. (In reality, the name only officially changed from Konstantiniyye seven years after the fall of the Ottoman Empire in

March 1930.) Unsurprisingly, the Ottoman capital moved, once again, to a new location, to a grander city. Constantinople was to be the fourth and final capital of the empire. Bursa, which had been the resting place of all the sultans before Mehmed II, would be the site of royal tombs no longer, a reminder to all that it was Mehmed II who had fulfilled the Hadith. According to the Prophet Muhammad's very own judgment, the twenty-one-year-old sultan was the ultimate general, the ultimate conqueror.

After the events of 1453, Mehmed II took his new title to heart and embarked on a highly ambitious campaign of expansion. The empire was now being referred to as the 'Eternal State'. Putting aside that glib label, it is clear that once Constantinople became part of the empire, there was no longer a distraction at the very heart of the Ottoman realm and, for the first time, the Ottoman regime could concentrate its full attention on securing its borders.

The first area to feel Mehmed II's new purpose was Serbia, a vassal state but a fickle one. In 1454 Đurađ Branković had to watch as Serbia was absorbed into the empire proper, no longer a vassal state. From there, Mehmed pushed further west and laid siege to Belgrade in 1456. Here we see another name from the time of Nicopolis, John Hunyadi, who led a fleet along the Danube and broke through the Ottoman navy, sinking three galleons in the process. After a two-week siege, he brought food for the defenders and fresh troops. Despite the setback, Mehmed II ordered the siege to continue and, on the night of 21 July, sent the Janissaries to capture the city. But John Hunyadi was waiting and hurled tarred wood, bales of hay and sticks – anything flammable – onto the troops, starting an inferno. The Janissaries were cut off from the rest of the army and, while they fought bravely, those who weren't roasted alive were brought down by the defenders.

The next day some of the local peasants sallied forth from the defences in search of loot from the Ottoman camp. Mehmed II still had most of his troops, so John Hunyadi decided to turn the trickle into a deluge, deploying all of the troops he had available. It was a high-risk strategy that caught Mehmed II unprepared. We know that the sultan himself fought in the thick of things and killed a knight in one-on-one combat before being wounded in the thigh by an arrow and falling unconscious. Despite Mehmed's personal bravery, John Hunyadi's unorthodox plan had delivered an unexpected defeat, so while over the next three campaigning seasons the rest of Serbia did fall to Mehmed, everything west of Belgrade remained independent. Although no one knew it at the time, the siege of Belgrade resulted in a western frontier between Ottoman lands and the Christian west that would last for nearly a half century. Undeterred, the Greek vassal state that Constantine XI had ruled before being emperor was next on Mehmed's list of vassal territories set to become permanently absorbed. By 1460, he had conquered all of the Peloponnese.

After this, Mehmed II turned to a new area of interest for the Ottomans. With Greece and the Balkans under his control, he could cast his net wider and new realms were now his target for conquest. A diplomatic spat had been brewing between the Ottoman court and a Turkish clan on the Black Sea coast of Anatolia. Mehmed attacked the city of Sinope with his army and navy, took it and secured more territory in eastern Anatolia. The reality was that this conquering sultan had more successes in the Peloponnese and Anatolia than he did in Europe. He had already been stopped at Belgrade, but now he faced a new challenge to his authority.

In 1459 Mehmed II sent two envoys to Wallachia, one of his vassal territories, to demand tribute from a prince who had grown up in the Ottoman court. The Ottoman diplomats were killed by having their turbans nailed onto their heads. The prince responsible was Vlad III, son of the dragon (Dracula), known to history as – yes, finally – Vlad the Impaler. This Vlad will always be remembered for his stunning acts of torture and violence, but he also excelled in another area that is often overlooked. Vlad III was excellent at guerrilla warfare or, in modern parlance, asymmetrical warfare. He knew that he had less of everything and that he couldn't possibly hope to match Mehmed II on the battlefield, so he used terror tactics and ambushes to stave off the enemy. As he had grown up in the Ottoman court, he could speak and read Turkish, and he knew the customs and practices of both the Ottoman military and the state's administration.

Vlad III used this knowledge against Mehmed II in classic insurgency tactics, which is how he managed to survive for so long. Having said that, his use of cruel and sadistic methods terrified his own people and he was twice deposed from his territory in Wallachia. However, when looking at him as the ruler who would do anything to push back the Ottomans, it's little wonder he is regarded as a national hero in the modern sate of Romania.

The killing of the Ottoman ambassadors could mean only one thing, but before Mehmed II could react, Vlad used his Ottoman armour and perfect Turkish to march up to a number of forts and order the gates to be opened so that each one, in turn, fell to him. It was a clever ploy, which further provoked Mehmed II. When a small Ottoman force was ambushed, the soldiers were all impaled on spikes, with the leading pasha placed on the highest stake as an 'honour'. This time the sultan was outraged and brought together a gigantic invasion force, said to have been second in size only to his force at Constantinople, to conquer Wallachia.

When Mehmed II marched on Vlad III, he melted away from the region, leaving behind a land denuded of resources. This classic scorched-earth policy would do little damage to a small force (like Vlad's), but it had serious food and supply implications for Mehmed's massive troop numbers. On 16 June 1462, Mehmed II and his army were camped outside the town of Târgovişte. That night Vlad III and his best soldiers raided the Ottoman camp, slipping in with their Ottoman attire and Vlad III's impeccable Turkish. Unfortunately for Vlad, he mistook the vizier's tent for Mehmed II's and attacked. When he realised his error, he simply disappeared from the scene of the attempted assassination. It was a brave move that, had it worked, would almost certainly have led to the collapse of the Ottoman forces, giving Vlad much-needed breathing space.

Mehmed II pushed on past the town towards a huge field where he and his gigantic army found a man-made hell of wooden staves. Each stake had at least one human impaled on it. A few were Ottoman soldiers, but the vast majority were local Wallachians. Mothers and children had been impaled. On some, as many as five people had been stacked, one on top of the other, in the style of a macabre shish kebab. Mehmed II had entered a forest of death containing an estimated 20,000 mutilated bodies – which explains, finally, why Vlad III is known as 'the Impaler'. Some accounts state that the great Ottoman host had to retreat due to the lack of food and water, a typical result of a scorched-earth policy. However, while it is conjecture, it is not unreasonable to think that arriving at such an unexpected horror might be another reason why the Ottoman army retreated; they had seen the devil's work. Either way, Mehmed II did not catch up with his would-be assassin that year. With Vlad III gone, the Ottomans made Radu their puppet ruler and left him to overthrow his brother. Vlad III managed to defeat Radu in several battles, but his draconian rule led to defections to Radu's side.

Vlad III needed an ally and approached the King of Hungary, Matthias Corvinus. While Hungary had every reason to want to fight the Ottomans, it was the wrong time and, after talks broke down, Matthias Corvinus had Vlad III imprisoned. Vlad returned fourteen years later and ruled, for a third and final time, for about a year. Again he fought tenaciously against Mehmed II, this time as the Ottomans were pushing into Moldova. However, in the winter of 1476/7, Vlad III and his Moldovan bodyguard were ambushed and massacred. One Italian ambassador said that once Vlad III's body was discovered among the dead, the Ottoman soldiers hacked his corpse to pieces in revenge for all the atrocities he had carried out. It was a fitting end to one of the most vicious men in history.

With all of this going on in the Balkans, you might think that Mehmed II didn't have the resources to fight another major war, but that would be wrong. In 1462, an Albanian slave fled to the Venetian fortress of Coron (Greece) with 100,000 silver aspers from the Ottoman treasury in Athens. The Ottomans sent an ambassador to the Venetians to demand the return of the slave and the money, but the Venetians refused on the fairly shaky grounds that the Albanian had converted to Christianity. In the winter of 1462, the Ottomans retaliated by attacking and nearly capturing the Venetian fortress of Lepanto. Then in the spring of 1463, the Ottomans succeeded in taking the Venetian-held town of Argos (again in Greece). It was these events that started the First Venetian–Ottoman War.

For nearly two centuries Venice had clearly been the more powerful of the two regimes. Mehmed I would have been insane to attack Venetian interests, so, as a consequence, all the sultans prior to Mehmed II had deferred to Venice and Genoa in diplomacy and trade. However, by the late fifteenth century the tables had turned and the apparent status quo was upended, something Venice failed to realise. Having said that, the war was by no means a short conflict; it lasted from 1463 to 1479. This would be the first of seven clashes over the centuries between the Venetians and Ottomans. On this occasion, as the Venetians rallied, they brought a war fleet to Greece; meanwhile, they counted on a diversionary assault on the Balkans by Hungary, to which Matthias Corvinus had agreed. The fighting spread all over the Ottoman Empire and resulted in Mehmed II successfully capturing Albania. When the Ottomans encountered fierce resistance at the siege of resolutely defended Shkodra, Mehmed II himself arrived to see if he could put some steel into his men's resolve. Despite overwhelming numbers and the use of cannons, the citadel withstood everything Mehmed II could throw at it. However, as he had conquered everything around the fortress, it was inevitable that Albania, as a whole, would fall to him.

For the first time, the Ottomans had to face amphibious assaults by the master seamen of Venice. Islands were attacked and ports besieged, but the Ottomans acquitted themselves well. There were so many battles on so many fronts that Mehmed II had to count on the effectiveness of the viziers and pashas around him to fight effectively in their own areas – and they did. The initiative shown by Mehmed II's generals was such that he could leave Europe and press the beleaguered Turkmen realm of eastern Anatolia. This culminated in the largely forgotten but extremely significant Battle of Otlukbeli, a titanic clash between the cream of the Ottoman forces (and their technology) and the last great army in Anatolia made up of traditional horse archers. This was the last stand of Uzun Hasan, who had already seen his power eroded in northern and central Anatolia because of Mehmed II's expansion. He had been approached by the Venetians (with their vast trade and spy network this wasn't hard), who convinced him to put up a fight as the Ottomans were busy waging war in Europe. It would prove to be his undoing.

While Mehmed II was famous for his cannons, Matthias Corvinus, King of Hungary, was famous for having a large number of troops armed with arquebuses, very early muskets. They were inaccurate, could occasionally explode and were useless in the rain, but they were loud, scary and, if they hit their target, far more deadly than an arrow since they could puncture light armour and a basic shield. Mehmed II was never slow to recognise the value of new weapons, and at the Battle of Otlukbeli he not only had horse archers and cannons but, for the first time, he had a large number of arquebuses. Horses are skittish creatures, and getting them to charge against cracking arquebus fire and the deafening roar of cannons was an impossible task. The Battle of Otlukbeli was a staggering victory for Mehmed II. While it showed that the old form of combat through horse archers was now obsolete, it also extended Ottoman power into eastern Anatolia and eliminated the eastern front of his war with Venice. A look at the Venetian strategy in this conflict reveals little to criticise; forcing an enemy to fight on multiple fronts should have worked to the Venetians' advantage. Also, fighting battles where they wanted, in the way they wanted, should have meant victory for the Venetian forces. The problem was that, while the strategy was faultless, the Ottomans simply refused to lose. The resulting Treaty of Constantinople, agreed in 1479, meant that Mehmed II now ruled an expanded realm. Most humiliatingly, the Venetians were forced to pay a 100,000 ducat indemnity and had to agree a 10,000 ducat annual payment in order to sail into the Black Sea. There can be no doubt that Mehmed II had won a decisive victory, one in which he had shown commendable eagerness to embrace new technologies and an impressive ability to adapt to changing circumstances.

There was one silver lining in this Venetian cloud: Genoa was licking its wounds too. Unbelievably, during all this fighting in Anatolia and Europe, another front opened up when the Crimean Tatars, led by Meñli I, asked for Ottoman assistance against Genoese outposts, and Mehmed II agreed. The Tatars were, culturally and ethnically, similar to the Turkish horsemen of Osman's time and saw the Ottomans as their southern cousins. They were the typical agile cavalrymen of the Asian steppes, and because of that they were unable to besiege the walled Genoese trading posts on the coast of the Black Sea. As great as Mehmed II was, he couldn't be in two places at once, and while he travelled considerable distances throughout this era (I have already mentioned him being in both Albania and eastern Anatolia), being too far away from the real fight was inadvisable. So Mehmed II decided to send Gedik Ahmed Pasha to the Black Sea. Gedik Pasha was a remarkable man who had fought in this war in both Europe and Anatolia and was now being sent to the Crimea. He would eventually become both a grand admiral of the Ottoman fleet and the sultan's grand vizier. He was the very embodiment of the capable leader that Mehmed II counted on to use his initiative and get the job done. With Gedik Pasha, Mehmed chose well, and within a couple of years all the Genoese towns were under Ottoman control.

Then Mehmed II did something that was practical but dishonourable: he had Meñli I of the Tatars taken hostage. He was not released until he swore an oath of loyalty to the Ottoman throne, and it was from this point on that an understanding was brokered that would last for centuries. The Tatars would remain semi-autonomous and would, in time, become the irregular cavalry of the mid-Ottoman period. In return they could rule their lands as they saw fit, with little interference from Constantinople. The coastal towns remained in Ottoman hands and continued to be important trade hubs, only this time the tax revenues flowed to the Sublime Porte (a term used to denote the Ottoman seat of power) and the Ottoman treasury, not to Genoa. With the expansion into Moldova, north-eastern Anatolia and now the Crimea, the Black Sea was rapidly becoming an Ottoman lake. Complete encirclement had yet to occur, but in just one generation Ottoman control of a sea was on its way to becoming total domination. But territorial gains were not all Conqueror Mehmed was interested in. As mentioned above, in the 1470s, the Ottomans wanted to wrestle Genoese trading outposts from Italian control. As the empire expanded, so did Mehmed II's ambitions – and chief among those was trade.

Bazaars

Today the Grand Bazaar in Istanbul has sixty-one covered streets and contains some 4,000 shops (one of which was owned by my father in the 1960s). This sprawling, free-market maze was founded by Mehmed II shortly after capturing Constantinople. It started small and grew over the centuries to become not only a market that sells almost everything, but an international tourist attraction as well. According to 2014 statistics, it was the most visited tourist attraction in the world, with 91,250,000 visitors. On average (depending on the time of year), it gets between 250,000 and 400,000 visitors daily. So a market started in the reign of Mehmed II is still going strong today.

Meanwhile, after the battle and the butchery of 1453, Mehmed II had to repopulate the city of Constantinople; even if he had taken it peacefully, the population was then only 10 per cent of its peak. So Mehmed filled his new capital with people from all over the empire, making it a melting pot of cultures and ethnicities. Even the Genoese, who had fled during the siege, were allowed to return to their homes. Mehmed of course wanted to put his stamp on the city, and to this end he authorised the construction of many new buildings, including mosques and madrassas, as any Muslim ruler would do, but he also understood that he ruled an empire composed of many different races and religions. Counterintuitively, he restored the seat of the Greek Orthodox Patriarch and that of the Armenian Christian Patriarch. Furthermore he installed a Jewish grand rabbi, a sign that all were welcome – as long as they contributed. Compare this to Europe, where the Jews had been exiled from France and England, and all Muslims and Jews were about to undergo ethnic cleansing in Spain and Portugal. Mehmed's plan worked, as shown in a census from 1478, which indicated a population of 80,000, of which 20 per cent was Christian and 10 per cent was Jewish.

Tuğrâ

Islam forbids the depiction of either human beings or animals, so decorations and ornamentation in palaces and mosques were always abstract. The restriction on the illustration of living things led to the development of elaborate calligraphy and geometric designs, which brings us to the *tuğrâ* (pronounced 'too-ra'). This is the calligraphy symbol, unique to each sultan and is the eastern equivalent of a western monarch's coat of arms. Every sultan had a *tuğrâ*, but it is under Mehmed II that we start to see familiar features become standard, with the massive loop on the left, three spike-like strokes at the top centre and a tapering line to the right. As a symbol based on Arabic, it was read right to left. Later *tuğrâs* would become far more elaborate but, while they were continuing a tradition that predated Mehmed II, all later ones were influenced by his.

Meanwhile, with an impressive imperial capital, a greatly expanded realm and numerous enemies either neutralised or absorbed, it was under Mehmed II that there were changes to the power of the sultan in particular, and to Ottoman society in general. Prior to Mehmed II, the Ottoman court, while evolving, was still steeped in the traditions and culture from the time of Osman. Mehmed II not only took on the title of Caesar, but also began to expand Kanun (non-religious Ottoman) law alongside traditional Sharia (Islamic) law. This allowed for a central bureaucracy. Mehmed II often chose to populate governmental posts not with members of the aristocracy, but with men from the *devşirme*, the collection of Christian boys who had once been used to fill the ranks of the Janissaries. Time and circumstances had moved to the point where they were now used to fill the bureaucracy. As individual Janissaries aged, some moved into governmental positions, but some of these administrators were also eunuchs. This means that there weren't many actual 'Turks' walking around the corridors of power in Constantinople. Ethnically, the Ottoman bureaucracy comprised an assortment of different groups, but every one of these men did his best for the good of the empire. Even if a man had been born in Albania, he wouldn't have thought twice about sending forces to suppress an uprising in his birth country (unlike the previously mentioned Byzantine and Balkan princes who grew up in the court). The empire was where his loyalties and his best interests lay.

Ottoman law was not the same as Islamic law. This has led some in the modern world to accuse the sultans of being 'un-Islamic' despite the fact that Western chronicles almost always frame the Ottomans in an exclusively Islamic light. The reality was that, just as the French Empire happened to be Christian, religion was not the only way that empire defined itself. The same thing was true for the Ottoman dynasty. They could be good Muslims when it suited them, but there were practical considerations as well. One of the pillars of Islam (tenets to be a good Muslim) is that all Muslims should go on the haj, the pilgrimage to Mecca, at least once in their lifetime, if able to do so. It is interesting that from the 1300s to the 1920s, no Ottoman sultan went on the haj. Instead of depending on Sharia law, as many other Muslim civilisations did (and still do), the Ottomans had three courts that ran parallel with (and later superseded) Sharia law: one for Muslims, one for non-Muslims and one for trade disputes. However, things weren't quite that simple (two Muslims might take a trade dispute to the Muslim court rather than to the trade court) and, obviously, the Muslim court was the largest of the three. While the equivalent of the high court was in Constantinople, there were regional courts as well. However, that the business sector had its own defined judiciary shows again just how important trade and the economy were to Mehmed II.

Many of the Kanun laws were far from admirable. Mehmed II made fratricide legal for new sultans. Having witnessed the chaos of civil war between Ottoman princes, Mehmed II thought the simplest solution was cold-blooded murder, so on the accession of a new sultan, all his brothers (and half-brothers) were to be executed by strangulation. It was a horrific law. When Mehmed III came to power (over a century later), his nineteen brothers were lawfully murdered, including those who were still children. It was said that as the nineteen coffins were taken from Topkapı Palace, weeping and laments echoed around the city. It is unsurprising that the next sultan, Ahmed I, banned the practice, but the law had remained in place for more than a hundred years, and dozens of young princes were strangled under Mehmed II's law.

You would think that after all this Mehmed II was an old man, ready to hang up his spurs, but he was young when he came to the throne and was now only in his late forties. He was ready for a new challenge, which presented itself in the island of Rhodes. There, right in the Aegean, was the naval base for the Hospitaller Knights, who had been conducting what amounted to religiously motivated high seas piracy against Muslims for nearly two centuries. Mehmed II decided to deploy a large fleet under Gedik Ahmed Pasha, the man who had so ably captured the Crimea, and another general called Mesih Pasha (in charge of at least 20,000 troops) to take care of this persistent threat.

The Hospitallers had world-famous fortifications but were always short of men. At this time in Rhodes they numbered around 500, supplemented by a few thousand French troops. What unfolded from May to August of 1480 was a flurry of bombardments, breaches and attacks, but, unbelievably, the knights hung on and repelled everything Gedik Pasha could throw at them. Eventually the Ottomans withdrew, which infuriated Mehmed II. But the pasha wasn't done. From Rhodes he turned his attention to the Italian port of Otranto, where a number of survivors from Rhodes had fled. Gedik Pasha reasoned that a victory here would ensure a toehold for any future campaigns on the Italian peninsula. After fifteen days of bombardments and assaults, Gedik Pasha captured the port and, for the first time, the Ottomans had territory in Italy. To say panic spread across Italy would be a gross understatement. Otranto is on the very heel of the country and only a little over 400 miles from Rome, a city that was far less well defended than Constantinople. There was a flurry of Christian visitors to Rome that summer as travellers assumed this would be their last chance to see the ancient capital as a Christian city. Pope Sixtus IV called for a crusade against the infidel, but nobody came to his aid. The warring territories of Italy stood little chance against the Ottomans in their prime. It really did look like an end to the era of Christian rule in Italy.

But then something most unexpected happened. While planning a new assault on Rhodes, Mehmed II died in 1481, at the age of forty-nine. His death meant that three sultans in a row had died of natural causes in their forties. When a monarch dies in battle, by assassination or as the result of unusual circumstances (for example, according to some sources King John of England died from eating too many peaches – not the noblest way to go), the details become a matter of record. However, before the era of modern medicine, some older monarchs were said to have 'died of old age'. Nobody dies of 'old age'. People die from heart disease, strokes and cancer, but age itself does not kill. However, for three sultans (who would have had the best medical attention of the age) all to have died in their middle years was unusual and suggests some kind of hereditary illness. And yet, contemporary Ottoman sources are frustratingly vague about the symptoms suffered by any of these three. So, quite simply, no more can be said on the matter.

The unexpected death of Mehmed II was terrible news for the Ottoman realm but a blessing for Europe. The Ottoman garrison in Otranto was forced to leave when the empire fell into a new era of civil war. Italy could breathe a sigh of relief and, unbeknown to anybody at the time, the Ottomans would never return with an invasion army.

6

A Sultan Blackmailed

While Mehmed II died at a relatively young age, he had started siring children in his teens. Consequently his eldest son, Bayezid, was already in his thirties when his father died, and while it might be assumed that the eldest son would inherit the throne there was no such official tradition at this point in the history of the Ottomans. Although the eldest usually had the strongest claim, this was a time when it was 'every prince for himself'. According to Mehmed II's new law, the next sultan was to have all of his brothers strangled and rule unopposed, but there was nothing to say that Mehmed's favourite son, Bayezid, would be that sultan.

When Mehmed II died, messengers loyal to different sons rode out to alert them to the situation. However, Grand Vizier Karamanlı Mehmet Pasha deliberately broke Islamic law to have Mehmed II's body brought to Constantinople, where it lay in state for three days. All of this was, allegedly, to give Mehmed's son Cem (a reminder that 'c' is pronounced as 'j' in Turkish, so it's 'Jem' in English, the man after whom the author was named), who was closer than Bayezid, time to get to the capital. While Bayezid had every reason to expect to be the next sultan, Cem had a technical argument in his favour: he was the first son of Mehmed II to be porphyrogenitus, a title bestowed on Roman imperial babies who were born in the purple room at the imperial palace in Constantinople. Porphyrogenitus literally means 'born in the purple' and indicates that the child is the rightful imperial heir, according to Roman/Byzantine law. Of course the reason why Bayezid wasn't porphyrogenitus is because he was born before

1453. So, while Cem had the weaker claim, he had nothing to lose by trying his luck. After all, according to the new law, it was either that or be strangled to death.

As the first-born son and an older prince, Bayezid had better connections to the regime than Cem. The Janissaries backed Bayezid and saw through the grand vizier's delaying tactics. They responded in the only way battle-hardened troops knew how: they killed (hanged) the grand vizier and rioted in the streets, raising fears of a breakdown in law and order. The empire, which had been on the rise for so long, was now slipping into chaos. Political murders, rioting, princes racing to the capital – none of this was good for stability. As it was, Bayezid arrived in the capital first, and he quickly donned Osman's belt and sword to legitimise his claim that he was the new sultan, Bayezid II. Meanwhile Cem was busy capturing towns around Bursa to shore up his support in Anatolia, but this was the wrong move, underlining Cem's lack of experience. Bayezid II raised an army and sent his newly appointed vizier to kill Cem and crush his younger brother's rebellion, but Cem met the vizier in battle and beat him. This gave Cem the breathing space he needed to set up his own Ottoman state from the old capital of Bursa, where he even had time to produce newly minted coins proclaiming himself sultan. In an attempt to settle the dispute, he offered Bayezid II a 50:50 split of the empire: Bayezid II could have Europe and Cem would have Anatolia. The offer wasn't even considered by Bayezid, who raised a new army, but this time he led it himself.

The two brothers met just outside of Bursa in a battle not only for control of the empire, but for the fate of the Ottoman state. Bayezid II won the day, but Cem managed to escape the field of battle and raced to the coast, where he got on a ship to the Nile Delta and the safety of the Mameluke state of Egypt. The Mamelukes welcomed Cem with open arms. Not only was this refuge a place where he could plot in safety, but it was also conveniently located for a pilgrimage to Mecca, so Cem was the only Ottoman prince to complete the haj (and as he's not considered one of the official sultans, this does not contradict my previous statement). After a year of planning, he returned to Anatolia with a new army, intent on renewing his quest for the throne. Bayezid II, however, was too smart for him, and while Cem was trying to regain control of his own area of influence around Konya Bayezid II caught up with his brother and, again, defeated him in battle. Yet again Cem slipped through his brother's fingers and managed to reach the safety of the sea. This time he went to the Hospitaller Knights on Rhodes, where the intrigue really begins.

During his lifetime, Cem was seen as something of a folk hero in Europe – and he is regarded as such nowadays in Turkey. He's seen in Anatolia in the same light as Robin Hood is in the West. He's a good story, but, unlike Robin Hood, Cem really existed; however, he was pretty much a total loser. To summarise so far: his claim to the throne was dubious at best. When the grand vizier tried to delay the announcement of a new sultan so that Cem could get to Constantinople first, he failed to do that. While he defeated the first force sent against him, on the two separate occasions when he needed to win a victory against his brother he lost, and then, twice in the space of a year, he was forced to flee his homeland. It's a little depressing to share a name with Mister Second-best-at-everything.

If all that wasn't bad enough, Cem was now in the hands of his ideological enemy. It shouldn't be forgotten that by this time the Hospitallers had been fighting against Islam for about 400 years and had been an effective thorn in the side of the Ottomans pretty much since the inception of the state. They were a religious order that reported directly to the papacy, an organisation whose knee-jerk reaction to any western expansion by the Ottomans was to declare a crusade (although, admittedly, many calls were ignored). The knights were not going to look after Cem in the name of Christian charity. Instead, Cem was to be used as a bargaining chip. Anytime Bayezid began to menace the West, the pope threatened to release Cem at the head of a crusade, a tactic that would combine military might with a claim to the Ottoman throne. So Pope Innocent VIII did the not-so-innocent thing of telling Bayezid II that he would happily keep Cem out of the way in return for a steep ransom of 120,000 crowns. To put that into context, it was roughly the same amount as the entire annual income of the papacy of that time. It was also agreed that Bayezid II would pay an annual tariff of 45,000 ducats for Cem's 'expenses'. And the ransom was not just about money – along with the ransom Bayezid II sent gifts, including the Holy Lance and one hundred Moorish (therefore Muslim and acceptable to the pope) slaves. All of this came flooding into the Vatican treasury at the same time as some of its most famous artistic commissions were being paid for. So, while it can never be proved conclusively, it's likely that at least some of the work on the Sistine Chapel was paid for by the ransom.

Cem had a very comfortable lifestyle in Europe. He was never a prisoner in the traditional sense of the word; his life was more like that of an honoured guest under house arrest, although he still wasn't out of the woods in terms of danger. Of his clothing that still exists, one silk shirt looks unusually bulky. That's because it has three layers: the outer and inner layers are silk, but the middle layer is steel mail armour. Another silk shirt is covered in mystical symbols, presumably designed to ward off evil spirits. The possibility of an assassination attempt must never have been far from Cem's mind. From the host's point of view, this was the first time any Ottoman family member had spent more than a few hours in close proximity to European gentry. As such, he was something of a novelty, and a number of books were written about him. Their illustrations are the first ever to show what Ottoman nobles wore rather than what Europeans thought they wore. It was a useful cultural exchange, and everyone who met Cem was impressed by him. It was also said that he had multiple affairs with European ladies looking for a little 'Turkish delight' (I am aware the euphemism is anachronistic and childish, but I like it).

As an ongoing threat to Bayezid II's reign, Cem's mere existence thwarted his brother's ambitions for fifteen years. Cem died in 1495 during the siege of Naples, where he fought on the side of the French King Charles VIII (proving Cem was more of a lover than a fighter). The news wasn't exactly rushed to Bayezid II as it meant the loss of some serious European leverage, but when the sultan finally heard, he declared three days of mourning across the empire. This was an admirable show of remorse and fraternal loss, but, in truth, this must have been the best news Bayezid had had in all of his long reign. Because of the pressure from the West while Cem was in captivity, Ottoman expansion into Europe was centred largely on mopping up Venetian strongholds in the Peloponnese. Bold campaigns to push into the Hungarian heartland or landing invasion forces in Italy weren't options as long as Cem lived. Following his death Venetian bases of operation in the Greek ports of Lepanto, Modon and Coron all fell in quick succession and were to develop into key trading sites and bases for the Ottoman navy. It was becoming a zero-sum game for Venice in their dealings with the Ottomans.

Meanwhile, Bayezid II ensured that his navy grew and that his ship designs included the most up-to-date refinements – and that they were well equipped with the latest cannons. All of this would have been extremely expensive. Naval warfare was always much more costly than funding armies, but the fact that Bayezid II invested so much in his navy was a sign of his intention to beat the Venetians where their strength lay. Eventually, in 1503, Venice signed a treaty of peace with Bayezid II. Once again they had clashed with the Ottoman state and lost, but the actions described here represented Bayezid's main activity against Western powers. Because of the situation with his erstwhile brother, Bayezid II concentrated most of his efforts in the East, where there was growing dissent in Anatolia.

The Qizilbash is a convenient catch-all phrase for the militant Shi'a groups that ranged from central Anatolia eastwards. For those not familiar with the doctrinal difference between Shi'a and Sunni Islam, the best way to describe it, although it is not a perfect analogy, is to think about it as similar to the split between Catholics and Protestants. While they both believe many of the same things, in the case of the Muslims, they disagree about the legitimacy of the Prophet Muhammed's successors and emphasize different aspects of the traditions, resulting in a lot of bitterness between the two sects. As the sultans were Sunni, the Shi'a were only ever going to rebel. They were largely based in the newer areas of the empire conquered by Mehmed II and had connections further east into the Shi'a heartlands of Persia (Iran). Their rebellion wasn't small in size or fervour, and the battles, though small in scale, were fought with vicious intensity. The Shi'a rebellion had a charismatic and effective leader called Ismail, but by now the Ottoman Empire was too large and too well ensconced for this rebellion to succeed. In the end the Qizilbash had either to move out of Ottoman lands or face annihilation. Ismail decided to move and took his followers with him to found a new Persian empire further east. This was the beginning of the Safavid Empire, which was to challenge the Ottomans in Asia for centuries.

What had been an uprising within the Ottoman Empire eventually became a war between two empires, one that also drew in the Mamelukes who, for the first time, clashed with Ottoman forces in Syria. The war lasted six years and ended with minor concessions from Bayezid II; however, his overall territory was expanding into what is now northern Iraq. The situation with the Qizilbash emphasized the need for Bayezid to clarify the place of Islam in Ottoman society, especially after the divisions between Shi'as and Sunnis turned into what was essentially civil war; but another event far to the west also highlighted the plight of Muslims in the world. In 1492 the Iberian peninsula witnessed two key events: one was the famous voyage of Christopher Columbus; the other was the equally important but less well remembered fall of Granada, the last Muslim realm in Spain, where Islamic rule ended more with a whimper than a bang.

Spain has done some interesting rewriting of its history. I have had first-hand experience of tour guides pretending their civil war wasn't worth mentioning, and controversial issues, such as the Spanish Inquisition, apparently never happened. Perhaps the biggest misunderstood moment in Spanish history is the 'Reconquista'. I go into this in more depth in my book on the crusades, but the simple fact is that some areas of Spain were under Islamic control for more than 700 years. Some areas of Spain, to this day, have been ruled longer by Muslims than by Christians. The Christian princes in the north had never had control of these areas in the past, so it was a 'conquest' and not a 're-conquest' – but the latter term played better with the other Christian powers. The climax of this conquest was the fall of Granada, after which Ferdinand and Isabella had total control of the Iberian peninsula. However, they were in the same boat as Bayezid II because they both faced a potential fifth column of people not aligned to the religious orthodoxies of the rulers. But there was one big difference: Bayezid II faced outright rebellion and fought against it with conventional means. The Jews and Muslims of Spain were not in revolt; they were simply ordinary people trying to get on with their lives under a new regime. There is no evidence that these groups tried to return former Muslim rulers to Spain. Instead, it was the new rulers who proved to be intolerant to change.

The decade in Spain from 1492 to 1502 is enough for a book of its own (and indeed has one, entitled *A Fraudulent Decade*). From a distance, we start to see Spain's rise as a superpower; closer up, we see its paranoia about the 'other'. Condensing a very complex situation, after forced conversions, religious pogroms and the use of all kinds of other nefarious methods, including the infamous Spanish Inquisition, the Spanish forcibly ejected everyone who was Muslim or Jew, or thought to be Muslim or Jew, from the country. There was no appetite for them to be accepted elsewhere in Europe either. France and England had expelled their Jewish populations centuries earlier. Venice had theirs in a semi-restricted area known as a 'ghetto'. Everyone in Europe 'knew' that Muslims were the enemy as the echoes from the crusades were still there in the sixteenth century. Where could the diaspora go? Who would welcome them and give them refuge? The answer was Bayezid II. Despite his difficulties with Shi'a rebellions, he had no problem welcoming these Sunni Muslims and Spanish Jews, whose fellows, already under Ottoman rule, were well integrated into Ottoman life. The prospect of new tax revenues didn't hurt either.

For a time Galata Tower was temporarily turned into a mosque for the arriving Muslims, and the Jews were allowed to practise their faith in safety, provided they paid the *cizye*, the tax for non-Muslims. This wasn't all philanthropy; the artisans of southern Spain were well regarded, and the new Spanish rulers had foolishly allowed many scholars and craftsmen to go to a foreign power. Bayezid II summarised the situation by saying, 'They say Ferdinand is a wise monarch. How could he be? He who impoverishes his country to enrich mine.' Now all that knowledge and expertise resided under Ottoman control. For example, the first printing press in Constantinople was built by immigrant Jews in 1493. Jewish communities cropped up in every major European city under Ottoman control. Regardless of the benefits to the Ottomans, compared to other dynasties of the day Bayezid's open-door policy showed remarkable broadmindedness. Given how much effort the West devoted to making the Ottomans seem 'other' and 'alien' during Bayezid II's rule, it's little wonder that he turned his back on his father's westernisation of the court. A Renaissance era painting of Mehmed II, by the Venetian painter Gentile Bellini, shows that Mehmed II had Western-style decorations in his palace in Constantinople. No such Western-style painting exists of Bayezid II, who ordered the removal and remodelling of the Western influences in the palace.

The need for ships to transport Jews and Muslims from Spain came to the attention of four brothers: Ishak, Oruç, Hızır and Ilyas. These men were ever alert to a money-making opportunity, and seized on this one. They came from Albanian/Greek stock (their mother's first husband had been a Greek Orthodox priest, so she had been, at some point in her life, Christian), but the sons were very much Ottomans, and on top of that they were pirates. The brothers (minus Ishak, who stayed at home) started off as privateers, plundering specifically for the Hospitallers. Success encouraged them to strike out on their own, and they became independent raiders. So now they were definitely pirates, specialising in plundering North Africa and Italy. Some time later they were attacked by their previous employers, the Hospitallers. Ilyas was killed in the engagement and Oruç was captured. He was held on Rhodes for three years before Hizir located him, crept into the Hospitaller fortress and set him free.

From here Oruç went from strength to strength. At first he was in charge of eighteen galleys, and then twenty-four galleys when he participated in the Ottoman naval expedition to Apulia in the Kingdom of Naples, where he bombarded several coastal forts and captured two ships. On his way back to Lesbos, he captured three galleons and another ship. By now, like every good pirate, he had a new name: Barbarossa ('red beard'), a nod to his less-than-Turkic heritage. After this he approached the Mamelukes and met their sultan, who gave him another ship to raid the coasts of Italy and the islands of the Mediterranean. In 1503, Barbarossa managed to seize three more ships as well as the island of Djerba in Tunisia. This location became his new base of operations, allowing him to conduct raids in the western Mediterranean. It was at this point that Hızır joined Barbarossa again.

The local sultan of Tunisia (the third Muslim power they had worked for) allowed them to use the port of La Goulette on the condition that one-third of their booty went to him. From here they terrorised Mediterranean Christian shipping. Papal galleys were plundered and a huge Sicilian warship, with more than 400 warriors on board, was captured by the two brothers. When not enriching themselves on the lucrative shipping routes, they raided the coasts of Calabria and Liguria.

All this was taking its toll on the European powers, while costing Bayezid II precisely nothing. Things were so good that Ishak finally joined in. In 1510, the three brothers raided Sicily and repulsed Spanish attacks on three different North African cities. By now they were not so much pirates as admirals of their own formidable fleet. In August 1512, however, during a battle in North Africa against the Spanish, Barbarossa lost his left arm. He had it replaced with a silver one and now went by the even more memorable name of Gümüş Kol, 'silver arm' (take that, Gold Finger).

For the next six years they attacked everywhere in the Christian Mediterranean. The European powers were always one step behind the brothers, and dozens of ships were captured or sunk. In 1516 they captured Algiers, and when Barbarossa proclaimed himself sultan, nobody dared to object. However, it soon became clear that the role of sultan brought different challenges to that of pirate captain, and Barbarossa was shrewd enough to realise that he had overstretched himself. So, in 1517, he offered Algiers to the Ottoman sultan. Suddenly, with no military effort or expenditure, the Ottoman Empire had expanded across vast tracts of the North African coast. Overnight Algiers became an Ottoman province. Naturally Barbarossa became the *bey* of Algiers and was also made *beylerbey* (Chief Governor) of the Western Mediterranean. The challenge now for the Ottomans was to hold the territory and protect it from the Spanish, who were flush with riches pouring in from the New World. So the Janissaries, with equipment that a pirate just couldn't afford, were brought in to stabilise the situation and resist any Spanish attack. A year later, the Spanish King Charles V arrived in North Africa to rid himself of the Barbarossa scourge. After a twenty-day siege at Tlemcen, both Barbarossa and Ishak were killed. However, the Barbarossa name lived on as Hızır took on the title and continued the fight.

The first thing Hızır did was recapture Tlemcen, and from there he went on and on. Not to be outdone by his brother, he, too, picked up another name: Hayreddin Pasha. To keep it short, he ruled Algiers for a time and became the most feared naval commander of the first half of the sixteenth century. He was so good that the French offered him anything he wanted to switch sides and lead their fleet. He declined, and in 1545 he retired. With a long list of victories under his belt, he had plenty to write about, and (as unlikely as it seems for someone who had been a pirate) he began work on his five-volume autobiography, which became essential reading for any naval officer at the time. His book is aptly named *Gazavat-ı Hayreddin Paşa* ('Conquests of Hayreddin Pasha'). In conclusion, Ottoman expansion in North Africa happened by accident. No sultan ever planned to expand the empire with Muslim pirates. This all started during the reign of Bayezid II but ended several sultans later, so back to Bayezid II.

A pious man, Bayezid II had a mosque built in his name in Constantinople. The mighty Bayezid II Mosque was his faith written in mortar and stone. In its time it was the largest mosque in the city, and today it is second only to another, later mosque. But this was just one of many dozens of madrassas, mosques and other religious projects Bayezid II paid for during his rule. Construction of the mosque was delayed as, in 1509, Constantinople was hit by a major earthquake. This was neither the first nor the last, but it was the first major one to occur under Ottoman rule. The quake (and the following tsunami) affected a 200-kilometre stretch along the north eastern coast of the Sea of Marmara (with Constantinople pretty much in the middle); the aftershocks went on for more than forty-five days. It is estimated that tens of thousands were made homeless on top of the estimated 10,000 who died. Countless buildings were demolished, and a hundred mosques were ruined. It was a truly devastating event, but one that Bayezid II poured everything into, using the resources of the empire to rebuild and rehouse his subjects.

The first Bayezid had the epithet of 'thunderbolt' because of his success in military campaigning. Bayezid II was not a great conqueror; instead, he became known as Bayezid 'the just'. He was a deeply religious (some would say superstitious) man. He increased the power of the Islamic courts (contrary to his father's plans) and made sure the rule of law was fairly applied according to Islamic principles. But more than anything else he was a consolidator, as seen in the way he put substantial money and effort into rebuilding the capital after the earthquake. His father had won many new territories in the course of his lifetime, but not all of those conquests were complete. It was left to Bayezid II to ensure that Ottoman rule went unchallenged within the empire's expanding borders.

It is ironic that, after all of this, Bayezid II faced betrayal by his sons, Selim and Ahmed. It was becoming apparent that, because the eldest son did not automatically inherit the throne, the prince who got to Istanbul first would become sultan. Ahmed was his father's favourite son, and as such was based nearer the capital, but he just couldn't wait for his father to die and set about capturing several Ottoman cities for himself. Selim did pretty much the same thing. Bayezid II was able to turn on Selim first, beating him in battle and exiling the rebellious son to the Crimea, where the Tatars could keep an eye on him. When he faced Ahmed and his army, he simply did not allow them to enter Constantinople – which left Ahmed at a loss as to what to do next. To attack the capital and imprison or kill his own father would be an inauspicious way to start his rule. This impasse was resolved when Selim made a spectacular comeback. He gained the allegiance of the Janissaries, and in 1512 arrived at the Ottoman capital, demanding that his father step down. Bayezid II carried out his son's wishes and headed off to retirement in Anatolia. However, he died en route, at the age of sixty-four, much older than his three predecessors.

Now in the seat of power, Selim I went on a purge to ensure he had total control. This meant having each of his brothers killed – except for Ahmed, who was out of reach but ready to challenge his younger brother. When the two met in battle, Ahmed lost and was executed shortly afterwards. He had barely had time to warm the cushion on the throne, but Selim had already proved to be both politically shrewd and decisive; however, the succession was surrounded by uncertainty and soaked in blood once more. Everything about it was needlessly messy. While all of Europe had settled on a system of primogeniture (the eldest son takes all), the Ottomans, by contrast, were regularly facing periods of conflict and potential civil war, times that external powers could exploit (an example is the story of Cem). Inadvertently, the Ottomans had set up a kind of Darwinian experiment; whoever could scrabble to the top of the heap in the Ottoman rush for succession was likely to be capable enough to rule. The problem with primogeniture is that sometimes the eldest son is inadequate to the role (think of Richard II or Henry VI in England). Also, inadvertently, Selim had created a precedent when he gained the backing of the Janissaries in his fight for the throne. Now the military elite had a hand in determining who would become the new sultan. It was an evolution of authority later sultans would come to regret.

Selim I was never meant to be sultan; he had achieved the throne the hard way. Nevertheless, he inherited the problems that Bayezid II had faced. First of all, the nascent Safavid Empire to the east was causing trouble, so Selim I rode out to face them in 1514 at the Battle of Chaldiran. Almost nobody remembers the name of this battle, and yet it had major consequences not just then, but today as well. At the time the Safavid ruler was Ismail I of the Qizilbash, who was then seen as an almost divine figure, an infallible prophet, but Selim I put an end to that image when he delivered a decisive victory for the Ottomans. Ismail I was wounded, nearly captured and had to watch with dismay as a number of his wives were captured and eventually married off to Ottoman nobles. It was about as ignominious a defeat as he could imagine.

The lasting importance of the battle was that it extended Ottoman influence into western Iran. It also brought Armenian and Kurdish communities under Ottoman control. Because the Armenians were a Christian community living on the very edge of the empire, they were always considered with suspicion by the Ottomans. Then there were the Kurds, a fiercely independent warrior race with their own distinct ethnicity, culture and language. They had long been allies of the Persians, but after this major Ottoman victory they switched sides to become loyal fighters in the Ottoman army – and would remain so until the end of the empire.

Selim was not known for his patience. He had so many viziers executed that a common curse of the time was 'May you be a vizier of Selim's'. When the dust had settled on the vanquished Safavids, Selim I looked next to the Mamelukes who ruled Syria, Palestine, parts of Arabia and Egypt. In less than two years, he routed an empire that had withstood both the crusades and the Mongols (at their peak), and, after 250 years, Mameluke rule in the Middle East was swept aside. At the Battle of Marj Dabiq, in August 1516, the Mameluke sultan was killed. All of Syria fell in just one battle when Selim I amassed an army that easily outnumbered anything the Mamelukes could muster. When the Ottomans got to Gaza, the Mamelukes made one last attempt to stop them from getting into the Mameluke Egyptian homeland at the Battle of Yaunis Khan. That also was an emphatic defeat (thanks mainly to the actions of Selim's grand vizier Hadım Sinan Pasha, a rare vizier whom Selim actually liked).

Mameluke Egypt was in crisis. A new sultan was hastily installed only for the Mamelukes to face a huge invading Ottoman army marching towards them. In early 1517, Selim won a battle at Ridaniya, the final stop before Cairo. Although Grand Vizier Sinan Pasha had died, the battle for Cairo was another emphatic Ottoman victory, and the Mameluke capital was thoroughly plundered as the conquerors indulged in an orgy of rape and vandalism that lasted for days. The comparative reserve demonstrated by Mehmed II at Constantinople sits in stark contrast to the destruction displayed by

Selim. Mameluke rulers (including the sultan) were hanged. Heads of Mameluke captains were put on spikes that festooned the city walls. Cairo was a macabre charnel house by the time Selim was finished with it.

There are some people, both at the time and today, who like to portray Islam as a force outside of Europe. It is an unwelcome 'other', which leads to an inevitable clash of civilisations. The reality is that many areas of Europe were under Muslim control for centuries: Portugal, Spain and Sicily, as well as the Balkans. It's a fact that Islam has been around in Europe longer than Protestantism, but many places have gone out of their way to pretend a country's Muslim past never happened. Additionally, as the Ottoman Empire is the most recent Muslim power to have ruled in Europe, it is portrayed as being obsessed with defeating Christian powers. The Ottomans did clash with many of these powers, and many of those clashes were bloody, but, as the destruction in Cairo shows, the empire was capable of carrying out lethal and destructive attacks on Muslims too.

The idea of the unifying force of religion doesn't hold up under scrutiny in any religion. After all, the princes and monarchs of Western Europe were all Christian, but their history is one of being at each other's throats for centuries. Practical realities always came before religious considerations. The Ottoman sultans regularly made treaties with Christian rulers, but these agreements were based on what was deemed to be of practical benefit – for both sides. In such matters, European rulers could not have cared less that they were doing a deal with the 'infidel', and the same was true of the sultan in Constantinople. An interesting side note to all this was that at the time of the Ottoman invasion, the Mamelukes were already at war with Portugal in the Indian Ocean. Selim wanted to protect his new conquests and continued the battle, so that now there were Ottoman vessels fighting off the coasts of Africa and India. This would lead later to the Ottoman capture of Aden and Yemen.

While there can be no doubt that Selim was a fierce man with a short temper, he had other sides to him as well. He was a poet who wrote in both Ottoman Turkish and Persian, and, perhaps surprisingly for a man capable of stunning violence and brutality, he had a humble side. Among the prizes in the conquered Mameluke territory were the three most important religious cities in the world to Jews, Christians and Muslims. Jerusalem was one, but Mecca and Medina also became his property. Mameluke sultans had called themselves 'Ruler of the Two Holy Cities', but Selim showed unexpected humility by taking the more pious title of 'Servant of the Two Holy Cities'.

The collapse of the Mameluke state coincided almost exactly with the timing of Barbarossa's gift of Algiers, so in the space of just a couple of years Selim had more than doubled Ottoman territory. This was one of the fastest expansions of a mature empire in history. However, despite such an astonishingly successful start to his rule, his time as sultan was to be cut short when, in 1512, he fell ill and died at the age of fifty. Some think the cause was an anthrax infection (not uncommon for men who rode on horses a lot); others believe that his death coincided with an outbreak of plague. Regardless, his legacy to his successor was a greatly expanded empire that had vanquished all neighbouring enemies. While it is tempting to ponder what he could have achieved had he been given more time, his son also proved to be remarkably good at the conquering business. His name was Suleiman.

7

A Magnificent Lawgiver

A great place to start with Suleiman is a full list of his titles, and they are fascinating: 'Sultan of the Ottomans, Allah's deputy on earth, Lord of the Lords of this world, Possessor of men's necks, King of believers and unbelievers, King of Kings, Emperor of the East and the West, Majestic Caesar, Emperor of the Chakans of great authority, Prince and Lord of the most happy constellation, Seal of victory, Refuge of all the people in the whole entire world, the shadow of the almighty dispensing quiet on the Earth.' I think we can agree that his business cards would have been awesome!

Let's break the list down. The first title is obvious, and 'Allah's deputy' implies his supreme Islamic authority without overstepping the mark (the word 'Islam' means 'one who submits'). The 'possessor of necks' harks back to his father Selim's practice of beheading even senior officials; anyone who displeased the sultan could expect to be beheaded for certain crimes. The next few titles are unexpectedly Roman; the Ottomans were aware that when they conquered Constantinople (in essence, the Eastern Roman Empire) the titles of 'emperor' and 'Caesar' still had importance. Claiming to be 'Emperor of the East and West' was not only an exaggeration, but also a direct challenge to the authority of Rome, which at this point was hopelessly outclassed by the Ottomans. 'King of Kings' may sound a little Biblical, but that's only because the Gospels took the title from the Persian emperors' *shahenshah*, literally, 'king of kings'. So, again, the Ottomans are challenging a major rival, but this time it's the Safavid Persians to the east. The next few titles are little more than showing off, but then we come to 'Refuge of all the people in the whole entire world', which shows that the sultans were well aware that their empire was multicultural and multi-faith, with Christians, Jews, Muslims and others all living together (not necessarily 'in harmony', but much better than anywhere else at the time). The ejection of the Jews and Muslims from Spain was still fresh in the minds of those living in the first half of the sixteenth century.

I hope the reader will be pleased to learn that this is the only time in this book that all of Suleiman's titles will be listed. In the West he has become known as Suleiman the Magnificent – and he truly was. Only two of his military campaigns failed; everything else he swept before him. When he wasn't in the saddle, he was sitting in his opulent palace in the largest city in Europe. His empire stretched for hundreds, if not thousands, of miles in all directions. If anyone should be called 'magnificent', Suleiman fits the bill perfectly. And yet, that is not the name he is known by in the East. There he is remembered as 'Suleiman the lawgiver', and, as we shall see, his effective running of the empire was to be much admired. Suleiman had every opportunity to be distracted by the wealth of an empire in its prime, but instead he was regularly hard at work, looking at finances, the legal system and legislation as well as fighting to expand his territories.

Suleiman's reign saw the start of a period when the harem merged into the wider palace and the political sphere. It is with Suleiman that we see the era of the 'Sultanate of Women', a time when the harem became the focal point of political power. If that wasn't revolutionary enough, Suleiman was the first sultan in more than two centuries to be officially married (though he still had several hundred concubines). His wife was formally Hürrem Sultan, but she was better known as Roxelana, and she was what we would today call 'Ukrainian'. Roxelana was most likely captured by the Tatars and then handed over to the Ottomans as part of their annual tribute. She was about fifteen when she arrived in the harem in Constantinople, a young girl in a strange land, surrounded by an unfamiliar language, religion and culture. Because of the sheer number of women in the harem, just being there didn't automatically mean you would ever meet the sultan, let alone catch his eye. But catch his eye she did, as we can see from the love poem he wrote for her:

Throne of my lonely niche, my wealth, my love, my moonlight.
My most sincere friend, my confidant, my very existence, my sultan, my one and only love.
The most beautiful among the beautiful...
My springtime, my merry faced love, my daytime, my sweetheart, laughing leaf...
My plants, my sweet, my rose, the one only who does not distress me in this world...
My Constantinople, my Caraman, the earth of my Anatolia
My Badakhshan, my Baghdad and Khorasan
My woman of the beautiful hair, my love of the slanted brow, my love of eyes full of mischief...
I'll sing your praises always
I, lover of the tormented heart, Muhibbi of the eyes full of tears,
I am happy.

The Topkapı Palace harem is vast and labyrinthine. Walking around just the few parts of the compound that are open to the public is incredibly evocative; you can almost hear the whispered intrigue as footsteps echo through the beautifully tiled corridors. One room has a gurgling fountain, strategically located so that conversations could not be overheard. The harem would have been a lively place, with children running around, unaware that only one of them would become the next sultan, to the lethal detriment of the others. As such, there was constant plotting and scheming as each mother of a son vied to position him to become sultan.

When Roxelana arrived, Suleiman already had two favourites in Gülfem and Mahidevran. Roxelana became known as Hürrem because in Turkish it means 'cheerful one'. Her outgoing personality and playfulness intoxicated the young sultan, and over time Roxelana became the sultan's favourite by knocking her two competitors down the pecking order. She was so favoured that she was allowed to have to more than one son, breaking a centuries-old tradition – and she broke another tradition when she married Suleiman. An Ottoman ruler hadn't been formally married since the days of Orhan, a very different time, and their wedding, in 1533/4, was as lavish and as opulent as it was surprising. After this,

Roxelana was given the new title of Haseki Sultan, 'chief consort'. This marriage and her new title set a precedent and explain why women were to hold such sway at court for the next 130 years. Roxelana's wealth and influence would have made her far more powerful than her contemporary, Queen Mary of England. This Ukrainian former slave girl influenced foreign policy and affairs of state for the largest empire in Europe and the Middle East. The sultan's wife now had more power than anyone but the sultan.

A fact not realised by most is that some women didn't spend their entire lives in the sultan's harem. Once a son came of age at sixteen, he was sent off to govern an area of the empire – and the mother went with the son. This meant the son had an ally he could trust, and it also stopped the harem from becoming a nursing home for older consorts. Again, Roxelana bucked the trend and stayed in the royal harem to be near her husband and sons, in the thick of imperial intrigue. Later in Suleiman's reign, Mustafa, the son of Suleiman's erstwhile favourite Mahidevran, rebelled. He was older than any of the chief consort's sons and, therefore, more likely to take the throne come the sultan's death, which meant he posed a direct threat to Roxelana's sons and her legacy. Up until his rebellion, Mustafa had been seen as capable and had even served as his father's grand vizier for a time. The interesting thing about this rebellion is that there seems to be no evidence for it other than hearsay, and that hearsay seems to have come from Roxelana.

Rebelling Ottoman princes were nothing new, so it could be that Mustafa had grown impatient to become sultan, or it could be that the whole thing was made up by Roxelana as a means to remove the main impediment to one of her sons becoming sultan (with all that this meant for her). If the latter was the case, then her scheming worked. Suleiman had Mustafa executed, and Mahidevran, with no son, lost her status and became an irrelevance in the power politics of the sultanate. While it's not hard to believe that Roxelana plotted Mustafa's fall, it could also be that rumours about her involvement were spread by her enemies (she had many). However, when considering '*cui bono*' (who benefits), this turn of events would seem to have most favoured Roxelana. Her links to other high profile executions seem to have been based more on gossip than this particular one.

Roxelana was concerned to build a legacy outside the palace as well as inside it. She paid for the construction of a women's hospital near the slave market in Constantinople, the famous Mimar Sinan's first architectural project in Istanbul; this wasn't a small project, either, as the hospital was the third-largest building in the capital at the time. All her construction projects were either of religious or practical benefit, and they stretched to all the great cities of the empire. In Jerusalem she founded a public kitchen to feed hundreds of the poor and had another of a similar size built in Mecca. Her legacy encompassed not just the politics of the age but impressive projects in bricks and mortar, many of which can still be seen today (such as a recently restored women's *hammam* in Istanbul). She died in 1558 in her mid-fifties and her mausoleum is adjacent to Suleiman's in Istanbul.

Pastry (Part 1)

A somewhat mundane fact from the reign of Suleiman is linked to what is possibly the most disgusting name for a cake ever, the so-called Roman Placenta Cake. I hasten to reassure the reader that placenta is not one of the ingredients in what is actually a delicious confection. The cake was originally a multi-layered pastry with cheese, covered in honey and bay leaves. The name is misleading as it is thought to come from the Greek 'plakous', meaning thin layer (the same root word for the term 'placenta'). It is mentioned by a few Roman writers, including Cato, so it was obviously well known in his day and delicious enough to write about. These Roman references attest to the ancient origins of this allegedly 'Turkish' pastry. By now you have probably realised that we are talking about baklava. There are some differences from the original version because today it's made with filo pastry, the cheese has been replaced with ground nuts and, while honey is still used, sugar-based syrup is far more common. While it is likely that baklava originated in the Byzantine imperial court, the recipe was also to be found in the sixteenth-century kitchens of Topkapı Palace. We know that it was first mentioned in English in 1650, so this exotic pastry has been known even in Western Europe for centuries.

Despite his complex domestic life, courtly intrigues and diversionary pastries, Suleiman meant business when, early on in his reign, he assembled the largest invasion force seen in the West for a generation. John Hunyadi had done an effective job of keeping the Ottomans at bay, and Suleiman had no equivalent to Cem lurking in Europe as leverage, but the new sultan showed what the pent-up ambitions of an empire could do in Eastern Europe.

In 1521 he arrived at the walls of Belgrade, the Hungarian fortress town that had withstood all previous Ottoman assaults. This time, after the walls were undermined and the population had withstood weeks of withering cannon fire, it fell in just over a month. As a result, Belgrade became a key mustering point for Ottoman forces heading west. The Hungarian king, Louis II, tried to retake the town by amassing a huge army of about 60,000, but in his haste to build an overwhelming force he forgot about supplies, and the army disintegrated due to lack of food and pay. Events culminated five years later, in the summer of 1526, with the Battle of Mohács. This was to be the last stand of the Hungarian kingdom, which had amassed an army of around 20,000 to Suleiman's more than 50,000. Louis II also had thousands of heavily armoured knights clad in plate mail armour, and their horses, also encased in steel, were the medieval equivalent of tanks.

This campaign was not only an indication of Suleiman's military strength, but of his diplomatic skills as well. The Ottomans were now threatening the eastern borders of Habsburg power, and as the Habsburgs were the enemies of France, the French King Charles V had signed the Franco-Ottoman alliance in 1525. The concept of 'my enemy's enemy is my friend' is a good explanation for why European states made all kinds of alliances, but a Christian king brokering an alliance with a Muslim sultan was seen as shocking at the time. Even so, this alliance, in one form or another, was to last for almost 300 years. (One of its first practical outcomes came a few decades later in 1553, still in the time of Suleiman's reign, when a joint Ottoman-French armada successfully attacked the Genoese-held island of Corsica in the western Mediterranean. This meant that Suleiman would face no crusade or need to fear a unified European army marching to the aid of Hungary.)

Because it had been raining, the two sides at Mohács (in southern Hungary, near the River Danube) did not clash until early afternoon. Suleiman sent in his lightly equipped Rumelian (from what was essentially the Balkans and part of northern Greece) troops, which were quickly routed by the Hungarian heavy cavalry. However, as the Rumelian soldiers retreated, the cavalry was lured into contact with the Janissaries and muskets, which either pierced armour or made enough noise to send the horses into a panic. Chaos ensued, so much so that some thought, incorrectly, that the battle was over. The Hungarians, however, must have fought on even after it became apparent that they had lost as we know Louis II only left the battle as darkness was falling (this was in high summer). During his retreat he fell from his horse in a river at Csele and drowned in his heavy armour.

Louis II had chosen to fight a battle with less of everything, hoping that obsolete heavy cavalry could withstand musket and cannon fire. He paid for his folly with his life – as did many of his troops. Meanwhile, Suleiman was so underwhelmed by the size of the opposing force at Mohács that he remained there for a few days, assuming he had only beaten the vanguard of a larger force. He was, for a time, unaware that what he had faced was the best Hungary could muster and that its king lay dead in the river. Once he realised that the path was clear to Buda and its twin town across the Danube, Pest (they weren't unified until the nineteenth century), he lost no time advancing on the two. Suleiman plundered Buda but, due to ongoing local uprisings, didn't finally occupy it until fifteen years later in 1541. The Battle of Mohács destroyed the Hungarian monarchy and opened the gates to the rest of the kingdom. After such an emphatic victory, it was only a matter of time before Hungary became an Ottoman territory.

Another great success early in Suleiman's reign was the second siege of Rhodes. The reason for the first siege in 1480, led by Mehmed II, was because of the losses to Ottoman shipping that had been inflicted by the knights based on Rhodes. Nothing had changed since then; the Hospitallers remained a perennial thorn in the side of the sultans. In 1522, Suleiman arrived at the island fortress of Rhodes with more than 100,000 men. This gigantic army faced less than a thousand knights, supported by roughly 5,000–6,000 troops (mainly Venetian and French), but the Hospitallers had spent generations perfecting their thick defence walls and keeping up to date with the latest innovations. Rather than vertical their walls were now sloped, which made cannon balls skip away, or at least reduced their impact. The normally effective

Ottoman cannons took months rather than weeks to grind down the defences. The regular infantry assaults were always pushed back by the courageous defenders, led by the Grand Master Philippe Villiers de L'Isle-Adam. On through the searing summer heat, one side resolutely defended while the other side hammered away with all the resources of a mighty empire. Then, on 4 September, a mine packed with gunpowder was detonated, and the walls were breached for the very first time. A colossal assault was thrown at the gap, but the Hospitallers were there, ready for hand-to-hand combat with the Janissaries. After desperate fighting in the breach, the Ottoman forces faltered and retreated.

Summer turned to autumn and still the bombardment from the Ottoman siege guns continued. More mines were detonated, further tunnels were dug and, in November 1522, another great assault charged into the breach, only to be countered by ferocious resistance that brought both sides to breaking point. By now Grand Master Villiers de L'Isle-Adam knew he had nothing left, whereas Suleiman had tried everything to crack the defences at Rhodes and failed. To make matters worse for the Ottomans, the perennial problem of disease was starting to spread through the camp. So, in December, Suleiman came up with an offer: Grand Master Villiers de L'Isle-Adam didn't just have combatants behind the walls; the base of operations was a town rather than a fort, and once the Ottomans entered the fate of the civilians would inevitably be death or enslavement. Because of this, it was the people of Rhodes who ensured that a truce was maintained while negotiations took place. Suleiman was obviously as impressed as he was frustrated by the defence of Rhodes, and the offer was so generous as to be a 'no brainer'. It was agreed that all the islanders who wished to go could take their belongings and leave at any time within three years; those who remained would be exempt from Ottoman taxation for five years, and the churches on the island would not be converted into mosques. Meanwhile, the Hospitaller Knights had twelve days to leave and could take with them their weapons, treasures, and religious icons.

On 1 January 1523, the remaining knights and soldiers marched out wearing their armour. The Ottoman forces watched as they walked towards their waiting ships with banners flying and drums beating. This was a show of strength; they had resisted everything the mighty Muslim empire had thrown at them. They might be retreating, but they had yet to be beaten. It would take the Hospitallers years to find a new home, and for a time they faced an existential crisis. However, they eventually settled, a little begrudgingly, on Malta, the tiny island archipelago just off the shores of Sicily, a midway point between Europe and North Africa. Malta is little more than a rock and is the only country in the world to have no above-ground rivers or lakes. It would be repurposed as a Hospitaller stronghold from which they would continue their high seas piracy against Muslim shipping, this time from the centre of the Mediterranean. In the short term, however, Suleiman had largely secured eastern Mediterranean shipping, with the journeys to the Levant and Egypt finally free from Christian piracy.

With these multiple blows against Christian buttresses that were, after all, designed to halt the spread of the Ottoman Empire, it's easy to see why Suleiman was portrayed with a mixture of awe and dread in the courts of Europe. He was the 'Great Turk', with Titian's portrait of him more about an unfeasibly large turban than about the man himself. This mix of awe and dread reached new heights in 1529, when Suleiman, after sweeping once again through the heartlands of Hungary, arrived at the walls of Vienna, the Habsburg capital. To be fair, he hadn't exactly 'swept' through the country. The summer of 1529 was a wet one, and the rivers in Serbia and Hungary were unusually high; the region's roads were muddy tracks. When the heavy Ottoman guns bogged down in the quagmire, Suleiman was forced to abandon the larger cannons as they were simply too heavy to get through the mud. While he had successfully beaten what little resistance there was in western Hungary, he didn't have all his usual weapons when he arrived at the gates of Vienna. The Ottoman Empire, even this far along, was thought of as being 'eastern' and 'exotic', but the Ottomans were now besieging Vienna, a city in the centre of Europe that is regarded as European in every way. That the Ottomans had fought their way to the very heart of Europe shows that they were every bit as much a part of European history as England is.

The siege of Vienna lasted just three weeks. The terrible weather in mid-October was only going to get worse, and it was apparent from their failure to wear down the Viennese defences that Suleiman needed those larger siege guns. The Janissaries were in near revolt, demanding that Suleiman either lift the siege or fully commit to it. This led to a few mass assaults that were beaten back by the Austrian and German defenders. Everyone knew they had been attempted before any proper breaches in the defences had been made and were, therefore, highly risky. So Suleiman headed for home, his point made. But that was not how the siege was explained by Ferdinand I, the Austrian ruler. According to his account, he had stoutly resisted an army of over 100,000, acting bravely as a bulwark of Christianity against the rising tide of Islam. Ferdinand's son built the Castle of Neugebaeude, allegedly on the spot where Suleiman had pitched his tent, so that no 'Turk' would ever again be able to do so. While, hyperbole to one side, all this was strictly true, the reality was that Suleiman had been frustrated, mainly by the weather, in his attempt to capture the city; he was not decisively defeated by a Christian ruler. But things got worse for Suleiman when snow began to fall as his army trudged back through freezing mud in the winter of 1529.

These events are well remembered in the West, where it seemed as if Suleiman was obsessed with expansion in Europe. However, by far the longest series of campaigns he fought were the ones in the East against the Safavids. These took Suleiman to Armenia, Georgia, Iraq and Iran, and led to the Peace of Amasya in 1555, agreed between Shah Tahmasp of the Safavids and Suleiman. Twice the Safavids had been reduced to burning the crops in the Euphrates River basin to try to slow Suleiman, and while this had frustrated him, it did not stop him. Although Suleiman's conquests in the East were not total, and the Safavids remained in power in Tehran, he gained what is now called Iraq (all of it) as well as western parts of Georgia and Armenia. In terms of square mileage, his conquests in the East rivalled his conquests in the West. Suleiman was an equal-opportunity conqueror.

Meanwhile, to the south, the important trading city of Aden was allied to the Portuguese. The Ottomans and the Portuguese had continued to butt heads after Selim's conquest of the Mamelukes, and Aden's alliance with Portugal was a consequence of this. In 1548, Suleiman sent his respected naval officer Piri Reis to capture the city; he succeeded, and four years on he captured Muscat, another key Portuguese trading outpost on the Arabian peninsula.

Maps

It is worth pausing to take a look at Piri Reis, one of the most famous Ottoman mariners, remembered for all the wrong reasons. 'Reis' is the Turkish word for admiral (it's not his surname), and he was one of Suleiman's most capable naval officers. He surely would have been the most celebrated under Suleiman had it not been for the fact that Hayreddin Barbarossa was still around and in active service until 1545. Piri Reis's story is much like that of any other effective naval officer of the time, but, unusually, he was also a cartographer and the second Piri Reis map is a magnet for all kinds of conspiracy theories. This particular map is one of the then known world, but it seems to show the Brazilian coastline (known at the time), with land at the bottom of the map. Some say this is a sign that he sailed to Antarctica. Others take this further and claim that the coastal outline shows the land under the ice. However, this can be comfortably dismissed through the facts.

Piri Reis's career is fairly well documented. We know he sailed all over the place, but there's no evidence (nor does he report) sailing far south enough to see Antarctica, and there aren't enough gaps in his career to suggest a secret voyage. Those pointing to 'uncanny accuracies' look past the monster embellishments and the stylised (and not uncannily accurate) depictions of European coastlines. The maps are good in terms in generalities but are hardly up to the standards of modern maps. Since the time of Ptolemy (born centuries before Jesus), extra land, called *Terra Australis Incognita*, has often been added to maps. The Piri Reis map is good as maps of the age go, but it does not prove hidden journeys to a lost continent – or aliens.

Back on the campaign trail, Suleiman's reach continued to extend ever further east. Aceh is now a sultanate in the modern country of Indonesia (which is also the most populous Muslim country in the world). In the late 1550s the sultan asked for Ottoman assistance against the Portuguese, so in addition to having maritime dominance in the Red Sea, the Persian Gulf, the Black Sea and the eastern Mediterranean, Ottoman ships were also operating off the coast of Indonesia. Britain and Venice are famous maritime trading powers, but the Ottomans at the time of Suleiman were similarly positioned – a fact that often goes unrecognised.

Among all these naval expeditions, there was one that had a dreadful foreboding about it. In 1551 an Ottoman fleet arrived off the coast of Malta, where the Hospitaller Knights were waiting. As the fleet was relatively small, the skirmishing led to a stalemate, so the fleet set sail to the second-largest island of the Maltese archipelago, Gozo, where every single occupant was rounded up and sold into slavery. It was a warning – and a sobering reminder of the power of the Ottomans. As a result, the Hospitallers' Grand Master, Juan de Homedes y Coscon, decided to spend their ill-gotten gains on building as many new fortifications as they could afford. A second warning came at the Battle of Djerba, just off the North African coast near Malta, where an Ottoman fleet annihilated a Christian one that consisted of Spanish, Venetian and even Hospitaller ships. More than half the Christian fleet was sunk or captured. The threatening Ottomans and the building Hospitallers were both still going strong in 1565, but now the knights were under a new Grand Master, Jean de Valette, aged seventy. It was during this year that Suleiman set his sights on the Hospitallers. He had long rued the day, all those years ago, when he had shown them such leniency on the island of Rhodes. Now was the time to rid the Ottomans of this scourge, once and for all.

Malta is, in essence, a giant fortress, with huge natural harbours and high cliffs. What had been an inauspicious start for the Hospitallers on the island soon changed when they realised they were in God's gift of a defensive setting. In May of 1565, the Ottoman navy, with nearly 200 ships of various sizes, arrived in a harbour that was 6 miles from the main fortifications. This was a long way to haul equipment and cannons, so it was decided that the big guns should remain where they were. Another problem for the Ottomans arose at the very start of the siege, when Suleiman split the leadership between Piyale Pasha and Mustafa Pasha – and ordered both of them to report to Dragut, yet another famous Muslim pirate of the age (he had managed to capture Tripoli for Suleiman). All this was happening under the blazing sun of a harsh Maltese summer, when the wind that comes off the Sahara Desert is hot rather than cool.

Almost immediately there was a drive by the Ottomans to move the fleet from its original anchor on the western edge of the bay through the fortified entrance of Marsamxett Harbour and closer to the main Hospitaller defences on the eastern side. The only thing that stood in their way was Fort St Elmo, and Mustafa Pasha became obsessed with its destruction. As dozens of siege cannons began pounding away, masonry cracked, walls shuddered and, over several days, the once proud fort was reduced to little more than a pile of rubble. However, every night de Valette had the wounded shipped out and reinforcements shipped in. After just a week, the knights in the fort requested total evacuation. De Valette refused and the final battle took place not two days later, but two weeks later. Thanks to the fact that the Ottomans had been unable to move their mighty cannons, this one small fort withstood a bombardment that would have flattened a larger town's walls. Meanwhile, over at the main defences, the bombardment was going nearly all one way – the other way, as the Christian cannons fired on the Ottoman besiegers, forced to hide behind their own palisades. Somewhere in these exchanges of fire, Dragut was killed; he was found with a piece of shrapnel lodged in his turban, whether from friendly fire or enemy fire, nobody knew. This meant that there was now no umpire between the differing views of the two pashas.

The final assault on Fort St Elmo was a close-quarters' nightmare. Eyewitness accounts describe wooden hoops covered in tar being set alight and thrown at the Janissaries, their robes catching fire as crude grenades, blocks of masonry and anything the defenders could lay their hands on were used as weapons. By the end of the bloody day of 23 June 1565, Fort St Elmo (what was left of it) had fallen to the Ottomans. However, while 1,500 Christian defenders died in the siege, so had some 6,000 Ottoman troops, including more than half the Janissaries brought to the Malta fight. I have been to the rebuilt Fort St Elmo; the reconstruction is, if anything, larger than the original, and still it was impossible for me to imagine 7,500 dead or dying men in such a confined area, a space so small the bodies must surely have been stacked one on top of the other. Other battles of the time had more casualties, but they were spread out over whole fields of battle. Fort St Elmo would have been a charnel house of rotting bodies bloating in the ferocious heat and flies laying their eggs in the black, coagulated pools of blood. Piyale Pasha could now anchor in Marsamxett Harbour, but had it been a price worth paying?

Unbelievably, things became even more horrific. Mustafa Pasha ordered that the bodies of the Hospitallers were not to be given honourable burials after such stout resistance but were instead to be decapitated and their bodies floated across the bay nailed to crucifixes. You might think that this automatically gave the Christians the moral high ground, but sadly not. De Valette, in turn, had all the captured Ottoman prisoners beheaded, their heads loaded into cannons and fired into the nearby Ottoman camp in retaliation. De Valette had been efficient and resolute in his defence of Malta and had ably withstood an attack where he was outnumbered perhaps by as much as 5 to 1. However, he also knew he needed help, so no matter how grim the situation he always made it sound even worse when he wrote to anyone who could offer assistance. Pope Pius IV had previously sent his finest engineers to work on the fortifications of Malta, but right now the pope was more interested in the Council of Trent than in saving the Hospitallers. Indeed, everyone in Europe sent de Valette their best wishes – but not much else. The irony was that the Ottoman forces were pinned down and even a small relief force could have won a spectacular victory against the Muslim 'Turks'. Instead, self-interest came before religious considerations. De Valette had done an impressive job of delaying the attackers and soaking up the punishment, but, with no outside help, how long could he last?

The Ottomans now looked to encircle de Valette by capturing the Senglea promontory, where an estimated one hundred small rowing boats and sailing ships were used as an amphibious landing force. Unfortunately, they happened to stray across the cannons at the base of Fort St Angelo, which, at point-blank range, shredded the small ships like so many matchsticks. With just two salvos, almost all the ships had been sunk and more than 800 Ottoman soldiers killed, with thousands more reduced to floundering in the sea – and all for no gain. The fort now came under heavy fire as the Ottomans began to grind down another Hospitaller defence; de Valette was running out of forts. This time either a gunpowder mine or a series of cannon shots made a breach in the walls, and de Valette was seen, sword in hand, adding some motivation to the tenacious defence of the gap that had appeared. It was a close-run thing, but the walls were still held by the Hospitallers, despite some of the defenders being gunned down by friendly fire at a critical moment.

There were serious discussions about abandoning the shattered fort, but de Valette would have none of it. However, it was now

September and Mustafa Pasha realised that, as the season was starting to turn, a safe base of operations was needed. To this end he ordered an attack on the capital, the centrally located Mdina. The force sent to take the town was small and exhausted from a brutally intense siege. As they approached, Mdina's skeleton garrison fired its one cannon. It was all they had, but it was enough to fool the attackers into thinking that resistance would be far more formidable than it would have been. Enough was enough. The two pashas, who had been vying for control, now agreed on one thing: it was time to go. They had lost about a third of their entire force for the gain of one obliterated fort. However, just as the Ottomans had finished embarking their siege cannons, a Christian relief army arrived. García de Toledo Osorio, fresh from his victory in North Africa, where he had recaptured Peñón de Vélez de la Gomera (think of a North African version of Mont-Saint-Michel), arrived with 8,000 troops, ready to take on the Ottomans. His forces easily annihilated the bedraggled and retreating Ottomans, who had already embarked most of their equipment. It was an ignominious end to an epic siege. The Great Siege of Malta (Malta would of course be besieged again in World War II, by the Axis powers) became a most celebrated moment in Renaissance Europe. Grand Master de Valette received donations from all over Europe, which allowed him to build even greater fortifications. When he died, the area around the great harbour he had defended so effectively became the new Maltese capital of Valetta, named in his honour. In the pithy words of Voltaire, writing centuries later, 'Nothing is better known than the siege of Malta.' The story was used as a rallying cry to show that Ottoman (and therefore Muslim) power had its limits. The Great Siege of Malta was the second significant siege that Suleiman failed to win. However, while these failures showed that there were limits to his power, they did nothing to diminish it. As mentioned in passing, the Hospitallers had been part of a significant maritime defeat in 1560 at Djerba. Piyale Pasha bounced back the following year by capturing the Aegean island of Chios, which had been a Genoese outpost for centuries and a reminder, once again, of the supremacy of the Ottoman navy in the eastern Mediterranean.

While Suleiman's military campaigns reflected power, his domestic reforms reflected good governance. He saw education as paramount and set up a network of free schools (madrassas, attached to mosques) all over the empire. These were open to Muslim boys from poor backgrounds and resulted in a rise in literacy, an amazing achievement when compared to education in the West in the same period. Suleiman recognised that some Christians in his empire had been reduced to serfdom and their rights disregarded, so he changed this to allow Christian farmers to move freely and to settle where they wished (again, compare that to England, where peasant farmers were still tied to the land). Similarly, he refined the legal system. He went through the decrees of all the previous sultans and compiled them into the Kanun-i Osmani (Ottoman Laws). He was careful not to place them above the Sharia laws but alongside them as a more workable set of laws. While all this affected Muslims in the empire, he didn't forget Christians and Jews. Suleiman officially decreed that the Jews did not conduct blood-libel (the myth that some Jewish ceremonies required the kidnap and murder of non-Jewish children). Again, put in the context of the age, random child murders in Europe were blamed on Jews, and some of these poor innocents were turned into saints simply because they were believed to have been killed by Jews. Even today there are anti-Semites and neo-Nazis who continue to believe the heinous lie of blood-libel. Suleiman made it clear that such poisonous accusations would not be tolerated in his realm.

Suleiman had another connection with the Jews, but one that is a little more surprising. Pictures of East (old) Jerusalem show the walls of the city and the gleaming golden Dome of the Rock. The dome was renovated by Suleiman (it was covered in gold leaf in the twentieth century). The re-tiling of the dome was a major undertaking, requiring nearly half a million tiles, so many that a temporary tile factory was set up next to the Al-Aqsa Mosque. Most people assume the walls around the city are Roman or possibly Jewish; they aren't. They were rebuilt by Suleiman and are only about 500 years old. The population of Jerusalem was not very large at the start of Suleiman's reign, only some 5,000–6,000, but his renovations and improvements made it a far more attractive place to live, and by the 1560s the population had grown to around 16,000. About 2,000 of these were Jews, many of whom were refugees from the West. Of course if he helped the Jews by rebuilding an important religious site, he did the same for Muslims by renovating the Kaaba, the building draped in black at the heart of Mecca, believed to have been built by Abraham and his son Ismail as a house of worship. It is the most sacred site in Islam, and all Muslims pray in its direction.

While all of the mentioned projects are worthy ones, Suleiman's greatest architectural achievement, designed and built by the brilliant Mimar Sinan, was his mosque, the Süleimaniye. The mosque was built in just seven years (compared to the century it usually took for a Western European power to erect a cathedral) in the 1550s. It references both the Dome of the Rock and the Hagia Sophia, but is very much its own powerhouse of Ottoman architecture. The main dome is 53 metres high, with a diameter of 27 metres. Its interior space measures more than 3,400 square meters and is painted white, with some distinctively Ottoman Iznik tiles and golden Islamic calligraphy in the dome's centre. The overall effect is minimalist, but impressive. The Süleimaniye isn't just a mosque but an entire religious complex, with an attached madrassa, *hammam* and royal mausoleum. It is here that Roxelana and Suleiman are buried, and, interestingly, after designing so many great architectural masterpieces, it is here that Mimar Sinan is also buried. Suleiman died in September of 1566, aged seventy-one, at the fortress of Szigetvar. While his body has always resided in Istanbul, his organs were left in Hungary. He had ruled the Eternal State for forty-five years.

8

The Architect, the Drunkard, the Diplomat and the Murderer

For generations after Suleiman's reign, there was a general perception that he represented the pinnacle of the Ottoman Empire before it went into a gradual and then precipitous decline. That is now largely debunked. While all empires crumble, the Ottoman Empire continued in good health for generations after Suleiman's death. One example of someone who underpinned Ottoman glory was the previously mentioned Mimar Sinan (Architect Sinan).

In the modern world we tend to specialise; a top architect in the twenty-first century will have spent many years training to be one. However, in the past most people famous for one thing turned out to have talents in other areas as well. So, while it's not especially remarkable that Sinan started out doing something else, it is a little odd that one of the greatest Renaissance architects in the world began his working life as an army officer and, yet again, a famous 'Turk' was, ethnically speaking, no such thing. While we don't know where he came from, we do know that he was conscripted through the *devşirme* system, which meant he was born a Christian and that Sinan wasn't his birth name. He wasn't some sort of civil engineer in the army, either, and he saw fighting in a number of diverse locales. He started off in Suleiman's household cavalry and was there in the thick of the fighting at the Battle of Mohács. His effectiveness in this battle led to a promotion, and he went on to serve in Suleiman's campaigns against the Safavids around Baghdad. From there, he participated in various Ottoman fleet raids in Italy and Corfu. All of this meant that by the time he started studying architecture he had already had a military career that matched that of a well-known general. It was during the campaigns in the East that he began to show an inherent knack for building bridges across rivers, and it soon became clear to Suleiman that he should lose a capable military officer in order to gain a talented architect.

As mentioned earlier, the most famous building in Istanbul is Hagia Sophia, a structure that predates Sinan by nearly 1,000 years, but he is still connected to it because he recognised that the main structure needed buttressing or the dome would collapse. The Byzantine Empire had added some buttresses but by this time they were failing, so it's thanks to Sinan's support work that the great structure still stands today. However, his work on this iconic building didn't end there. One of the things that makes Hagia Sophia (a Byzantine Church) look like a mosque are its minarets. Sinan designed and built most of them, meaning that what we see today is the very best of both Byzantine and Ottoman architecture.

Without going into too much detail, Sinan thought of his architectural career as being split into three stages. The work on the Hagia Sophia is an example of his apprenticeship period. The Süleimaniye Mosque is from what he called his 'qualification stage', and he did not regard it as his best work. Best of all in his view was the mosque he built for the next sultan (who, as we will see, certainly did not deserve anything better than his father), the Selimiye Mosque in Edirne. This is an example of his master stage.

Born a few years before Suleiman, Sinan outlived him by more than twenty years, dying almost a generation later in 1588, at the age of nearly one hundred. But his legacy didn't stop with his death. As his fame spread, an architectural school grew up around him, leading to his status as one of the most influential Islamic architects in early modern history. Not only are his constructions works of great beauty, but apprentices working under him went on to design and build some of the world's most famous buildings on different continents. Sinan said, 'It is my sincere wish that kind-hearted people will look at my works until the end of time and see the honesty and hard work in my efforts.' He certainly had a point, and his legacy lives on with the Stari Most, the old bridge in Mostar (now in Bosnia). This beautiful stone bridge was commissioned by Suleiman to replace an existing suspension bridge spanning the Neretva River. Built in Sinan's lifetime, it is a classic example of the utilitarian but aesthetically pleasing constructions carried out by Ottoman architects from Sinan's school. The Stari

Most Bridge spanned the river from the 1560s until 1993, when it was deliberately destroyed by Croat artillery during the Croat–Bosnian war of the 1990s. The bridge became a symbol of the wanton destruction of that war, and it was carefully reconstructed and reopened in 2004. It is now a UNESCO World Heritage Site.

Then there is one of the most famous buildings in the world, the Taj Mahal. The official architect is the Safavid Persian Ustad Ahmad Lahauri, but the design has an undeniably Sinanesque quality to it. The main dome is said to have been designed by Ismail Khan, an Ottoman architect, which does not seem unreasonable, given that there were regular diplomatic and cultural exchanges between the two most powerful Muslim empires at that time, the Ottoman and the Mughal. The memorial may be India's most iconic building, but its designs were a mixture of Ottoman and Persian, the structure has Quranic calligraphy engraved in its façade and it was paid for by the Mughals (who, in terms of ethnicity, religion and culture were definitely not Indian Hindus). It's interesting how something so multicultural is now considered so emphatically to be of one country. The Taj Mahal was completed nearly a century after Sinan's heyday in the mid-1600s.

While it's easy to talk about an empire in terms of its military might (and there are more Ottoman successes in war to come), there are other indicators to check the health of any regime. Is it politically stable? Does it have a trade surplus or deficit? And what of its broader cultural influences? If it is still influencing and/or building world-class structures, it isn't on the wane. It is safe to say that Ottoman culture still had clout well beyond Suleiman's reign.

By the last few years of Suleiman's rule, only two serious heirs to the throne were left, both sons of Roxelana: Şehzade Bayezid and Şehzade Selim (Şehzade is an Ottoman title that refers to the sultan's male heirs). It is conjecture to say that Bayezid seemed the more likely heir and probably showed more potential, but Selim managed to provoke his brother into rebelling against their father – and Selim (very conveniently) 'saved' the day on the sultan's behalf. Bayezid was now on the wrong end of a rebellion against a mighty empire and was forced to flee. He ended up in Safavid territory with not much in the way of anything to offer, so, after some lengthy negotiations, the Safavids strangled Bayezid at Suleiman's request. Selim was, quite literally, the last man standing at the time of his father's death.

One reason that Suleiman was seen as the apogee of the empire, with nothing but a downward spiral afterwards, was that his son and successor, Selim II, became known as Selim the Sot (or drunkard). Some monarchs get to be called 'the Great' or 'the Magnificent', but then there are the ones known as 'the Unready', 'the Bald' or 'the Fat'. If the best summary history can give to a monarch's endeavours is that he was 'the Drunkard', it's probably fair to assume that things didn't go well for him and that he was not an effective ruler. So far the Ottomans had been lucky with their rulers. There had been a number of civil wars at the time of succession, but no sultan had been downright incompetent. This Selim was, however, an example of how power politics could go wrong. With no clear hereditary tradition for the Ottoman throne, able sons died, sometimes through illness or accident, sometimes due to courtly intrigue – and sometimes thanks to the law which required them to be strangled.

Selim II was, in many ways, exactly that oriental despot you have in your mind when you think of the words 'sultan' and 'harem'. Every sultan so far had been diligent in his duties, attending to the affairs of state and leading armies into battle. However, Selim was diligent only when it came to self-indulgence, interested only in the state of affairs in the harem. He was barely seen for the first two years of his reign. Instead, everything was left to his Grand Vizier Sokollu Mehmed Pasha. Fortunately for the empire, Sokollu Pasha was a highly capable administrator and, once again, a product of the *devşirme* system. Earlier in his career he had been an admiral of the fleet and the governor of an entire region. He had been appointed to the exalted position of grand vizier at the end of Suleiman's reign, continued in his post right through Selim II's rule and carried on into the time of Selim's successor, Mehmed III. To have been grand vizier for three sultans makes him one of the most impressive administrators in a long list of grand viziers. Perhaps surprisingly, even after decades of duty, he did not retire or die in his bed, but was still working on the sultan's behalf when he was murdered in 1578 by a mad dervish (really, this section of Ottoman history ticks all the boxes of Western clichés about the Ottoman Empire).

As such, while Selim the Sot lived up to his name, with heavy drinking and equally heavy fornicating with his hundreds of concubines, the empire itself was in safe hands. Nevertheless, it still needed direction and leadership as the grand vizier could be an effective caretaker, but not a policy maker. The day-to-day truth of Selim II's reign was that Grand Vizier Sokollu Pasha was the de facto ruler of the Ottoman Empire, and during his tenure he had a mixed record. As a man who understood diplomacy and treaties, he brokered a very favourable deal with the Habsburgs. Maximilian II knew he didn't have the resources to push back the Ottomans and may well have feared a second siege of Vienna, so he agreed to an annual 'gift' (it was, specifically, not 'tribute' – but was 'tribute' with a face-saving name) of 30,000 ducats. Also, for the first time, the treaty recognised Ottoman authority in Moldavia and Wallachia, which acknowledged the reality that had been evident for about a century. This was a major coup for the Ottomans, allowing them to concentrate on other areas.

The first area of interest was the fortified town of Azov at the mouth of the River Don where it ran into the Russian exterior; it also sat on the shores of the Sea of Azov, the smaller sea that is part of the Black Sea. The Ottoman assault failed and, for the first time, Ottoman forces faced a military setback with a new, previously unmentioned, power in the Tsars of Russia. At this time Russia was ruled by Tsar Ivan IV, who also had an epithet, 'the Terrible' (although some have argued that a more accurate translation would be 'the Awesome', 'terrible' is a more accurate description of his power and use of it). While the immediate impact was a slowing of expansion around the coast of the Black Sea, there were other far-reaching and more ominous implications. With established imperial enemies to the east and west, the Ottomans now had a growing empire to the north of their lands. If these powers were ever to attack simultaneously, the empire could not effectively defend its borders on three different fronts.

But there was some good news in 1571, when a massive Ottoman armada set sail for Cyprus. The fleet consisted of 350–400 ships, with 60,000–100,000 men. The landing was unopposed and the Ottomans headed immediately for the centrally located capital of Nicosia. Cyprus was then a Venetian possession, so it was they who fought to defend the island against the Ottoman threat. The Venetians had, quite correctly, anticipated an eventual attack from their old enemy and had spent a fortune turning the medieval walls of Nicosia into a star fort. The walls, rather than having been constructed of solid stone, were merely capped in stone but had a core of earth. Further, the angular points on the walls acted to deflect cannon fire. For its time, it was one of the most modern defences in the Mediterranean and had been deliberately designed to give the Ottoman cannons a hard target.

The Siege of Nicosia lasted for seven weeks, until 9 September. The cost of the walls was money well spent as they withstood furious and continual bombardments. Dozens of assaults were thrown at the defences; all were thrown back. However, the leader of the Ottoman forces, Lala Mustafa Pasha, dug trenches towards the walls and gradually filled the surrounding ditch, enabling the Ottoman sappers to inch their way closer to the walls, all the while protected by musket and cannon fire. On that final day the Janissaries pushed through the defences and a massacre ensued. Nothing like it had been seen since the time of the first Selim and his conquest of Cairo (although that had been worse). Frustratingly for Venice, a combined Christian fleet of 200 vessels composed of Venetian, Papal, Genoese and Spanish ships had nearly made it to the island as a relief force, but it turned back when it received news of Nicosia's fall. The fight was not yet over but most of the island capitulated. The one town that resisted was Famagusta, its defence led by the Venetian Marco Antonio Bragadin. It resisted for eleven months, which showed not only the bravery of the defenders, but also how well the Venetians had built their defences. Also in its favour was the fact that Famagusta was a port, so it could be resupplied by sea, something the Ottoman navy was never able to completely prevent.

As the siege wore on, Sokollu Pasha offered to concede a trading station at Famagusta if the republic would cede the island, but the Venetians refused. However, with the defenders exhausted and out of ammunition, they eventually surrendered. This time the Ottomans allowed the Christian residents and Venetian troops to leave the town unharmed, but when Lala Mustafa Pasha learned that some Muslim prisoners had been killed during the siege he had the Venetian leader, Marco Antonio Bragadin, flayed alive and his officers executed. Bragadin's skin was then paraded around the island before being sent to Constantinople. Cyprus, the last major Christian holding in the eastern Mediterranean, was now under Ottoman control. This was a victory of significant strategic importance to the empire, and the island would remain under Ottoman control for centuries. But Selim II had another reason to celebrate: it was said that Cyprus was where his favourite wine was produced.

The battle for Cyprus was, however, only part of a wider war the Ottoman Empire was now waging with Venice, and this culminated just a few months later in the Battle of Lepanto. For a number of reasons, this battle is seen as one of the most important in naval history. Taking place on 7 October 1571, Lepanto was simply the largest naval battle in Western history. From the Christian perspective, it marked a brief moment of unity not seen since the time of the crusades as Spain, the Papal States, the Hospitallers, the Republics of Venice and Genoa and some other of the Italian powers came together to fight the Ottomans. Europe was still recovering from its religious wars between Protestant and Catholic states, so Lepanto was a chance to show that Catholic power was still relevant and, more importantly, potent. Despite the combined might of these European powers, the Ottoman fleet was still bigger (212 ships versus 250), while 100,000 men (and at least one woman) were involved in this epic clash. There is a lot of bias to the descriptions of this battle from both sides, and sources need to be treated with caution. It was said that, as the two sides met, the Ottoman soldiers belly danced to show how confident they were – which smells like Christian propaganda to show the decadence of the East. In truth the Ottoman forces took this battle as seriously as their Christian counterparts, and anyway Muslim men don't belly dance. While most accounts of this battle refer to the men fighting at Lepanto as 'Turks', we now know that Ottoman forces comprised many ethnicities.

Bravery and skilled seamanship were demonstrated on both sides, but it seems one of the deciding factors was the six Venetian galleasses (essentially, galleys on steroids) among all the hundreds of galleys on both sides. This was the last naval battle to feature galleys as the main weapon of war, so ending a 2,000-year-old chapter in maritime history and starting a new 'age of sail'. The galley was a huge row boat with a central sail. Its basic design had been enlarged and refined over centuries, but its ancestors were the galleys and triremes of ancient Greece. The era of the 'ship of the line' (a warship with sails) had yet to come to the Mediterranean.

The galleys had cannons fitted to the front so that as they approached the enemy they could fire, but if the galleys were boarded from the sides their cannons were useless. The Venetian galleasses were designed and built in the legendary Arsenal shipyards, where all of Venice's ships were produced (at its peak Venice had a global fleet of 3,000). These new warships were higher-sided galleys with cannons fitted stern, aft, port and starboard, meaning that if surrounded by enemy vessels (which is what happened), they could attack all of them, while being almost impossible to board. The careful manoeuvring turned into a messy melee as hundreds of ships collided and, interspersed with cannon and musket shots, vicious hand-to-hand fighting took place on the decks. It was said that the Janissaries fired so many rounds there was nothing left for them to do but throw oranges and lemons at the enemy (again, this is likely to be Christian hyperbole). However, what isn't disputed is that the crux of the fight occurred when the two flagships (the Spanish *Reale* and the Ottoman *Sultana*) met, and a vicious fight broke out when the Christians boarded the *Sultana*. Accounts reported that one Spanish soldier's lover, Maria la Bailadora ('The Dancer'), dressed in armour and pretending to be a man, led the charge (this is plausible as there are other cases of women who pretended to be men and fought in battles).

The Janissaries fought with skill and fury as the fighting ebbed and flowed across the deck, but the Spaniards were able to cling on and, eventually, the Ottoman admiral was killed. In addition to the usual state and domestic allegiances, both side's flags had significant religious meanings. The *Real* flag had been blessed by the pope, whereas the Ottoman flag was said to have come from Mecca. With the fall of its admiral, the Ottoman flagship lowered its flag, a gesture that would have deflated the Ottoman forces. This, combined with the Venetian galleasses ripping through enemy vessels, was enough to tip the battle in favour of the Christians.

The casualty figures were enormous. It was said that the Mediterranean was red with men's blood, and with more than 16,000 killed there is no reason to think this was an exaggeration (although a significant amount of the dead would have drowned, which meant that the site would also have had corpses floating around the sinking hulks of the galleys from both sides). The

Ottomans lost fifty galleys, while the Christians lost just seventeen, and the Christian victory meant they achieved both practical and political advantages by capturing 137 ships, a significant addition to their naval power. Further, the Ottoman galleys contained 12,000 Christian galley slaves, all found and freed. Had their Christian souls been saved from Muslim hell? Well, yes and no. The situation was far more nuanced than that.

Slavery (Part 1)

As mentioned in other places in this book, many Ottoman subjects had once been Christians, having been enslaved at an early age. After converting to Islam they had diverse opportunities to serve the empire, and some rose to the top of the pecking order. Galley slaves were considered the lowest of the low, but most converts settled into their new lives, recognising that they were probably materially better off as a result of the lives that had been forced on them. An obscure example would be Samson Rowlie, an Englishman captured in 1577 by Muslim pirates. He was taken to Algiers (an Ottoman territory), where he was castrated to become a eunuch and forced to become a Muslim with the new name of *Hassan Ağa*. *(Ağa is a title of respect; the ğ is silent.)* All of this sounds dreadful, so you would expect that when he had the opportunity to return to England, he would have jumped at the chance, but no. By the time the opportunity presented itself, he had become a pasha in control of the treasury in Algiers. He had made a new life for himself with more power and influence than he could ever have imagined. (This explanation is not meant as a defence of slavery.)

The Battle of Lepanto was a great success for the Christian coalition, which celebrated by almost immediately dissolving and returning to the good old days of bickering and infighting. Such an emphatic victory is noticeable for its lack of follow-up. The Christian fleet did not sail further east, nor did it capture any Ottoman ports; it just drifted into history. Some historians have claimed that had the battle gone the other way the Ottoman Empire would surely have struck further west, but this again sounds like propaganda, implying that the Catholic powers had saved Europe from the Muslims. This sounds good but doesn't bear close scrutiny. Although the Ottomans had been halted at Malta, they ruled the east coast of the Adriatic. If they wanted to attack Italy, it would have been easy.

In the meantime Selim II was doing his best to spin the defeat by pretending that the battle meant nothing, arguing that if you shave your beard it grows back again. Indeed, all the lost vessels were replaced; however, the plan had not been to lose, and rebuilding the fleet was expensive (although the Ottomans had learned something and built eight galleasses of their own). They had been lucky that this decisive defeat happened at a time when they had the resources and the money to rebuild their fleet. More importantly for the Venetians, it was the biggest victory in their war with the Ottoman Empire (the fourth such war out of seven); however, in 1573 Venice had to sign yet another humiliating peace treaty. This time they had to ratify the Ottoman conquest of Cyprus as well as give away rich farmland along the border between the two powers in Dalmatia (modern-day Croatia) – and, to add insult to injury, they had to pay an indemnity of 300,000 ducats for the privilege. The victory at the Battle of Lepanto did nothing to stop these punitive terms from being agreed and implemented.

A Famous Writer

There is an unexpected connection between the Battle of Lepanto and a famous writer. Miguel de Cervantes had been ill with a fever on board one of the Spanish galleys, but was determined to fight and went on deck, where he was shot three times in the battle (an indication of the ferocity of the fighting). He lived, of course, but when he retired he wrote *Don Quixote*, considered to be the first modern novel and one of the greatest works in literature.

If it feels like Selim has been largely absent from the story of his own reign, it's because he *was* largely absent. It's worth mentioning that he wasn't only referred to as Selim the Sot; his other epithet was Selim the Blond. This is hardly surprising as his mother was Ukrainian and his father came from a long line of men whose mothers were Russian, Ukrainian, Bulgarian and Greek. Dressed in the robes of a European noble, any observer would have assumed him to be German or English rather than a 'Turk'. While Selim did ride out against his brother in the early days, it didn't lead to battle. After that he gave up the active military role played by his predecessors, and he was the first sultan never to show his presence in an imperial campaign. This was later to become the norm – not just in the Ottoman realm but across Europe. Selim II was a lover and an alcoholic, but he was not a fighter, and, probably as a result of staying close to home, he showed more kindness in his reign than many before him. His mother's rival, Mahidevran, was given back her wealth and her son, Mustafa, was honoured with a new tomb. Roxelana would not have been happy, but Selim was willing to mend fences. His Ottoman subjects seemed to genuinely love him for his gentle and generous soul (despite his ruthless bid for the throne). He probably should never have been sultan, but after eight short years the matter was resolved. He drunkenly slipped on the wet marble floor of a harem *hammam* and died from a head injury.

Selim II's successor was his son Murad III, and he started his reign in complete contrast to his father by having his five brothers strangled where they lived in the Topkapı harem. Under the laws of the time, this was not only legal but almost mandatory. Murad III was twenty-eight at the time of his coronation, which meant that he had grown up during the reign of his grandfather, Sultan Suleiman. Sokollu Mehmed Pasha was his grand vizier for the first five years of his reign (until the pasha was murdered by the mad dervish), so Murad III was not only well prepared for the throne, but had time to ease himself into the role. This was still the era of the Sultanate of Women, and Murad III had two very forthright women in his life.

The first was his mother, Nurbanu Sultan, who had been Selim II's chief consort, which was no small feat as Selim II had spent a lot of time in the harem 'getting to know' the hundreds of women who lived there. This strong relationship implies that Nurbanu was beautiful (or she would have been unlikely to catch Selim II's eye), smart (or she would have lost out to others in the power politics of the harem) and cunning (once she gained power and influence, she kept it). When her son became sultan, she became the *valide* sultan, the title of honour for the sultan's mother, who was automatically the most powerful woman in the harem, and for the first few years of Murad III's reign she and Sokollu Mehmed Pasha ran the empire.

During her nine years of regency (from 1574 to 1583, when she died), her outlook was so pro-Venetian that many, including the Venetians, thought her to have been born there. Although we don't know where she came from, this bias was enough to make her a hate figure in Genoa. She did, however, make a connection with many Western powers, including France (whose queen at the time was Catherine de Medici) and England, which was then ruled by Queen Elizabeth I. France continued its alliance with the Ottomans because it was a useful counter-balance to Habsburg power. Queen Elizabeth pointed out that because she was a Protestant and Murad III was a Muslim, they were both outsiders in the eyes of the Catholic powers. Some of her letters even go so far as to point out how important Jesus is in both religions, as if Protestant Christians and Sunni Muslims were almost the same thing. They weren't, but these were political niceties used to emphasise similarities rather than differences.

While Nurbanu Sultan and Sokollu Mehmed Pasha were running the show, officially all correspondence came from Murad III. Some of the Ottoman letters were sprinkled in gold dust as if to say 'we have wealth to spare' – and compared to the fiscally challenged Elizabeth, they did. The political niceties did lead to various trade agreements, but no practical military aid came Elizabeth's way.

Nurbanu Sultan retained her influence over her sultan son until she died in 1583. With her passing, though, there was a female-shaped hole in Murad III's life. This was filled by a second strong woman, his ever faithful wife, Safiye Sultan. Unusually, they had a monogamous relationship, much to the distress of his mother when she was alive. Nurbanu had known that the more her son concentrated on one wife the more likely it was that she would oust the *valide* sultan from her position of power. Nurbanu insisted that Murad sleep with concubines, as the succession was too fragile with only one son, little Mehmed. Murad III resisted his mother, who then flat-out accused Safiye Sultan of using witchcraft to beguile her son and make him impotent. Eventually Murad III relented, and he certainly got the hang of things considering he sired nineteen more sons and twenty-seven daughters. While this presumably kept his mother happy, he maintained that he was still loyal to his only true wife.

On the military front, Murad fought lengthy and inconclusive wars against the Habsburgs in Hungary. One of these conflicts is remembered (quite aptly) as the Long Turkish War. Blood was spilt; sometimes the Habsburgs won and sometimes Murad's forces, but no overall advantage was gained by either side. However, Murad's preoccupation with the West was seen as an opportunity by the Safavids out east. Because the empire had grown so large, Murad now had to worry about conflict in Hungary and the Caucasus, two fronts that were more than a thousand miles apart. The Ottoman–Safavid War soon broke out, eventually lasting for over a decade. The most interesting moment of the war occurred during the night-time Battle of the Torches (at Derbent in the Caucasus, near the Caspian Sea), so called because it was just that, a night-time battle fought by torchlight. The Battle of the Torches was an emphatic Ottoman victory, and, with the Safavids pushed back, Ottoman influence now stretched from North Africa to the Caspian Sea. But events beyond Murad's borders were causing problems at home. Spain had been bringing in tons of gold and silver from the New World for nearly a century. This led (particularly in the case of silver) to inflation and a debasing of currency as silver was in far more plentiful supply throughout the Continent than before 1492. This didn't affect only the Ottomans, but it came at a time when Murad III was fighting two lengthy wars and was also upgrading his army's equipment.

Murad III, like his father, never went on campaign. He was the head of state and dealt with issues that affected a vast empire. Constantinople was increasingly the hub of a network of communications that stretched over three continents. Had he gone on campaign to either front, he would have been too far away to make decisions that affected the rest of his empire. Murad III was a smart and pragmatic man, but while it was the right decision to remain in the capital, there were less noble reasons behind it. Murad III was obsessed with plots against him, and he was particularly fearful of a revolt by the Janissaries. Because he had settled into an isolated existence, he was not seen in public (including at Friday prayers in the Hagia Sophia) for two years. His personal physician, Domenico Hierosolimitano, describes his routine:

In the morning he rises at dawn to say his prayer for half an hour, then for another half hour he writes. Then he is given something pleasant as a collation, and afterwards sets himself to read for another hour. Then he begins to give audience to the members of the Divan on the four days of the week that this occurs, as had been said above. Then he goes for a walk through the garden, taking pleasure in the delight of fountains and animals for another hour, taking with him the dwarves, buffoons and others to entertain him. Then he goes back once again to studying until he considers the time for lunch has arrived. He stays at table only half an hour, and rises once again into the garden for as long as he pleases. Then he goes to say his midday prayer.

Then he stops to pass the time and amuse himself with the women, and he will stay one or two hours with them, when it is time to say the evening prayer. Then he returns to his apartments or, if it pleases him more, he stays in the garden reading or passing the time until evening with the dwarfs and buffoons, and then he returns to say his prayers, that is at nightfall. Then he dines and takes more time over dinner than over lunch, making conversation until two hours after dark, until it is time for prayer. He never fails to observe this schedule every day.

And so Murad would have continued into his dotage had it not been for a unique moment in history. Given that Murad III never saw battle, his death from a volley of cannon fire was most unexpected, especially considering that it was 'friendly fire'. In 1595, Murad III was going about his daily routine in Topkapı Palace, when a pane of glass was shattered by a noisy salute from Egyptian ships entering the harbour of Constantinople. The noise and the sudden breaking glass led him to suffer a massive heart attack, and he died from the shock.

As soon as Mehmed, Murad III's eldest son, learned of his father's death, he set out on a coldblooded flurry of murder. He was one of twenty brothers and half-brothers, and according to Mehmed the Conqueror's law there could be only one survivor. Because no royal blood could be spilled, the male heirs were strangled by deaf mutes who could, therefore, never speak of what they had done. All nineteen of Mehmed's brothers (some little more than toddlers) were murdered according to the tradition. It was this procession of nineteen coffins that led to lamentations across the capital. Mehmed III had done what was legally right, but it was clear to all that it was morally wrong.

Mehmed III inherited the ongoing war in Hungary (it was called the Long Turkish War for a reason), and it was at this point that the Ottoman frontier began to slip back. Even worse, Michael the Brave, Prince of Wallachia, had been raiding with his forces all over Rumelia, even coming within a day's march of the capital. This was completely unacceptable. In the same year as his accession, the Habsburg Holy Roman Emperor, Rudolf II, had managed to get the Ottoman vassal states of Transylvania and Moldavia to rise up with the already rebellious Michael of Wallachia. Things were looking grim for Mehmed III. One of his viziers, Sinan Pasha, was sent at the head of an army that numbered 100,000 to annihilate Wallachian resistance once and for all. The Ottomans crushed Michael and the Wallachian army but, when Sinan Pasha concentrated on the capture of key forts rather than finishing off the army, its remnants, including the prince, retreated in good order. The Ottomans would come to regret that in October 1595, when they reached the Danube and found a large allied army waiting for them. The Battle of Giurgiu (in modern Romania) was a surprising victory for the Christian alliance, one that threw all the recent Ottoman victories into doubt. The uncertainty led Mehmed III to strap on a sword, don armour and lead an army on campaign, making him the first sultan to do so since Suleiman.

Almost exactly a year after the embarrassing defeat at Giurgiu, Mehmed III met a similarly sized Christian force at the Battle of Haçova (in Hungary). This had not been the plan for either army. Mehmed had originally set out to capture the Hungarian fortress of Eger, but, after hearing that Christian forces had captured the Castle of Hatvan, massacring not just the garrison but their families as well, Mehmed III felt compelled to meet them and remind them what an Ottoman army led by a sultan could do. As he marched his army through nearby marshes, Mehmed III came out onto the plain of Haçova, where he found Christian defensive earthworks with trenches and palisades. The Christian side was a veritable 'who's who' of Catholic power, with forces from the Holy Roman Empire, Spain, the Papal States, Transylvania, Saxony, Serbia, Bohemia, Walloon (Belgium), French mercenaries and even Polish and Cossack cavalry. Both sides had scores of cannons and thousands of muskets, but only the Christians had defensive cover – and they had turned the ruins of a medieval stone church into a firing platform. Equally, both sides had been exhausted through marches, sieges and worsening autumn weather. Mehmed III faced what was clearly going to be a tough slog of a battle.

Wave after wave of Ottoman troops, from poorly equipped leveed troops to the highly trained and well-equipped Janissaries, charged into battle amid the din of cannons and musket fire. The Christians poured their fire into the oncoming troops, with the Austrian position being particularly effective in dishing out the carnage. With its mud trenches and brave dashes across no man's land to the thunder of artillery, the whole scene could almost have been from the First World War rather than one from the late sixteenth century. After nearly two days of fighting (25–26 October 1596), Mehmed III had failed to dislodge the Christian coalition forces and had run out of ideas. Some Christians, sensing that the Ottomans wavered, broke from their positions and began plundering the Ottoman army camp. Christian soldiers were supposedly seen dancing jigs of delight as they began helping themselves to the money Mehmed III had brought to pay his troops. Mehmed III wanted to order a general retreat and despondently turned to his personal advisor, Hoça Sadeddin Efendi (*hoça* is the title given to a teacher/ religious leader) to ask what he should do. The *hoça* replied that he should keep fighting until the battle was over. Meanwhile, the non-combatants of the Ottoman camp, the cooks, grooms, stable boys, bakers and others, armed themselves with whatever they could find and charged at the plunderers. The Christian forces were caught off guard and fled.

A cry went up that the Christians were fleeing. The forces of both sides, still engaged in the battle at the trenches, could see what was happening. The Christians became confused and wondered if there had been an order to retreat, while the attacking Ottoman forces saw a sight that gave them fresh resolve. All of this, combined with a well-timed salvo from the Ottoman cannons, led to chaos in the Christian ranks. The Janissaries either pushed through the centre or came in from the flank, and what had looked just minutes earlier like inevitable defeat for Mehmed III turned into a hard-fought and unexpected victory.

This victory against a major Christian coalition force meant that Mehmed III returned a hero. A great celebratory procession in Constantinople coincided with four ships of sugar arriving from Egypt, so it was said that they 'sweetened the victory'. As the whole capital erupted into wild celebration, Mehmed III must have breathed a sigh of relief. He knew how close he had come to total disaster. But that was a high point. In 1601, at the Battle of Guruslău, the Transylvanians fought against an Austrian/ Wallachian army and lost, which took Transylvanian suzerainty out of the Ottoman sphere of influence. Meanwhile, Anatolia erupted in a revolt that was less about Mehmed III and more about the system. The aforementioned inflation meant money was tight in poor communities ánd this, plus increased taxation (to fund the war), led to Anatolian peasants feeling that they had nothing to lose. Another spark to the revolt was the evolving *devşirme* system. Now that some lands had been Ottoman for so long, many local populations had converted to Islam and it was therefore harder to find Christian boys to fill the *devşirme* quotas. Under the circumstances, Muslim boys were now allowed to join the Janissaries – an honour, no doubt, but one that was not welcome at this time of so much financial pressure.

The revolt was led by some of the feudal forces who had once been the backbone of the old Ottoman army (particularly the Sipahis, local Anatolian lords who were light cavalry) but who, while dealing with rebel peasants, were themselves feeling ostracised from the traditional power base. The Janissaries (already a lightning rod for the revolt) were sent in. Some rebel groups banded together to form a rag-tag army, exactly what the Janissaries wanted as they could easily defeat a poorly trained, poorly equipped force whereas an insurgency was much harder to stamp out. The leaders of the rebels were rounded up, a noticeable number of whom were Qizilbash Shi'ites, and while a link to the Safavids can't be proven, it was strongly suspected at the time. The revolt was put down by force, but it meant more instability, expense and distraction than Mehmed III needed. The outcome further bolstered the position of the Janissaries as they had protected the sultan from revolt. They had long since become more than a military force; they were now a political force as well.

The war in the West culminated in the hard-to-pronounce Peace of Zsitvatorok, which ended fifteen years of war between the Ottomans and the Habsburgs but by no means represented a capitulation by either side. Matters weren't helped by the fact that the Hungarian and Ottoman versions of the treaty had a subtle but important divergence. The Hungarian version offered 200,000 florins as a one-off tribute, whereas the Ottoman version stated that the payment was to be repeated after three years. That aside, the most important consequence of these events was that, for the first time in Ottoman history, the outcome of a campaign resulted in a reduction of territory rather than an overall increase. It was hardly the sign of a crumbling empire, but the days of western expansion were over. The Habsburgs had got the measure of their Ottoman counterparts, and, while neither side had the ability to destroy the other, the Ottoman Empire had reached its limit in the West. It is worth noting that despite all the agreements on trade and taxation in Hungary (and the 200,000 florins that were gratefully accepted by the Ottoman treasury), the Ottomans never complied with the agreed terms.

Mehmed III never signed the Peace of Zsitvatorok because he died in 1603, at the age of thirty-seven, after reigning for just eight years. Shortly before his death he heard rumours of a conspiracy to poison him. The culprit? His eldest son and natural heir to the throne, Şehzade Mahmud. Mehmed III had his son thrown into prison, where he was tortured in order to extract a confession. He said nothing. Was it wrong to have his son strangled? (Remember, this was a man who had had nineteen siblings strangled on his accession.) Mehmed III sought advice. Both his grand vizier and mufti (Muslim religious leader) said that without a confession it would be wrong. More time passed, but Şehzade Mahmud remained silent. In the end Mehmed III snapped and ordered four deaf mutes to strangle his eldest son – which left the succession up in the air. According to one source Mehmed III died from melancholy just a few months later, having never recovered from his decision to have his favourite son murdered (which begs the question that if that's what he did to his favourite son, what would he do to anyone else?). With war in the West, revolt in the East and court intrigue all around, it may well be that this last fateful decision was simply one too many, resulting in his early demise.

9

The Empire Unhinged

Mehmed III's son Ahmed became the new sultan at the age of thirteen. Even at this young age he made a significant impact on Ottoman imperial protocol: he did not have his brother strangled. Instead, his eleven-year-old brother Mustafa (a perennially unlucky name in Ottoman history) was quietly tucked away in a palace, essentially under a very luxurious house arrest. Ahmed had yet to hit puberty, so it was best for all that, in this case, there was an heir and a spare. However, his decision was written into law, and from now on no more coffins would be carried out of Topkapı Palace on the accession of a new sultan.

For one so young, Ahmed had a lot on his plate. First he had to finish the war in the West that his grandfather had started, and so it was a sixteen-year-old sultan who finally ratified the Peace of Zsitvatorok a few years later. Then there was the war with the Safavids. This ended badly for Ahmed, but, fortunately for him, the Safavids recognised that they couldn't hold on to their new conquests, so the peace agreement returned everything they had won to the status quo before the war – with the added bonus of 200 camel loads of silk a year thrown into the bargain.

Ahmed knew the importance of the dynastic line, and once he reached an appropriate age he met Kösem, a girl in the harem who was only a little older than he was. Better known to history as Kösem Sultan, she arrived in the harem at exactly the right time. Ahmed's mother and grandmother, both women of immense power and influence, would not have shared Ahmed with this new girl, but they both died relatively early in Ahmed's reign. Kösem, having caught the sultan's eye, now had to keep it. Whatever she did worked spectacularly well as the year she gave birth to the boy who would later be sultan was the same year that Ahmed's other consort, Mahfiruz Hatice Sultan, was beaten by the eunuchs, a sign that Kösem Sultan remained at the top of the pecking order. She was the wife of one sultan, the mother of two more and was still around to wield power for her grandson.

Sultan Ahmed was mainly interested in poetry, architecture and religion. He renovated the Kaaba in Mecca (the first time since Suleiman) and, while he was a talented poet (and was able to write in a number of languages), he shunned art, going so far as to destroy some European art he thought idolatrous. His crowning achievement was the Sultan Ahmed Mosque, also known as the Blue Mosque, in Istanbul (the exact point at which Constantinople started being called Istanbul is up for conjecture but, as we are at roughly the halfway mark in both Ottoman history and this book, the name now changes). A big difference between this mosque and the Selimiye or the Süleimaniye was in the financing. The latter were enormously expensive, beautiful constructions to show the power of a sultan, paid for by the spoils of war. The Blue Mosque, however, was paid for by the official treasury because there were no spoils of war. While the Sultan Ahmed Mosque is huge and magnificent, it is desperately trying to compensate for a sultan who paled in comparison to the sultans of a century earlier. Interestingly, his mosque was built on the site of a Byzantine palace that had fallen into ruin. If Ahmed couldn't dominate the Christians on the battlefield, he could at least erase traces of them in his capital city.

Minarets (and Eggs)

It's worth taking time to tell a fun story about why this mosque has six minarets (even the Selimiye and the Süleimaniye mosques have the far more common four). According to folklore, the architect, Sedefkâr Mehmed Ağa, misheard the sultan's request for '*altın minareler*' (gold minarets) as '*altı minareler*' (six minarets). It's a good story, but the real reason seems to be one of intent. Sedefkâr Mehmed Ağa was a pupil of Mimar Sinan, and the influence is clear to be seen, but this mosque is determined to out-Sinan Sinan. It has five main domes and eight secondary domes. It has more than 20,000 Iznik ceramic tiles and over

200 stained glass windows. The upper sections are painted blue (rather than the more traditional white), hence the unofficial but more common name for the mosque. Quite extraordinarily, there are ostrich eggs on the mosque's chandeliers. They are not there as some sort of exotic adornment, but they are there to prevent cobwebs because it is believed that spiders can't walk on them. I saw no cobwebs on my visit, so either the cleaners had just been in or the trick works.

In its haste to be better than any other mosque in the capital, some (including architectural historians) believe it to be a little less impressive, a little less elegant than the mosques of Mimar Sinan. It is probably fair to say that most mosques are examples of a minimalist architectural style, their interiors restrained and uncluttered, but the Blue Mosque is the architectural opposite. It was horrifyingly expensive and its construction was resented by the tax payers of the empire. This would not be the last time a weak sultan tried to make himself feel important by constructing impressive buildings with his people's money. It was a flawed plan, and while other sultans had also faced financial crises, they had spent their money on equipping the army or rebuilding the navy. Istanbul already had a number of giant mosques; of what practical use was another one?

Then, bad news: in 1615, the Safavids didn't send their 200 camel loads of silk. This failure was one of the most exotic reasons to declare war in history. Ahmed, busy with poetry and mosque building, sent his grand vizier to win another victory for the Ottomans, but the campaign was a disaster, and the Safavids made good progress in the Caucasus and Iraq. Worse news: Ahmed caught typhus in 1617 and died from internal bleeding. He was just twenty-seven years old, and although he had a young son, the Ottoman court, quite correctly, feared what message a boy ruler would send out to the empire's enemies. This was a critical moment for the empire. Enter Mustafa, the brother who had been quietly tucked away since Ahmed's coronation. Mustafa may have been born with a learning or mental disability, which would not have been helped by years spent in the 'cage', a windowless set of sumptuous rooms in the harem, where the sultans' male heirs lived out their young lives. The decision to gird Mustafa with the sword of Osman was not a popular one, and many in the court objected, including the chief black eunuch. However, despite the failures of many Mustafas in the past, this Mustafa finally broke the family curse to become sultan. With the impossible choice of a boy sultan or a mad one, the court picked the mad one. Unsurprisingly, this didn't go well and, unfortunately, he has been remembered by history as Mustafa the Mad.

By now the argument for an empire in decline is valid. The reality of the situation was twofold. The first problem was that the empire was now facing regular pressure on different continents from competitive empires the Ottomans had been unable to defeat. While the Safavids and Habsburgs were never likely to capture the Ottoman capital, the lands that bordered their empires were simply closer to their own capitals of Tehran and Vienna than that of the Sublime Porte. Further, Russia, which has barely been mentioned so far, by the 1600s was a new power to the north, eager to expand and flex its military muscles. Its ambitions would eventually lead to the Ottomans losing Ukraine and the Crimea.

As well as external threats, the Ottomans were now suffering from a run of ineffectual rulers. Any dynasty can survive one disastrous ruler, and, as Selim II's reign showed, the empire could keep going (with talented help) even though the sultan was distracted. But by now there had been five sultans in as many decades – Selim II, Murad III, Mehmed III, Ahmed I and now Mustafa I – and they had all been terrible rulers. The empire constantly faced new challenges and needed the strong leadership that had been lacking for decades. Had another Suleiman stepped into the fray at this time, the empire could well have recovered, but now the pressures of government rested on Mustafa, a man who had spent no time out in the real world and knew nothing of the harsh realities of politics. Now, for the first time in the history of the Ottoman Empire, a brother rather than a son came to power. With so many brothers waiting on the sidelines, this set a dangerous precedent. The whole plan was poorly thought through and hints at the desperation in the upper ranks of the Ottoman court at the time. Some have suggested Mustafa's madness was invented to justify his later deposition. However, if he had been of sound mind there would have been little debate in the first place. The fact that discussions were so heated and that even the chief eunuch objected tells us his mental instability was real and likely to be a serious issue.

Mustafa lasted three months. He was seen at the royal arsenal, made a few public appearances, waved to the crowds a bit and then was unceremoniously dumped back in his palace. The reason was that a powerful new cabal in the government preferred Osman, who was Ahmed's eldest son. So a fourteen-year-old was girded with Osman's sword and became Osman II. As the original Osman (and founder of the dynasty) was never a 'sultan', this Osman should have been Osman I, but as the entire dynasty was named after Osman it was decided to keep things logical.

The story of Osman II echoes that of a number of boy rulers such as the earlier Edward V of England and the later Louis XVII of France. Had Osman II reigned in a time of stability (say, immediately after Suleiman), then he would have been allowed to grow and forge his own future, but this Osman was unlucky. After his father's death and a decade of scheming, there were too many vested interests to give him a chance. He was meant to be the figurehead put in power by the anti-Mustafa cabal rather than a leader in his own right. As such, Osman II was a pale imitation of his namesake. He was a teenager surrounded by hungry wolves, with no power base of his own. The Janissaries, always alert to the machinations of power politics, began to scheme, while Kösem Sultan plotted from the harem. Osman II was not her son. If he were allowed to build a power base – or, worse for her, marry and announce his own Haseki Sultan – then her influence would evaporate.

Osman II took his responsibilities seriously, and, aged sixteen, even led his army into battle during the campaign against the Polish–Lithuanian Commonwealth in Ukraine (it's complicated and made all the more so by the fact that the enormously destructive Thirty Years' War was raging in Europe at the time). It ended indecisively, with Ukrainian borders unchanged; however, as both sides had managed major successes, both returned home to claim victory. This particular conflict showed that the Ottoman army, far from being an exotic outlier, was now much like a European army, with the same strengths and weaknesses. It was by no means a spent force, but neither did it have the advantages in weaponry it had enjoyed a hundred years earlier.

Despite his early promise as a military leader (unlike other more recent and older sultans) and the four years he spent trying to suppress the intrigue in his own court, Osman II was finally outmanoeuvred. The Janissaries seized the sultan and imprisoned him in Yedikule Fortress in Istanbul. A short time later Osman II was strangled, and Mad Mustafa was brought back to be a puppet for the ruling elite. It was a sad and premature demise for a young sultan who had showed surprising guile and effectiveness in his short reign. It was also a sign that, rather than doing what was right for the empire (allowing Osman to develop in the role), in their greed the elite would enable a madman to further weaken the empire. Finally, it was a sign that the system at the very top (rather than the government in general) needed change. In most histories this would lead to a change of dynasty (Chinese and Roman imperial histories are fragmented among many different ruling families), but the thought never seemed to occur in Istanbul, where whoever sat on that throne had to be a descendent of Osman, even if he was mad.

Interestingly, Mustafa did not take the news of his return to power in the way you might expect. As the heads of the various powerbases conveyed the news of his nephew's death, Mustafa was clearly making mental notes, and every one of the men involved in the plot, including the grand vizier and the head of Janissaries, was executed under his orders. Later he was seen wandering the corridors of the palace looking for Osman, crying out for him to relieve him of the burdens of being sultan. It was a like a scene from a Shakespeare play. The executions were probably the only thing Mustafa did in his second reign that were his own idea. He was still his mother's puppet, and behind the scenes Halime Sultan was vying for power with Kösem Sultan. It remained to be seen just which of the harem mothers would come out on top.

Meanwhile the Sipahis, who had been swept up in the earlier revolt, now had a new cause: to avenge Osman II. The focus of their ire was their main rivals to military power, the Janissaries. Thousands of Sipahis marched on the capital, armed and angry. The whole fabric of the empire was starting to unravel and at the head of it was a lunatic. Had this all happened at a time when Europe wasn't tearing itself to pieces over what had started as a war between Protestants and Catholics, substantial headway could have been made against the Ottoman territories in Europe; instead, it seems the 1620s were to be a time when the whole continent went mad with bloodlust and fury.

Kösem Sultan brought instability to a close (in the short term) when she won the battle for power in the harem. Mustafa gratefully stepped down again and was allowed to live out his days in the old palace, while Kösem Sultan's son became by far the youngest sultan at just eleven years of age. In the future Murad IV would become one of the greatest dichotomies in Ottoman history, but in the meantime Kösem Sultan was regent to the young sultan. She was all too aware that nature would take its course as her son matured, and that there was every possibility she could be superseded by her son's wife, just as she had herself had usurped her mother-in-law's power in earlier years. So Kösem Sultan came up with a cunning plan: she would ensure Murad IV was gay. While this is speculation, there can be almost no other reason for her to have had attractive male teenagers regularly paraded in front of her son. To say that her ploy led to Murad's strange attitude to women is something of an understatement. On one occasion he ordered the personal guard on his barge to attack washerwomen on the shoreline. Their crime? Singing. On another occasion he ordered all the concubines into the swimming pool where they had to tread water to stay afloat, while he fired a slingshot at any woman who tried to get out. Some of them drowned.

Random violence wasn't aimed only at women. Later in his reign, on hearing that his grand vizier had beaten his mother-in-law, Murad IV ordered his execution. He also liked to fire arrows at fishing boats on the Bosphorus if they strayed too close to the palace perimeter. None of these are signs of a stable monarch. When he came of age he brought in draconian laws. He banished alcohol (which, for a Muslim state, seemed understandable), tobacco (which, to the modern reader, seems smart) and coffee (the fiend!). The first two were felt to be 'un-Islamic', and banning coffee stopped the Janissaries from gathering in coffee houses where they sat around plotting. The punishment for breaking any of these rules? Death. But Murad IV was a hypocrite, known to regularly drink himself into a stupor, a practice that later led to his death from cirrhosis of the liver.

Murad was a giant of a man, so it was just as well that he was girded as a boy because, as a man, Osman's belt probably would not have been big enough. He was also an incredible warrior, and his weapon of choice perfectly suited his size and prowess: Murad IV liked to wield a mace, a weapon with a wooden shaft and a blunt

Above right: 1. An engraving of Mehmet II, the conqueror of Constantinople and one of the greatest Ottoman Sultans. (Courtesy of the Metropolitan Museum of Art)

Right: 2. The statue in Uzbekistan of Emir Timur, Tamerlane, the conqueror of the early Ottoman Empire. (Courtesy of Francisco Anzola under Creative Commons)

Below: 3. The walls of Constantinople stood for 1000 years before falling to The Ottomans in 1453. (Courtesy of Carole Raddato under Creative Commons)

4. The imposing outer gate and wall of Topkapi Palace. The home of the Ottoman Sultans for centuries. (Author's collection)

5. The Ottoman Harem, a small village where around 300 concubines and their children lived. It was a palace within the sultans' palace of Topkapi. (Author's collection)

6. The grand Bazaar in Istanbul. Founded by Mehmet II over 500 years ago and still a thriving centre of commerce. (Author's collection)

7. The Hagia Sophia, a Byzantine church that became the blueprint for mosques around the world after it was converted into one by Mehmet II. (Courtesy of Leandro Centomo under Creative Commons)

8. Interior of Hagia Sophia. Today it is a museum. (Author's collection)

10. A contemporary western portrait of Suleiman the Magnificent, arguably the greatest of all Ottoman Sultans. (Courtesy of the Metropolitan Museum of Art)

11. The Ottoman Tughra was the equivalent of the Sultan's coat of arms. Each one was different but the overall composition was the same. This one is Sultan Suleiman the Magnificent's ... and it's pretty magnificent. (Courtesy of the Metropolitan Museum of Art)

12. A 1600s sketch of the Great Siege of Malta in 1565 detailing the Turkish assault. It was to be a rare a defeat for Suleiman the Magnificent. (Courtesy of Rijksmuseum)

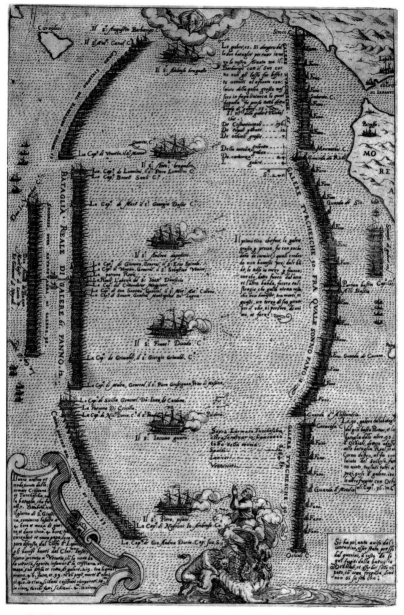

13. A European interpretation of the Ottoman conquest of Cyprus in 1570, one of the campaigns of the Fourth Ottoman Venetian War. (Courtesy of the Rijksmuseum)

14. A contemporary illustration of the Battle of Lepanto 1571, the last great clash of galleys. (Courtesy of Rijksmuseum)

15. Image of Sultan Osman II on parade with the Janissaries, the elite guard of the Ottomans. (Courtesy of Ashley Van Haeften under Creative Commons)

16. The Ottoman Empire was a forgotten ally in the multiple alliances created to stop Napoleon. In this British cartoon, the Ottomans are shown to be strong but barbaric. (Courtesy of the Rijksmuseum)

17. Dolmabache palace, the horrifically expensive white elephant that became the home of the sultans in the 19th and early 20th century. (Author's collection)

19. The Allied landings at Gallipoli 1915. The Ottoman troops were to be much tougher defenders than anticipated. (Courtesy of Archives New Zealand)

Above left: 19. An Ottoman military procession through Istanbul in the 1900s. (Courtesy of the Rijksmuseum)

Left, below left and below: 20, 21, 22. The three pashas were the only men in the Ottoman Empire's history to run the empire who were not part of the Ottoman dynasty. They led the empire to annihilation in World War One. (Courtesy of Cassowary Colorizations under Creative Commons)

metal head, perfect for causing damage to armoured opponents. His mace still exists and weighs an impressive 60 kilograms, which pretty much guarantees that whoever was on the receiving end of a direct blow would die instantly; even a glancing blow would ensure broken bones. Knowing about his size and physical prowess makes the following account hard to believe, but Murad apparently liked to dress as an average citizen and wander the streets of Istanbul of an evening to see if his bans were being observed. It would have been hard for such a large, well-built man to walk around incognito, but he probably got away with it because no one was expecting the sultan to appear in person.

Family (Part 1)

Murad IV also had a zero-tolerance policy where court intrigue was concerned (his mother was the exception). The merest whisper of a threat was immediately 'neutralised', no matter who was involved, an example of which comes from my own family. By the time of Murad IV, the Duducu clan was doing well. The head of the family was Duducu Hasan Pasha, a former governor of the province of Konya, who was now the senior general in charge of the Eastern Ottoman army (as opposed to the other senior general in charge of Ottoman lands in Europe). He had had the family tree recreated on silk-backed parchment and stamped with the sultan's seal to show it was a true copy of an earlier (degraded) original, but this was a family tree that showed a connection to the Prophet Mohammed. Would Duducu Hasan Pasha use this connection and his powerful army to threaten the sultan? Was he to getting too big for his boots? The mutterings of the court reached the sultan's ear, and Murad decided it was time to pay his general a visit. Duducu Hasan Pasha was based in Manisa (northeast of Izmir), far away from the machinations of the Ottoman court. He was a loyal general who was not plotting against the throne and felt honoured that his sultan was coming. But the visit was not what he expected, and the pasha found himself accused of crimes he hadn't committed. He was beheaded on the spot. When a senior official was disgraced, everything that bore his name was destroyed and his family was cast out. The Duducu clan's fall

---

from grace lasted for generations. My ancestor was just one of scores of senior officials and even members of the imperial family who died during Murad IV's reign. After so much uncertainty over such a long period, Murad IV wanted everyone to bend to his will; he wanted his word to be law. This was the dichotomy: Murad IV was an unstable and paranoid tyrant, but the paranoia was not without foundation. He had stepped into dead men's shoes, and he believed that a fierce, totalitarian grip was needed to bring the empire back in line.

Meanwhile, when there was another uprising from the Sipahis, it was crushed and the leader, unusually, was not executed but exiled to the European lands of the empire, where he had no supporters. Murad was bringing order from the chaos, usually by brute force. In the meantime the Safavids had, for years, been pushing the Ottomans back in the East. Murad believed it was time to act and rode out at the head of his mighty army, a sight that reinvigorated his troops. He could afford to turn his attention away from the West because Europe was still mired in the vicious Thirty Years War, and the Ottomans weren't high on anyone's list of priorities. Georgia and Armenia had been making moves towards independence, but it was this campaign, led by Murad IV, that brought them to heel. His invasion of modern day Iraq rolled back all of the Safavid gains, and he rode triumphantly into Baghdad. The great city, which had been lost for about a generation, had again become an Ottoman possession and would remain as such until 1917. The Treaty of Zuhab recognised all of Murad IV's conquests and determined what would become the present border between Iraq and Iran – not that this stopped any future fighting along the border. This campaign resulted in the first major expansion of lands and the first string of victories for more than a generation. Murad was a genuinely powerful ruler who brought stability at home, while crushing his enemies abroad. Respect had been restored to the title of Sultan of the Ottoman Empire.

Apart from being a hypocritical, paranoid, homicidal, tyrannical misogynist, Murad IV had one other flaw, though this was one over which he had no control: he sired eleven sons, but all died in infancy. Most of his daughters did, too. Despite the hundreds of fertile women available, he was failing to secure the bloodline. So, when Murad IV died unexpectedly of cirrhosis of the liver in 1640, aged just twenty-eight, all of his hard work to bring stability was undone. Murad IV had come to power after a mad predecessor and now, once again, power was back in the hands of a madman. Murad IV's brother and the son of Kösem Sultan, Ibrahim, had lived his entire life in the 'cage', from which there was no escape. Such a strict confinement was likely to drive anyone mad, but mad or not, Ibrahim had the strongest claim to the throne. Unfortunately he thought the ceremony of his accession was an elaborate hoax on the part of his dead brother, and he resisted being girded with Osman's sword and belt. To be fair to Ibrahim, Murad IV had killed men for far less, but Ibrahim couldn't believe he was sultan until he was allowed to see Murad IV's body. Fortunately for everyone, Murad IV had ended his reign (after various bloody purges) with the highly capable Grand Vizier Kara Mustafa Pasha, who was able to run things efficiently (at least at the start of Ibrahim's reign). It was Kara Mustafa who made a serious attempt to bring the expenses of the court under control and was largely successful in expelling the various court factions responsible for corrosive scheming and waste due to inefficiencies. After a decade of Murad IV and Kara Mustafa Pasha, things were decidedly on the up for the empire even if the sultan was rarely seen and constantly complaining of headaches. It seemed the personal power of the sultan was once more on the wane.

Kösem Sultan was in a bind. While she had always struggled to put her own power before the health of the empire, there was no doubt that heirs to the throne were becoming thin on the ground. While she did not want to lose out to a younger woman, she had to make sure that Ibrahim had children. Ironically, Ibrahim sired a record number of sultans: three. This is probably unsurprising given that he spent most of his time in the harem, which, to be fair, was the only home he had ever known. For a time one of his favourite women was Şekerpare Hatun, whose rise to power coincided with Kösem Sultan's loss of influence. However, Şekerpare Hatun ended up in a power struggle with Kara Mustafa Pasha, and the grand vizier was executed in 1647. It was his replacement that Şekerpare Hatun would go on to marry.

Before these events, however, a new round of hostilities broke out between Venice and the Ottomans, resulting in the Fifth Ottoman-Venetian War, known at the time as the Cretan War. Crete is one of the largest islands in the Mediterranean and was Venice's richest overseas territory (after it lost Cyprus). The Venetians didn't trigger the war; that was the Maltese Hospitallers (now known as the Knights of Malta) who, in 1644, attacked an Ottoman convoy full of pilgrims on their way to Mecca. On board were many important people from the Ottoman court, including the exiled chief black eunuch of the Topkapı harem, who was killed along with several other high-profile passengers, and 350 men and thirty women who were taken into slavery (a reminder that it wasn't just Muslim pirates doing all the enslaving in the Mediterranean). The Ottomans were furious that innocent pilgrims had been attacked and turned their rage on Venice for allowing the Hospitallers to use its harbour in Crete following the onslaught. The Ottomans sent an invasion fleet but misled the Venetians by appearing to head for Malta (the obvious target), which allowed the Venetians to lower their guard. At the last opportunity, the Ottoman armada turned south rather than west and landed on Crete in 1645.

It was said by Homer that Troy was besieged for a decade, and the marathon siege of Leningrad in the Second World War is often referred to as 'the 900 days', but both of these are fleeting compared to the longest siege in history: the siege of Candia, a Venetian trading port and the fortified capital city of the island of Crete. When the Ottoman forces arrived they were unopposed, not only because the Venetians had been misled but also because there was no attempt to hinder them. This was partly due to Cretan overreliance on Venetian maritime power, but nature also played a part. At the start of the siege, Candia was ravaged by an outbreak of plague. This would have made conditions for the Ottoman forces as grim as for those in the capital, but they were undeterred. In a mammoth tactical error, the Venetians allowed a landward siege to continue over the next three years until all but one of the Venetian forts on the island was captured.

Candia was always going to be a tough nut to crack; the Venetians had poured money into the city to give it the very latest defences. It had thick walls with the angular sides and protrusions of a classic star fort, with an added moat to make things even more difficult for besiegers. What neither side anticipated was the sheer dogged stubbornness of the other side. The Venetians were the principal defenders, but the Knights of Malta (who had started the whole thing) and the French also supported the cause over the *decades* of fighting. Changes of leadership on both sides didn't help, but the main reason Candia lasted so long was the continuing naval success the Venetians had in hampering Ottoman attempts to encircle and blockade the port. Although Venetian maritime power was past its prime, it was still an intimidating force. At one point Venice had a fleet of fifty-eight warships off the coast of the Dardanelles, where they planned to bottle up Ottoman shipping to stop reinforcements getting to Candia. It was here that they met an Ottoman fleet of double that size. The ensuing battle raged for three days, with the Ottoman fleet faring far worse than the Venetian one. While Venice achieved a tactical victory, it failed to ensure a strategic one, and what remained of the Ottoman fleet escaped to Crete. The siege of Candia had spread its tendrils out across the eastern Mediterranean.

I doubt the reader of this book would want a list of every naval action that happened during this lengthy siege, but they exist (there were four Battles of the Dardanelles alone). Militarily, the problem was that neither side could land a satisfactory knockout blow. Losing ships is an expensive business, and the Ottomans were better placed to absorb such costs than were the Venetians, with their substantially diminished revenues. From 1658 to 1664 Ottoman efforts were distracted by renewed hostilities with the Habsburgs. More men and materials were poured into this land war than the ongoing siege, but just enough support was given to keep the siege going, and by now Venice had run out of ideas to crack the virtual encirclement of their capital on Crete.

The Habsburgs and the Ottomans brokered a peace deal in 1664, so a couple of years later, in 1666, the focus was back on Crete. With Hospitaller and French backing, the Venetians won a few more victories at sea, but they were Pyrrhic victories that further denuded the West's resources without stopping the Ottomans from resupplying and bringing fresh troops. The final wave of Ottoman forces arrived in the winter of 1666/7, when 70,000 troops landed on Crete, backed by over 30,000 slaves and conscripts brought in to dig tunnels, raise earthworks and finally bring this epic struggle to an end. This Ottoman army would still be there two years later. The entire siege lasted for twenty-one years, four months and twenty-six days. That means a child born as fighting broke out would have reached adulthood by the time peace arrived.

After so many years of bruising effort, neither side could afford to lose; to do so would surely mark a turning point for either empire. The Ottomans began to waver, and in 1668 they proposed that Venice keep half of Crete. But the Venetians heard rumours of renewed turmoil at the Ottoman court and, furthermore, had just had reassurances of French reinforcements. They refused the deal, and in June and July of 1668 the defenders became attackers. With a combination of cannons firing from the city's walls and more firing from anchored Christian ships, thousands of cannon balls rained down on the Ottoman forces. Then the gates were flung open and thousands of warriors jumped into the Ottoman trench lines, where fierce hand-to-hand fighting broke out. Twice the attackers tried to soften up the besiegers with furious artillery salvoes, and twice they descended on the earthworks to break the siege once and for all. It was now a matter of honour. Would the West prove that Ottoman power was finally on the wane? Or would the Ottomans prove that Venice was in terminal decline?

The fighting was intense but achieved little except more death. The Ottoman sappers had ensured subterranean refuges in the event of cannon fire, and the hundreds of Christian cannons and thousands of cannon balls therefore failed to soften the Ottoman army. On both occasions the attackers who sallied forth from Candia were thrown back after suffering large numbers of casualties. Worse still, during one of the bombardments, *La Thérèse*, a 900-ton French flagship, accidentally sparked its powder store and exploded. The sight of such a huge warship being torn to pieces, combined with the failures of their attacks, greatly reduced the already flagging Christian morale. The Venetians were desperate, so desperate that recent discoveries in the Venetian archives have shown that there was a plan to hurl liquid derived from the spleens and buboes of plague victims into the Ottoman camp in order to spread deadly plague. While this would not be the first time in history that an attempt was made to spread illness (sometimes diseased animal carcasses or, occasionally, dead plague victims were hurled over walls), this was the first time there was a semi-scientific attempt to refine the potency. The Venetians were willing to try anything if it meant saving their city.

The French had had enough. Their assistance was costing a small fortune for no practical gain, and now they had lost one of the biggest warships in their fleet. The French evacuated

Candia in August 1669. At this time the leader of the defences was the highly capable Venetian Francesco Morosini, who now had fewer than 4,000 troops to defend the walls, not to mention that he was also out of allies. He accepted terms and surrendered to the Ottoman grand vizier, Ahmed Köprülü, on 27 September 1669 – before being given formal permission to do so from Venice. Although this meant that he was discredited for a time, it was generally agreed that the terms were good. A few Venetian ports in the area were allowed to continue to operate, and all the inhabitants of Candia who wished to leave could do so, with all the goods they could carry. It was said that Pope Clement IX collapsed on hearing the news of Candia's fall, and died two months later.

The Siege of Ceuta between Morocco and Spain lasted longer (thirty years in total), but there were points when the siege was lifted. The twenty-one years at Candia were unbroken, so it holds the dubious record of the longest continual siege in history. From the Ottoman point of view, only an empire in its prime could lay siege for so long and not risk being counter-attacked by another force. The siege spanned multiple sultans' reigns and was a convincing reminder that the Ottoman war machine was still a force to be reckoned with. While they had lost ground on the Dalmatian coast (modern-day Croatia), the capture of Crete was arguably the greater prize, and to have finally won such a lengthy siege brought new respect for as well as fear of the Ottoman Empire. This was truly a unique event in history.

There is a final point to make about this before returning to Ibrahim: Francesco Morosini was to make another (unwanted) mark on history. During the later 'Great Turkish War' (more on that to come), Morosini led a Venetian fleet to attack and capture Athens. The Ottoman governor put the gunpowder supplies in the Parthenon, assuming that the Venetians would never target a building of such historical importance. While what happened next is undisputed, the reasons for it are hotly contested. Whether deliberate or not, a Venetian mortar round went through the roof of the Parthenon and detonated the gunpowder, turning the venerated monument into the ruin we see today. Even worse, when it became clear that the Venetians would have to evacuate, there were discussions about blowing up what was left. Fortunately that course of action was never taken. Francesco Morosini was a brave

The Sultans

man, a highly capable general and one of the worst cultural vandals in history.

Meanwhile, back in the 1640s, Ibrahim the Mad was living up to his epithet as his decadence ran out of control. He raised not one but *eight* women in the harem to the title of Haseki Sultan. Of the eight chief consorts, Hümaşah Sultan became his bride. The blockade of the Dardanelles during the war with Venice had reduced the amount of goods flowing into the Ottoman capital, leading to scarcity and inflation. Even though high taxes were needed to pay for the war effort, Ibrahim's wife, who had been given the treasury of Egypt as a dowry, felt no need to curtail her lavish spending. Ibrahim was also a profligate spender, and perhaps most decadent was his order that the palace be carpeted in sable furs as a gift to his wife. Although it was less damaging to the economy, he increased tensions in the harem when he made his own sisters and niece subordinate to his concubines, taking away their lands and jewels and making them serve Hümaşah Sultan as if they were slave girls. There was also a rumour that Ibrahim had all 280 of his (lesser) concubines sown into sacks, weighed down with rocks and thrown into the Bosphorus; there is no specific account of this and it seems to be an exaggeration of an already insane situation. There are echoes in this era of the late Roman Empire when everyone in both empires agreed that, despite the ongoing uncertainties at the very top, the systems were robust enough to hold the empire together. In both cases, the systems simply worked better with an effective ruler in charge, otherwise stagnation set in and the empire began to fray at the edges as the power on the frontiers slowly eroded. The barbarians were far from the Ottoman gates, and the empire was by no means finished; to underestimate the empire's resources at this time would be a serious mistake, but the earlier energy of an expanding young empire was gone.

In 1647, Kösem Sultan, as well as the grand vizier, began plotting Ibrahim's overthrow. Unfortunately for them he got wind of the palace coup and acted first. The grand vizier was executed and Kösem Sultan was banished from the capital, but these moves only slowed the wheels of revolt. Once again the Janissaries rose up, and this time they were supported by the general population. Everyone had had enough. While Ibrahim was handing out sable coats, the price of food and other goods was constantly rising. There didn't seem to be much to lose for the average Ottoman citizen. A mob

158

moved against the new grand vizier, Ahmed Pasha, Ibrahim's mouthpiece and sycophant, and tore him to pieces (which is why he became known as 'Thousand Pieces'). If you have lost track of the number of grand viziers whose lives were cut short through violence, don't worry – there are more to come. Aside from the sultan, this was the most important role in the land and the only one open to someone who was not a member of the royal family. The job always seemed worth the risk.

With turmoil at the top once more, Kösem Sultan was brought back to work out what to do. Ibrahim's reign was now untenable, but a successor had to be chosen before an uprising turned into a revolution – or even civil war. Kösem Sultan and the new grand vizier, Şofu Mehmed Pasha, agreed that the best plan of action was to have Ibrahim executed and install his six-year-old son Mehmed as the new sultan. The solution was far from satisfactory, and shows how desperate they were. Before they made their bold move they consulted the grand mufti, the most senior Muslim cleric in Istanbul, to determine if the plan could be justified on theological grounds. The grand mufti, perhaps realising that desperate times required desperate measures, gave his consent.

It was Sultan Ibrahim's chief executioner who, in accordance with the long tradition that no royal blood should be spilled, strangled him in front of a window so that court officials could bear witness. Ibrahim ruled for eight years and had been one of the worst sultans in an increasingly crowded field of inept Ottoman rulers.

10

Peaks and Troughs

With his father dead, Mehmed IV was the newest and youngest sultan. In a time of complete chaos in the Ottoman court he was an unexpected stabilising influence, exactly what the empire needed. Later in life he became known as Mehmed the Hunter, a sign that he enjoyed more physical and martial pastimes than his insane and decadent father. Ibrahim had never seemed to warm to his son; a scar on Mehmed's head was allegedly the result of an incident when Ibrahim threw him down a well, and the eunuchs had had to save him.

It was during the reign of Mehmed IV that Candia fell, and the Ottoman Empire could finally claim another victory over Venice. It was under this sultan that Ottoman power arrived at one of the most unexpected places in Europe – in 1655, a force of forty Ottoman ships captured the Isle of Lundy in the Bristol Channel. That's right; technically speaking, the Ottoman Empire spread as far as the British Isles. Lundy is the largest island in the Channel and is roughly equidistant from England to the south and Wales to the north. For five years the Ottomans used this island as their official naval base in the North Atlantic – and less officially as their base for privateering operations in the same area. The base in Lundy was abandoned around 1660, when Ottoman ships were seen sailing along the east coast of America, particularly around Newfoundland and Virginia. It is widely believed that the Ottomans only ever got as far as Vienna (nearly), but their ships certainly travelled much further west.

Mehmed IV's reign brought an end to Kösem Sultan's power. She was not a blood relative, and Mehmed's mother, Turhan Hatice, feared the scheming woman might well make a move against the boy sultan. While this was thought unlikely, it didn't prevent her execution in 1651 (there is no proof, but some said that this had been ordered by Turhan), when she was strangled with her own hair. Her execution was a bold move and her death brought to a close the many decades of influence she had wielded both in the harem and the sultan's court. It was the end of an era, but not a particularly good one.

As well as the capture of Crete, other things were also going well for Mehmed IV. In 1663, at the age of twenty-one, he led an army against the Habsburgs (in what was just another of the many clashes that took place over the centuries) and, later, against the Polish–Lithuanian Commonwealth in 1672. (The word 'led' in this context means that he rode out at the head of the army but only went part of the way on the campaign trail. The rest was up to the grand vizier and his generals.) Both of these central European opponents were the perennial enemies of the Ottomans, and his victory over the Poles pushed Ottoman influence into central Ukraine. Even the age-old insubordinate vassal state of Transylvania was brought, once again, under Ottoman control in 1660. It was under Mehmed IV that the Black Sea became an 'Ottoman lake', as virtually all lands around the sea were either Ottoman territories or vassals to the Ottomans. But these achievements were to prove ephemeral. This was less to do with Mehmed IV and more to do with Köprülü Mehmed Pasha, who was one of the longest-serving grand viziers in the Ottoman Empire.

Köprülü Mehmed Pasha was from an Albanian family that rose to prominence in the seventeenth-century Ottoman court and provided six grand viziers over the years, and, as we shall see, his story reflects the story of the empire at this time. On his deathbed he is said to have advised Mehmed IV 'never to take advice from a woman, never to appoint a minister who was too wealthy, to always keep the treasury full, and to always keep the army on the move'. Aside from his comment about women (which, in the context of the harem, is understandable), his advice pretty much stands the test of time. Mehmed IV was easily distracted by his love of hunting, and although he lacked the talents to be a great sultan his flaws were papered over by an effective government, and he was a competent (if not exceptional) leader. It was a sign that a mature empire had the systems in place to allow the smooth running of government – as long as the sultan checked in now and again.

The Messiah

While things were mostly ticking along, there was one truly unique moment in Mehmed IV's reign, when he met the Messiah. Sabbatai Zevi was a seventeenth-century Jewish spiritualist who took things rather too far. Theologically speaking, the big difference between Christians and Jews is that the Christians have had their messiah, while the Jews are still waiting for theirs. So imagine the excitement when a young Jewish Sephardic rabbi and kabbalist announced that he was the long-awaited Messiah. Zevi's family had settled in Smyrna (modern-day Izmir), where it had built up a business. The son, however, had no interest in the commercial world; Zevi was a religious and pious young man. The *Zohar* is a Jewish mystical manuscript full of subtext and code-like clues and was believed to prophesy that the Messiah would appear in 1648, when he would lead the Jews back to Israel. In that very year, young Zevi began to preach that the texts were true and that all the clues pointed to him as the greatly anticipated Messiah. The local rabbis unsurprisingly cast doubt on these revelations, but Zevi was not only a devout Jew who observed all the rituals of the faith, but also a charismatic individual who could speak persuasively to the faithful. After so many centuries of hostility, uncertainty, displacement and worse, his words were like a glass of water in the desert. He ousted the local head of the Jewish synagogue and became the epicentre of a cult-like messianic following. From Smyrna he travelled to the major cities of the empire, including Salonica, Cairo and Jerusalem, to spread his message.

Jerusalem was a flourishing city under Ottoman rule. The overlords may have been Muslim, which stopped the building of any new churches or synagogues, but all faiths were tolerated. The Orthodox Christian Patriarchs of both Istanbul and Jerusalem still held their posts at this time. For the past 150 years, Jews had settled here and prospered under the Ottoman state, where they developed a large trade and banking economy within their community and where they were free to practice their faith. As such, Jerusalem exerted a strong pull for Zevi not only because it was safe, but principally because of all the religious connotations associated with this holy city. Everywhere he went he demonstrated his understanding of scripture and led a modest life, with days devoted to fasting and chanting. He was often watched by hushed crowds who genuinely believed they were looking at the Jewish Messiah.

Zevi caused a sensation as Jewish communities throughout Europe and the Middle East began to believe the good news. Many Jews even planned to relocate to be near the new Messiah. The excitement cannot be overstated; in the 1660s, Sabbatai Zevi was as famous as Moses and King David among the Jews of Europe and the Middle East. The resulting religious hysteria was causing a commotion which did not go unnoticed by the authorities. In 1666, Zevi was summoned to Istanbul. The Jews were ecstatic. Was the mighty Ottoman Empire about to become a Jewish Empire? Was the sultan about to convert? Well, no. Zevi was immediately arrested under the orders of Grand Vizier Ahmed Köprülü. His imprisonment was little more than house arrest, and Zevi's rich followers made sure his surroundings in 'prison' were sumptuous. Nevertheless Zevi was the sultan's prisoner and Grand Vizier Ahmed Köprülü gave him three choices:

1 Demonstrate his divinity by proving himself immune to the arrows fired by Janissary archers (if the archers missed or the arrows didn't pierce him, then he was the messiah)
2 Be impaled on a spike
3 Convert to Islam

The next day Zevi met Sultan Mehmed IV. It was decision time, and his pronouncement had the potential to rock the Ottoman Empire to its very core. When Zevi came before the sultan, he removed the symbols of his Jewish faith and put on a turban before converting to Islam. Mehmed IV was so delighted that he made Zevi a palace doorkeeper, gave him the title of Effendi and authorised a large salary for his troubles. Two things happened after that. The first and obvious result was that Zevi's followers were horrified; their euphoria turned to embarrassment and, later, to hatred. Zevi (who died in 1676) is a name that came to bear the dark mark of cowardice and apostasy. He is rarely mentioned by Jewish scholars and his story is largely forgotten, which is understandable. However, the other thing that happened was that a few devotees continued to follow him, believing the conversion was a trick. Their dedication led to the formation of the secretive Sabbatean and Dönmeh sects, whose followers are outwardly Muslim, but who secretly practice Judaism. They still exist today.

Meanwhile, back in Istanbul, things were definitely on the up for the empire; it felt as if the tide had turned. Thus buoyed, Mehmed IV decided to attempt the one major conquest that had eluded Suleiman the Magnificent: the capture of Vienna. If the Ottomans succeeded, it would shatter Habsburg power and credibility. It would also ensure dominion over Hungary and the Balkans as they would simply be too far away from Christian support.

Vienna was a prime target, and now that Belgrade was in Ottoman hands this city of the Holy Roman Empire, ruled by the Habsburgs, was once again within striking distance. With the Danube running through it, it was the perfect location for trade to flow in and out of Europe from the Black Sea. But the Ottoman intent to strike Vienna was known for about a year beforehand, giving the city time to gather together a coalition to fight the imminent Ottoman threat. Apart from their failure to keep their plans secret, Ottoman preparations were foolproof. Nobody underestimated the task ahead of them, so when the army marched out it was over 100,000 strong, far larger than any army the European powers could put in the field. When the Ottomans arrived and set up camp, it was so large and the tents were so well ordered that some onlookers thought the Ottoman plan was to set up a rival city beside the old one. It seemed that the Ottoman numbers were so great and the camp so magnificent that they would win through sheer scale.

While the Ottomans set up camp, the Crimean Tatars (Ottoman allies) headed further west, raiding and pillaging and generally making life miserable for those who lived in a wide swathe around the capital. While this was plunder for the Tatars, it was also an opportunity to scout the countryside to see if there was a relief column on its way. There wasn't. Leopold I, the Holy Roman Emperor, did not have the power to protect his own subjects, and he 'bravely' left the city before the besieging army arrived. One of his generals further weakened the city by moving 20,000 men to Linz. Leopold may not have been in Vienna, but the marvellously named Count Ernst Rüdiger von Starhemberg was there as the commander of a 15,000-man garrison, which was effectively outnumbered 7:1. With his emperor having fled the city, von Starhemberg had every reason to sue for peace and save his own skin, but this was a man in his forties, a seasoned veteran who had fought in multiple conflicts. Von Starhemberg had the experience and energy to carry out a vigorous defence and counted on his Polish–Lithuanian Commonwealth allies to provide a relief force before his defences crumbled.

Von Starhemberg did everything he could prior to the siege. He added about 50 per cent to his forces' numbers by equipping volunteers to become a militia, and it turned out that gamekeepers from the local forests were excellent snipers. He had also taken the logical, if draconian, measure of demolishing many of the houses and buildings outside the city walls. This allowed a clear field of fire for his more than 300 cannons targeting any oncoming Ottoman assaults. Kara Mustafa Pasha countered by ordering his forces to dig long lines of trenches directly toward the city. He also had great earthworks erected, manmade hills so that Ottoman artillery could fire directly into Vienna.

Suleiman had largely failed at the first siege because of abysmal summer weather. His siege cannons had got bogged down in mud, and the weather continued to be uncooperative, which meant that his bombardment never reached the intensity he needed. Kara Mustafa Pasha was aware of this and did everything he could to protect his troops from enemy fire, while also ensuring that there were enough good firing positions to grind down Vienna's defences. Von Starhemberg had anticipated that the Ottomans would try to undermine the walls, so he had tree trunks buried in the soft ground in various likely positions to hamper the advance of the Ottoman sappers. The whole siege was a series of moves and counter-moves. While von Starhemberg had been able to stockpile food, Vienna was a large city with a significant population, and Kara Mustafa Pasha was able to surround it completely, ensuring there was no way they could get additional supplies, either by land or the River Danube. As days turned into weeks and weeks became months, the defenders were slowly starving. When Kara Mustafa Pasha tried probing the defences with frontal assaults, it was usually at night. The constant bombardment, mixed with night-time attacks and little food, led to exhaustion on the part of the defenders. Men collapsing through fatigue became so common that von Starhemberg ordered any soldier found asleep on watch to be shot where he lay.

In an attempt to disrupt the Ottoman assault, there were multiple night-time attacks from the defenders. The first achieved complete surprise and slowed Ottoman preparations. Fires were started and various Ottoman stores and mines were set alight. But the Janissaries were alert to subsequent attacks, and with each new sally forth from the walls the raids steadily became less successful and more costly in defender lives. One defender reflected the frustration at the zeal of the Ottoman siege, saying, 'It is beyond the powers of human comprehension to grasp – just how obstinately the Turks defend themselves – it is easier to deal with any conventional fortress and with any other army than with the Turks.'

In early September the Ottoman sappers positioned their mines of gunpowder to explode and create breaches in the walls. Von Starhemberg countered with moves by his own sappers to intercept the Ottoman tunnels as they reached the walls. (It was common practice for tunnellers to stop occasionally to listen for any tell-tale sounds that might indicate a nearby enemy tunnel; sometimes they broke into each other's systems, leading to vicious and claustrophobic close-quarter fighting by candle light.) By 8 September, despite von Starhemberg's best efforts, some of the lower outer walls had fallen into Ottoman hands. There were a number of reasons why the defenders kept fighting. An honourable one was that if Vienna fell it would be used as an Ottoman base for further operations west, just as the fall of Belgrade had offered a launching point into Hungary. A less noble but more immediate motivation was the fear of a massacre. The atrocities of the Thirty Years War (between fellow Christians) were still often repeated in the West, and the knowledge that the Ottomans were more than capable of massacring a whole population would have been something in the minds of everyone in the city.

Then a miracle – or a disaster, depending on the point of view. The Crimean Tatars had not been scouting the areas around Vienna as they should have been, and had failed to spot a huge relief army before it swooped on the Ottoman camp. The Ottomans had grown complacent in their defences over the eight weeks they had been *in situ*. The Siege of Vienna turned now into the Battle of Vienna as an army of over 50,000, a mixture of Holy Roman and Polish–Lithuanian forces, descended on the Ottomans. The battle started in the most spectacular way imaginable, when King John III Sobieski led a gigantic cavalry charge down the slope towards the Ottoman camp. He was at the front of his 3,000 Winged Hussars, cavalrymen wearing plate armour and full-face steel helmets (at the time this was an anachronism, but John had learnt that the heavy armour worked well against the Ottoman light cavalry). Each one of these men had a metal frame on his back with large white feathers attached. The Hussars looked like a flock of steel birds swooping down on the enemy, the sight of which inspired the allied army to charge straight through the panicking Ottoman forces. John's Winged Hussars, plus the thousands of other allied cavalry charging into the fray, made this the largest (recorded) cavalry charge in history. Thousands died; thousands more were captured. Kara Mustafa Pasha had been badly let down by his allies, who had recognised a lost cause and didn't even engage in the final battle, despite the fact it had been the job of the Tatars to ensure nothing like this could happen. Kara Mustafa Pasha was able to escape with a portion of the army, but Vienna was to remain eternally out of reach of the empire. On his return to Belgrade, Kara Mustafa Pasha was strangled on the orders of the commander of the Janissaries. It had been the Ottoman Empire's worst ever defeat in a single battle, and the leader of such a disastrous campaign could not expect to survive the consequences. King John III Sobieski's spectacular cavalry charge became a legend. It was said afterwards that he had played on the words of Julius Caesar and, rather than saying, 'Veni, vidi, vici' (I came, I saw, I conquered), he changed it to, 'Veni, vidi, Deus vicit' (I came, I saw, God conquered).

The king and his soldiers had the first look at the spoils in the Ottoman camp, and they were wondrous. Kara Mustafa Pasha's tent (along with some others) is still in a Polish museum, where it is occasionally put on display. The grand vizier's tent is a stunning example of the use of textiles, with intricate geometric patterns woven in vibrant colours. Such detail in a campaign tent would have seemed extraordinary to Christian onlookers who saw the Ottoman encampment as a potential new city.

There are many books about the significance of this siege and the final battle of Vienna, said to have changed the face of Europe. No longer would central Europe fear Ottoman invasion; now it was the turn of the sultans to see an erosion of their power in Hungary and the Balkans. That much is true, and it is also true that the siege was followed up with other major Christian victories, but it is easy to read too much into events with hindsight. The siege was a close-run affair, and had the Tatars done a better job of scouting there would not have been a surprise cavalry attack. The simple fact was that most of the areas under Ottoman rule in 1683 were still under its rule in 1783. There were significant consequences for Hungary, which would forever shake off its Ottoman overlords, but it had always been a bit of a hinterland, positioned as it was between two empires and never, in reality, a docile subject to Ottoman governance. The Ottoman Empire was far from finished, but it had suffered a devastating blow. The Eternal State didn't look quite so eternal any more. It was not the death of Suleiman the Magnificent that marked the end of the golden era of the Ottoman Empire but the second siege of Vienna. Mehmed IV has the unenviable legacy of being the sultan who stopped the erosion of Ottoman power at the start of his reign, only to have it erode even more precipitously in his last decade.

Pastry (Part 2)

As a result of this siege, something new was created and it needs to have its moment in the spotlight. After the Ottoman forces were repelled, Vienna celebrated. Church bells rang out, people danced and cheered in the streets, and as supplies came flooding back into the city, one baker in particular wanted to commemorate the battle with a simple pastry in the shape of the Ottoman symbol: a crescent. The result was the croissant, made to celebrate the victory of the siege of Vienna in the 1683. So croissants are Austrian, not French as most people assume.

Meanwhile, back in Hungary and less than a month after his victory at Vienna, John III was leading his troops against the Ottomans at the Battle of Párkány, which was another (if minor) victory. This was the last clash in a campaign that had been an unadulterated disaster for Mehmed IV. The siege of Vienna was the opening salvo in what would become known as the Great Turkish War (mention of this was made earlier). In some ways the war showed the strength of the Ottoman Empire at the time. To the north the empire had to fight John III Sobieski of the Polish–Lithuanian Commonwealth and Peter the Great of the Russian Empire; the latter was rapidly becoming a regular competitor in the quest for territory in Ukraine and on the shores of the Black Sea. To the west, Mehmed IV faced the Holy Roman Empire, Venice, Hungary and rebellions from many areas of the Balkans and Greece. While the Ottomans were beaten and beaten emphatically, who else could take a beating from so many and remain in the fight for another 250 years? The term 'sick man of Europe' was not then in use, but the idea that the Ottomans were falling behind and in irrevocable decline began during this era.

Another eerie echo of Suleiman's reign and his failure to capture Vienna came after the second siege of Vienna, when there was a second Battle of Mohács in 1687. The first battle had been an emphatic victory for Suleiman and opened up Hungary to Ottoman domination. The second battle happened in roughly the same place, but this time the outcome was the exact opposite. It was an overwhelming defeat for the Ottomans and closed the door on any further attempts to recapture Hungarian land. The new grand vizier, Sarı Suleiman Pasha, fled the field of battle, fearing for his life. His fears were well founded, and when the remains of the army caught up with him another grand vizier's life was cut short, another small tragedy in a sea of many. The army was now in revolt. It had suffered defeat after defeat; its losses had been substantial. The tactics and organisation of the forces were old-fashioned and needed modernisation. What was the solution? Depose the sultan, of course.

The absolute rule of the Ottoman sultans had many perks, of which the harem and luxurious living were two, but on the downside it meant that when things went wrong it was the sultan who became the focal point of discontent. Decades of stability and a number of military successes were all forgotten in the midst of uprising and revolt by everyone from lowly foot soldiers to those who walked the perfumed corridors of Topkapı. Mehmed IV was put under house arrest in 1687 and barred, at first, from leaving his palace. His brother became Sultan Suleiman II, another sultan with a name from an earlier, more successful time. But Suleiman II was nothing like his namesake. This Suleiman was a man of frail health, with little experience in the affairs of state. He had spent thirty-nine years of his life in the cage in the harem, where he had devoted his time to copying elaborately illuminated calligraphy from the Qur'an. This was a worthy spiritual pastime but not the sort of study that would help him run an empire. When the court learned how ill he was, there were mutterings about bringing back

Mehmed IV. Suleiman agreed and asked on more than one occasion to be sent back to the cage, the place he called home and where he felt safe. However, it turned out that, sick or not, Suleiman II was a better sultan than anyone had expected. After a brief siege in 1688 the Ottomans lost Belgrade, but it was only a few short years later that Grand Vizier Köprülü Fazıl Mustafa Pasha returned with an army and recaptured the city. (Belgrade was to lurch between Austrian, Ottoman and, later, Serbian nationalists for over a century.) So Belgrade was an Ottoman city again, and the seemingly unstoppable push from the Christian alliance in the West was, for the first time, reversed.

The Great Turkish War ground on but now seemed less of an existential threat than it had before. The economy, which had been in a desperate state, was overhauled (along with the coinage) by Suleiman and his grand vizier, and inflation was coming down. The only negative in Suleiman II's short reign was that Peter the Great was starting to push back the Tatars in the Crimea, and the Ottomans didn't have the resources to come to their aid. Overall it was a pretty good record, but three years into his reign Suleiman's illnesses caught up with him. He was spirited away to Edirne, where he died in 1691. His predecessor, Mehmed IV, who by contrast had had a long reign of thirty-nine years, also died in isolation a couple of years later in 1693.

For reasons known only to the Ottoman court, the next sultan was yet another son of Ibrahim the Mad. He was Ahmed II, and things did not start well for him. He came to power when his armies were already fighting to the north of Belgrade, so there wasn't much he could do to influence events, but he did suffer an unfortunate loss when Grand Vizier Köprülü Fazıl Mustafa Pasha, the hero of Belgrade, was shot and killed at the Battle of Slankamen. While the Ottoman forces were about 50 per cent more numerous, the imperial forces of Louis William, Margrave of Baden-Baden (known as Türkenlouis, 'Turkish Louis', for his many victories over Ottoman armies) had entrenched themselves in a prepared defensive position. The Ottoman Sipahis charged bravely but pointlessly into musket fire and grapeshot. Then, as the Ottoman numbers dwindled (and despite their own lack of water and other supplies), Louis's cavalry and foot soldiers charged out from behind their defences to rout what remained of Ahmed II's army. An estimated 25,000 men, about half of the Ottoman army, were killed or wounded. This was said by commentators of the age to be the bloodiest battle for generations.

Economics

As has been already mentioned, the Ottoman currency fluctuated in value in the sixteenth and seventeenth centuries. This was due in part to the influx of silver from the New World, but also to changes in trade. As Ottoman interests turned westwards, contacts with Indonesia and the Mughal Empire waned (plus they had their own troubles). For centuries the Ottoman *akçe*, silver coin, could be found in the purses of traders around the Mediterranean and Asian coasts, but over time its value diminished. When the coin was first introduced in the reign of Mehmed the Conqueror each one had nearly a gram of silver, but by 1600 that had dropped to about a third of a gram. By the end of Mehmed IV's reign, the silver content had dropped further still to about 15 per cent of a gram.

The 'circle of justice' is a Middle Eastern concept dating from as far back as the tenth century AD and describes the relationship between the state and its people. The four key elements are the sovereign, the army, the wealth of the state and the peasant farmers. When each of these works successfully, everyone benefits – so the sovereign (or sultan) is all powerful, but he has a duty to protect (the role of the army) the peasants, who provide the agricultural produce and pay the taxes (the wealth of the state). About 40 per cent of the population of the Ottoman Empire were peasants who produced according to regions. The Balkans raised sheep and sold wool, Greece was famed for its olives, and Egypt's wheat continued to make it the breadbasket of the Mediterranean, a role it had held for more than 5,000 years. These areas were particularly sensitive to increases in taxation, which happened whenever the sultan went to war. In earlier centuries the increases were offset by the revenues that flowed from victories, which meant that there was less need to raise taxes, but when times were hard the taxes became more punitive – or were felt to be more punitive. Due to the poor quality of arable land, tax demands in the heartlands sometimes meant near starvation for local populations. Sultans knew only too well that they lived in 'the circle of justice' and that it would be foolish to break it for no valid reason.

While various exotic trade routes have been mentioned, recent research shows that more trade was conducted inside the empire than outside it. This is unsurprising given that the empire covered the mountains of Romania, the steppes of Ukraine, the deserts of Arabia, the coasts of Greece and the cities of Istanbul and Baghdad. It is thought that the reason why Ottoman trade was successful for so long was because everyone adhered to the unwritten rule that the empire benefitted all of its ethnicities through the use of one currency and one system of trade. That's not to ignore the importance of international trade. The Ottoman Empire straddled Asia and Europe and multiple seas. Any trade between these two continents required the approval of the sultan and his ministers. Favourable trade deals and taxes derived from these would continue to bring in healthy revenues right up to the end of the empire. Even today the Bosphorus, which ran through the heart of the empire and now through modern Turkey, is one of the busiest and most important shipping lanes in the world.

The main problem for the sultan was that his personal revenues came from the shared booty of successful military campaigns, and they were becoming fewer and fewer. If anything, the cost of these campaigns (such as the capture of Candia) was becoming far greater than any income from plunder. Newer parts of the empire contributed to the royal purse through direct tax, so Crete and Baghdad became considerable sources of revenue, but as time went on and some of the sultans' tastes for luxuries grew ever more extreme, these were not enough to cover costs. The financial arrangements for court officials were poorly defined. The jobs didn't come with salaries; instead, a grand vizier could expect revenues from specific towns or estates. It was common for the general/pasha/vizier who captured a town to become the beneficiary of the revenues from that town. Janissary captains might expect to be rewarded with the largest houses, and so forth. This worked well when the empire was expanding but did nothing to satisfy those in high positions in times of strife and contraction. (It was quite convenient for grand viziers to have a high mortality rate as their holdings would be transferred to the new occupant of the role.)

Slavery (Part 2)

Given the ubiquitous role of slaves, it is not unfair to say that the Ottoman Empire was built on slavery. On behalf of the Ottomans, pirates in the Mediterranean regularly carted off whole Christian villages, and one Barbary pirate (a Dutch Muslim convert) enslaved the entire population of Baltimore in Ireland – not a place where you'd expect that kind of thing to happen. The fishermen of Spain or the peasants of Italy must have been terrified when they saw the sails of an Ottoman raiding party appear on the horizon. The fact that little, if anything, is known about the fate of many of these people is, in its own way, the story of slavery.

Virtually all of the women in the harem were slaves, which meant that the sultan himself was the son of a slave. The women were, in turn, protected by black eunuchs who were also slaves. Many of the ministers, including the grand viziers and all of the Janissaries (up until the mid-seventeenth century) were slaves. Slaves rowed the Ottoman galleys, which expanded the empire and shipped goods across the seas, and it was slaves who worked the land on some of the larger agricultural estates. When we talk about the slave trade today we tend to think exclusively of black slaves from Africa being shipped to the New World, where they could expect nothing but back-breaking work. The Ottoman Empire took a more nuanced approach, with different types of slaves, many of whom had opportunities for advancement. A poor Christian girl would (probably) happily trade her freedom to be the wife of a peasant farmer for the chance to become a *valide* sultan in the harem. Many of the famous 'Turks' in this book (apart from the sultans) were actually ex-Christian slaves who went on to achieve remarkable things in this cosmopolitan empire. While capturing Christians (especially children) and forcing them to convert to Islam scandalised the West, Westerners were, if anything, more avid slavers than the sultans, and offered far fewer opportunities to rise to high positions. This is not a defence of Ottoman slavery, but it is important to understand the context of the times and the role of slavery at the very heart of the empire.

Back at the palace, Ahmed II lasted about as long as Suleiman II, reigning for just three years – at which point Mustafa II, another brother, was installed. This means that since Mehmed II's reign of relative stability (until he was deposed) there had been four sultans in ten years. It also means that three of them had been brothers, with none of their sons having come to power. Fortunately, Mustafa II recognised that a period of calm was needed after the tumultuous events both within the empire and outside it, and he lived long enough to ease the court back into a steady routine after its murderous series of plots and coups.

Chios (or Sakiz, as the Ottomans called it) is an island in the eastern Aegean that had been lost to the Venetians during the Great Turkish War. It was small but profitable, so the Sanjak Province of Sakız was worth fighting over. Mustafa II just happened to be the man in the seat of power when it was recaptured, and although this didn't make up for all the other reversals it was much welcome news after the western frontline had become deadlocked just north of Belgrade. The war had reached a stalemate for all concerned, and it was apparent that the Ottomans were never going to be able to recapture all of their lands north of the Danube. They had tried to carry out what would be their one last push into Habsburg territory but suffered a crushing defeat at the Battle of Zenta in 1697. So that was that, for now at least. As for the Habsburgs, their earlier dashing successes and relatively unhindered advances with their allies were now a decade old; too much blood was being spilt and too much of their treasury was being depleted for no discernible headway. Zenta had been a great victory for the Habsburgs, but it was on the back of three successive defeats in two years by the Ottomans. In the circumstances there was an appetite on both sides to finally agree peace, and it was Mustafa II who signed the peace treaty that ended the Great Turkish War, which his father had started more than fifteen years earlier.

The Treaty of Karlowitz is an important, if largely forgotten, peace agreement in European history. Signed in January 1699, it was the first-ever treaty the Ottomans agreed that conceded a significant loss of territory. After centuries of Ottoman rule, the Kingdom of Hungary was now an independent entity and, as Hungary is not a small country, this was a considerable loss to the empire. At the same time the Polish–Lithuanian Commonwealth gained lands in central Europe, and for the first time the Russians were part of a major European treaty against the Ottomans. Peter the Great lived up to his name by gaining the Azov region, which gave the Tsar access to the Black Sea from the River Don, a hugely significant development in the northern Black Sea. Venice won critical areas of the Dalmatian coast, so securing their diminished trade routes through the Aegean. All of these concessions were at the expense of the Ottoman Empire. It was a humiliation and a sign that the empire was well past its prime – and yet, the victory was not total. The treaty also recognised that Belgrade was still an Ottoman possession. Similarly, it acknowledged that Wallachia and Moldova, despite their yearning to be free of Ottoman hegemony, were still very much part of the empire, and there was nothing their Western allies could do about it.

Throughout this period the Ottomans were clearly reeling, and the Safavids, who had clashed with the empire so many times, could have easily attacked from the east and acted as a figurative knife in the back of the empire. The Safavid ruler, Suleiman I, was even approached by European powers to do just that. At the time the Safavids were not at war, and while they would soon face a revolt in the east of their own empire, that was still in the future, and there was then no rebellion on the home front to hamper any plans for war elsewhere. The Ottomans, as Sunni Muslims, were the ideological enemy of the Shi'ite Safavids. Had they gone to war at this time the Ottoman sultans would have faced war on three fronts: north, east and west. It's unlikely that any empire could survive such an onslaught. It therefore begs the question: why didn't the Safavids use this golden opportunity to attack and bring down the Ottoman Empire? The answer is a little underwhelming. Suleiman I of the Safavid Empire was, like some of the lesser Ottoman sultans, more interested in the pleasures of the harem than in running the empire. While he had capable ministers and generals, they wouldn't have dared go to war without the express permission of Suleiman – and he was too busy enjoying himself. Safavid Suleiman died in 1694, leaving it to the next generation to expand the empire's territory at the expense of its old foe.

The Safavid Succession

Before we leave the Safavids, there is a strange story from their court that bears re-telling. As Suleiman lay dying he asked his court eunuchs to choose the next ruler from his two surviving sons. Suleiman explained that if they wanted peace and quiet they should pick the older son, Sultan Husayn, to be the new *shahenshah*. However, if they wanted war and territorial gains, they should choose the younger son, Abbas. The eunuchs went for an easy life and chose Sultan Husayn, who earned the nickname of Yakhshidir (Persian for 'very well'), the response he gave when asked to decide on matters of state. The choice of Sultan Husayn was one of the single biggest strategic blunders in history, and the Safavids paid for it when he was ousted from power and the empire collapsed.

Meanwhile, back in Istanbul, there was a sting in the tail to Mustafa II's reign. From 1688 to 1699 the Venetians were, once more, fighting the Ottomans. They were drawn in initially by the Great Turkish War but continued fighting after everyone else had signed peace treaties. This was an obvious attempt to bolster their power with the forces of Western allies in order to finally claw back some of the holdings they had lost over the centuries, and the ploy worked. By the end of what was later called the Sixth Ottoman-Venetian War, the Venetians had reclaimed a Greek area of the Peloponnese (Morea) and expanded their territory in the region of the Dalmatian coast. It had been the Venetians' sixth war, but it was their first clear victory (a case of sixth time lucky). The interesting thing is that the Ottoman Empire is seen from this point onwards as falling behind its competitor empires. However, thanks to a few quirks of history, the sultans survived them all.

Early in his reign, Mustafa II declared, 'We have prohibited ourselves pleasure, delight and comfort.' It was a statement of intent to return to a more responsible, conscientious and diligent form of government. He was aware that the sultan had gradually become a figurehead rather than the focal point of power, and recognised that, if things were allowed to continue to slide, his bloodline could end up like that of Safavid Suleiman I. By the late 1600s, the grand vizier was the real power, usually backed by a dominant woman in the harem. Mustafa II wanted to bring things back under the sultan's control. To this end he moved his court to Edirne for a number of reasons, but principally because it took him away from the established court. The immediate effect was that he could avoid any sneers about the Treaty of Karlowitz. The treaty ensured that there was less bad news flowing into the capital on a regular basis, but it had been an expensive and unpopular war. Mustafa II tried to lower taxation, but it remained onerous and a useful rallying cry for opponents.

The move meant Mustafa II could surround himself with men who were loyal to him rather than sit in the nest of vipers, which is what the court in Istanbul had become. It also kept him separate from the Janissary high command, which, over recent decades, had become a source of political activism rather than the sultan's unquestioningly loyal vanguard of Ottoman military power. The move was not popular. It ruffled all the feathers that mattered. Edirne also gave him the chance to create his own power base. The Sipahis had always been a fundamental part of Ottoman society, right back to the time of Osman. They were an embodiment of Ottoman culture every bit as much as the Janissaries, but the Janissaries were now a byword for rebellion and insubordination. Mustafa II decided to make the position of the Sipahis hereditary. This meant that their lands and titles couldn't be handed out by the grand vizier, which instantly made a large part of the army loyal to him and him alone. This idea had merit – except for two problems. First of all, the Sipahi light cavalry was (like Osman's glory days) a thing of the past. It was an anachronism on the field of battle, so Mustafa II had chosen the wrong part of the army to back. Secondly, the Sipahis' lands were spread out across the empire. If there was trouble in Istanbul, it would take a long time before he could expect a response from the Sipahis near Basra or Cairo. There was a reason why the Janissaries had become involved in the politics of the court: their headquarters was in the capital, and they had been the backbone of the army for centuries. Mustafa II had picked the wrong horse.

To aggravate the situation, Mustafa II went back on his word and, in the early 1700s, began to spend more time hunting than he did on the affairs of the state. The palace had had enough. It was clear that if allowed to continue he might well come up with another, perhaps successful way to re-establish and concentrate power on the sultan, and, as such, Mustafa II was unceremoniously deposed in a coup in 1703. It was (as expected) the Janissaries who rose up, complaining of 'overdue pay, and of the sultan's absence'. While both of these things were true, they were a veneer of legitimacy on something far more cynical. The Janissaries were busy whipping the capital's populace into a revolt. After spending years trying to avoid such an outcome through various attempts to nullify the power of his own court, Mustafa II ended up suffering the very fate he had tried to avoid.

Exactly one hundred years rather neatly separate the start of the reign of Murad III and the reign of Mustafa II and provide the historian with easy demarcations to look at how things had evolved for the sultans and the empire over a century. Murad III was the twelfth sultan and Mustafa II was the twenty-second, showing the veritable procession of rulers in that time. The reality was that almost all of the problems faced by Mustafa II were the same ones that Murad III had faced – except that, after a century of mismanagement and vicious political plotting, the court (and therefore the empire) was in a far worse state to endure it. At the time of Murad III it would never have occurred to the court that they could either depose the sultan or pick a son or a brother (due in no small part to the fact that they were still murdering the sultan's male children during Murad III's rule). However, by the time we get to Mustafa II, it had become a regular occurrence to depose the sultan. It happened to him and it had happened again to his namesake, Mustafa the Mad, as well as a number of others.

What was really needed was an opportunity to wipe the slate clean and start again. The empire still had a lot going for it: robust trade, good and plentiful agricultural land, a large navy and control of some of the most populous and politically important cities in the world. In Western Europe, when a dynasty failed to live up to expectations, or a new and popular concept of government came about, there was a full-blown dynastic change. It had happened in France, Spain and Germany; even England had had a civil war during which republicans had publicly executed the monarch. As an empire, the Ottomans can be legitimately compared to the Roman Empire, another example of a civilisation that replaced dynasties of rulers when they weren't effective. With the Ottomans, however, although there was the same level of scheming, none of the conspiracies ever took that final step of overthrowing Osman's family, the Ottoman family itself.

Mustafa II would never have wanted power to go to another family, so when everyone recognised that the system was no longer working he tried to restructure government. What is interesting is that, despite all the rebellions, palace coups, deposed sultans and murders in the harem, it never seemed to occur to anyone to take the role of sultan from the family of Osman. No matter the cost, another member of the family was always installed – and so it went on for more than six centuries. This is why it is always remembered and accurately described as the 'Ottoman Empire'.

11

The Tulip Era

After so many sultans in the preceding century, the good news for stability in the empire was that the next sultan, Ahmed III, was to rule for twenty-seven years. He was the son of Mehmed IV and was just what the empire needed after so many cruel, absent or insane rulers of the recent past. The story of Ahmed III's reign starts with an alliance that looks almost comical, between the Ottoman Empire and Sweden. The Swedish Empire is a truly forgotten empire (except in Sweden). At its peak it covered about half of Norway, a few areas of Finland, most of the eastern Baltic States and areas of what is now northern Germany – as well as having virtual dominion over all of the Baltic Sea.

The reign of Peter the Great, Tsar of Russia, can be defined in two words: modernisation and expansion. His army and the Russian aristocracy were forced to shake off the old ways and become more 'European', both in outlook and in military tactics. Once Sweden's technological and strategic advantages were neutralised, Russia, in the long term, was always going to defeat Sweden as it had far more men and resources. Even so it took the best part of a century and Peter's steely determination to defeat the Swedes. Peter was not only eyeing the Baltic States, he was also looking for a way to break into the Black Sea, tantalisingly close now that he had been able to secure the port of Azov with the Treaty of Karlowitz. So both Sweden and the Ottomans now had to deal with the rising power of Russia, but as Swedish and Ottoman territories were so far removed from each other, the two empires could work together without threatening each other's interests.

In 1700, Charles XII of Sweden managed to beat an allied force of the Polish–Lithuanian Commonwealth, Norway and Russia, which showed the effectiveness of the small Swedish fighting force. For Sweden and Russia, however, the critical clash came in the summer of 1709, at the Battle of Poltava (in modern-day Ukraine). Charles XII of Sweden had decided to invade Russia and capture Moscow, a move that would neutralise the threat on his borders, but, due to an unusually severe Russian winter and the scorched-earth policy conducted by the Russians, Charles XII was forced to turn south (if this sounds familiar, it's because both Napoleon and Hitler tried their own variations on this, which proved, over and over again, that the Russian 'General Winter' was an unbeatable foe). The Battle of Poltava was a devastating defeat for the Swedes and justified all of the changes Peter had introduced in his army. Charles XII was seriously wounded in the battle, and, even worse, lost more than 90 per cent of his troops, killed, wounded or captured. Add to all of this the fact that he was more than 500 miles from friendly territory, and things looked decidedly grim for the Swedish king. But Charles was close to Ottoman territory, and, using the logic of 'my enemy's enemy is my friend', fled to Bender in Moldova, close to the Black Sea coast. The King of Sweden was now an unexpected guest of the Ottoman Empire.

Peter the Great, having annihilated his Swedish foe, now wanted to finish the job. Forceful demands were sent to the court of Ahmed III demanding Charles XII be released to Peter. There was nothing in it for Ahmed III. If he carried out the Russian's wishes, he would have betrayed an ally and increased the status of his enemy. Exasperated and frustrated, Peter attacked Moldova. This was a chance to capture yet more Ottoman territory and get the Swedish king as a bonus. At this point it would be fair to assume that there would be a Russian victory, with yet more Ottoman territory being lost to a rising European power. But that's not what happened, showing yet again that there is rarely a straightforward narrative when it comes to history.

Led by Peter the Great, the Russians, along with Moldovan rebels, captured the Ottoman fortress of Brăila after two days of fighting. However, the Russian/Moldovan army met a large Ottoman force, led by Grand Vizier Baltacı Mehmet Pasha (unusually, a grand vizier of a Turkic rather than Christian heritage), in the Battle of Stănileşti, which is not well recorded. Its obscurity is strange because the battle lasted for four days (which is already unusual) and saw the legendary Peter the Great surrounded and forced to surrender. Numbers of forces are unknown; casualties were likely high but, again, the numbers are unknown. What we can say is that pretty much everything that had happened to Charles XII in 1709 happened to Peter the Great (except being wounded) in 1711. The so-called Pruth River Campaign (also known as the Russo-Ottoman War of 1710–11, of which the above battle was a part) was an unmitigated disaster for the Russians and reminded all of Europe that the Ottoman army was far from finished. The result was the humiliating Treaty of Pruth. Critically for the Russians, Azov, the hard-won port so close to the Black Sea, was returned to Ottoman suzerainty after less than twenty years of Russian ownership. The treaty also formally curtailed any Russian interference in the affairs of the Polish–Lithuanian Commonwealth.

Ottoman power again echoed through Europe, and in 1714 Charles XII returned to his homeland. The stay of the Swedish king in Moldovia was a complicated affair. In one sense he was entertained as an honoured guest, but he was nevertheless kept under a kind of house arrest. He knew he was vulnerable so far away from his power base, but, despite the Janissaries' wish to shoot him and despite a myriad of plots around him, the monarch was well treated and received a hero's welcome on his return to Sweden. Ahmed III had managed to accrue enough authority to ensure the safety of a fellow monarch and ally, and had seen off a genuine Russian threat. Charles XII got home just in time for yet another round of fighting in what became known as the Great Northern War. This conflict ran concurrently with another clash of European interests, the so-called War of the Spanish Succession. Virtually the whole of Europe was involved in fighting one of these two wars, which took the pressure off Ahmed III's western and northern borders and allowed him to settle an old score.

In their sixth war with the Ottomans, the Venetians had finally got their way and had recaptured Morea in Greece. Correctly assessing that no European powers would come to their aid, Ahmed III's court came up with a provocation for war (hiding a rebellious archbishop and illegally confiscating an Ottoman vessel) and invaded Morea. The Venetians had had more than twenty years to build up Morea's defences, and the territory was scattered with forts. The port was an obvious target for Ottoman attack, but, as Candia had shown, the Venetians could be tenacious defenders when they put their minds to it. Surprisingly, the area's forts and walled towns had not been upgraded. Many were still medieval in design and vulnerable to cannon fire. The defences of the region were also lightly garrisoned, with Venetian troops bolstered by mercenaries. It was almost as if Venice had given up on Morea as soon as they had won it. The truth was that, compared to what it had been a century earlier, Venice was now a shadow of its former self. It simply didn't have the resources to invest in its newly won prize. Putting it simply, the Venetians had won Morea with the aid of other Western powers, and without them it was only a matter of time before they lost it.

Up against the motley crew of Venetian defenders was an army of about 70,000, supported by eighty warships. Only a miracle could save Morea. The Upper Corinth fort, which was meant to be avoided, was attacked by the Janissaries, who killed or enslaved virtually everyone in it. This action illustrates two hard truths about the state of the Ottoman army. Firstly, the Janissaries traditionally had been brave fighters as well as loyal and unquestioning members of the army, but by now they had overthrown multiple sultans. They fought only when they wanted to, usually when they saw profit in the situation. That was not the kind of army anyone needed. But there was a second, more practical reason for their actions, which gives us the second hard truth: the Janissaries' pay was woeful. Janissaries needed to bolster their salaries with booty, so if there was an easy target, suitable for plunder, that's where they went in order to make the expense of the campaign worthwhile.

The attack on the fort was a cruel and bloody start to a campaign that was seen by many locals as liberation. It turned out that not only had the Venetians done little with the defences, they had also done nothing to endear themselves to the Morean population. As such, many yearned to return to a time of Ottoman rule (a concept that might sound strange to some, but which reminds us that this was still an age before nationalism, when local communities would naturally prefer whatever system worked best for them). Effective resistance crumbled as the Ottomans marched south, and in less than a hundred days the entire southern Peloponnese had been re-taken by the Ottomans. But the Ottoman sweep of Venetian possessions didn't stop there. Other small Venetian outposts on various islands were captured. Corfu was also besieged, but when the Venetians resolutely defended its walls the Ottomans went no further.

By now the Habsburgs were on the warpath again, and Ahmed III turned his attention to this more dangerous opponent. As for Venice, it was soundly thrashed in the seventh and last war with the Ottomans, so, in the space of about 300 years, Venice had only once (in the sixth war) come off better than the sultans. It is safe to say that the Ottoman Empire was the definitive nemesis of the Venetian Republic.

The world was changing – or, rather, Europe was changing. We are now in the realm of John Churchill's revolution of military logistics. This was the time of the political philosophies of Hobbes and Bossuet – and then there were the mathematics and science of Leibniz and Newton. The Ottoman Empire had no such equivalents. Ottoman armies were still large, still brave and still winning (sometimes), but they also had one foot in the past. A Janissary in 1700 would have been fighting a very different Habsburg soldier from his predecessor of 1600, but in the meantime the Janissary had barely changed.

Across the empire, however, things were changing in a different way. The core of the empire around northern Greece, southern Bulgaria, the capital, Anatolia, Syria and Palestine had been Ottoman for centuries, and by the 1700s it is estimated that a third of the Ottoman ministers in Istanbul were of Greek Orthodox Christian birth. The core of the empire (as mentioned at the time of the Venetian capture of Morea) was quite happy to be Ottoman, but as central power waned there were moves by the far-flung territories, the ones that were difficult and expensive to defend, to have their own border rivalries with neighbouring states. This low-level warfare can be seen in the pillaging by the pirates from North Africa and the regular skirmishes in the Balkans (which have led to an apparent everlasting enmity) between different ethnic groups.

It wasn't just the sultans who played political games. The Russians were Orthodox Christians because of Byzantine influence. This meant there was always a spiritual connection with the Greek Orthodox Church in Ottoman lands and, specifically, with Hagia Sophia in Istanbul. The tsars pretended that they had a moral obligation to protect all Orthodox Christians, which made them not only imperial enemies, but also ideological enemies of the Ottomans. It was in the early 1700s that the vanguard of nationalism first appeared. This was an evolving idea that wasn't much of an issue at the time but one which only grew in intensity over the decades, culminating in some highly convoluted reasons for war in both the nineteenth and twentieth centuries. The concept of nationalism would, ultimately, undermine the basis of any empire. Once people started to see a unity in ethnicity, rather than in the artificial construct of empire, the empire was bound to fracture. An example of this evolution of ideas can be seen in the American Revolutionary War, which was about the legitimacy of rule and the right to raise taxes rather than about creating a separate nation; a few generations later, almost all revolutions were about national identity, whether in Greece or Bolivia.

Sultan Ahmed III was aware of these ideological changes and understood the difficulties they presented, but there were limits to what he could do. When Suleiman the Magnificent had failed to capture Vienna, it hadn't occurred to anyone to plot a palace coup. However, in the decades between Suleiman's rule and Ahmed III's reign, too much central power had eroded. The sultans now had to be aware of the moves by the women in the harem (although that influence had faded with the demise of Kösem), the ministers of the court and the eternally unruly Janissary corps. The loss of Morea was just what the Habsburgs needed to use their alliance with Venice as an excuse to go to war with Ahmed III, and the incredibly effective Holy Roman general, Prince Eugene of Savoy, led an army into Ottoman territory. In 1716 the two sides met at Petrovaradin, where there was a titanic clash of arms. The Ottomans had gathered an army of over 100,000 versus a Habsburg army of about 80,000.

Petrovaradin was already a fortress town, but Prince Eugene added further defences to protect his army. Grand Vizier Silahdar Damat Ali Pasha was leading the Ottoman force, bolstered with Crimean Tatars. He recognised all too well the formidable obstacles Prince Eugene had created for anyone trying to capture the town, so he held his army back. When Prince Eugene ordered his forces, including those in the town itself, to attack, it took them a long time to get past the gates of the defensive curtain wall. The wings of the attack ferociously drove past the Ottoman flanks, but the central attack was too slow in coming and an effective frontal assault by the Janissaries pushed the Habsburg troops back into the town. However, they were now at risk of being surrounded in a pincer move. This was the perfect time for the fast cavalry of the Tatars to attack and pin back the Habsburg flanks, but they did nothing and later slunk away from the field of battle, leaving their erstwhile allies in a critical situation. The Janissaries were engulfed by enemy troops, and the Habsburg army pushed on towards Ali Pasha's encampment, where the rear guard fought fiercely but was hopelessly outnumbered. Ali Pasha was one of the estimated 30,000 Ottoman dead, with tens of thousands wounded. The Ottoman casualties in that one day were similar to the British casualties on the first day of the Somme offensive – but this was in the era of the musket and cannon.

Prince Eugene pushed on and, despite fierce resistance, captured the major Romanian town of Timișoara. However, by then he had lost his momentum and his own casualty list was mounting. The result of this brief war with the Habsburgs was the Treaty of Passarowitz, which was another humiliation for the Ottomans in all but one respect. The Habsburgs had, once again, pushed back Ottoman holdings in the Balkans, and most (but not all) of Serbia was now independent. A few other areas were also ceded by the Ottomans, but all of the territory that Venice had lost was now formally recognised as Ottoman. Even the Holy Roman Empire couldn't support Venice's case for its lost territories. It was after this war that Ahmed III began to urge westernisation on his court. Alliances with Sweden had been forged, and it was time to look to other Western powers to create a counter-balance to the ascendant Habsburgs.

Puckle

The Puckle gun was one of the strangest inventions of the era and reflected what the West thought of the Ottoman Turks. The first prototype was built in 1718, and this British invention was one of the most innovative and bizarre guns ever created. It was a single-barrelled flintlock weapon, with a manually operated revolving cylinder of seventeen gunpowder charges and musket balls. It was revolutionary in design (an example of a very early Gatling gun) and was intended as an 'anti-boarding' weapon for ships. However, it's the different ammunition depending on the *religion* of the enemy that makes it really weird. The design of normal musket balls was created for use against Christian enemies. The second design was for square bullets to be used against the Muslim Ottomans. Square bullets were considered to be more damaging and painful, and they would, according to the patent, 'convince the Turks of the benefits of Christian civilization'. Quite how being maimed by square bullets would convince you to convert was never satisfactorily explained and, as a tool of conversion, it completely failed to work.

The Puckle gun attracted few investors and never achieved mass production or sales to the British armed forces. As with other designs of the time it was hampered by 'clumsy and undependable flintlock ignition' as well as other mechanical problems. Putting aside the two types of ammunition, the revolving mechanism was just slightly beyond the technology of the day and proved unreliable. A leaflet from the period sarcastically observed of the venture that 'they're only wounded who hold shares therein'. Production may have been as few as just two guns. It was, however, a physical manifestation of the fear of Islam 'infecting' the Christian West that was still prevalent in the eighteenth century.

Meanwhile, back in Istanbul, Ahmed III and his court entered what became known as the Tulip Era (1718–30), a period of relative peace, when the sultan encouraged the empire to look to the West, when Ottoman scholars took inspiration from their Western counterparts, when the arts flourished and when the empire's aristocratic society developed a craze for growing tulips. It was in this period that the subjects of the empire were encouraged to cultivate their own tulip gardens as a sign of symbiosis with the West. Printing presses had existed before but now there was mass production of books in Turkish (rather than Greek or Hebrew), although disgruntled scribes managed to get the presses shut down for a time. The sultan himself built a summer palace that looked west, rather than east, in its architectural style, and there are places (today) in Topkapı Palace where Western-style wallpaper is framed by Islamic Iznik tiles. Western-style carriage clocks, with Arabic rather than European numbers, sit on marble tables and strike an incongruous note. Most of the extant décor comes from a slightly later period, but the overall effect is almost the same as it would have been during the time of Ahmed III.

Tulips
The fashion for tulips in Europe occurred almost a hundred years before the Ottoman Tulip Era, when flowers that are indigenous to some areas of the eastern Mediterranean arrived in Europe, where they proved to be very popular (there was even a phenomenon known as 'tulip mania' in the Netherlands, when tulip bulbs fetched extremely high prices). Although tulips represented something 'good' from the Ottoman Empire, not everyone realised that's where they originated.

Meanwhile, the irony was that as the Ottomans looked to the West, Ahmed III's greatest successes came in the East. The Safavid Empire was crumbling, and the collapse of the dynasty was messy and violent. When attempts were made to forcefully convert everyone to Shi'ite Islam, the Sunni and Kurdish communities turned to the Ottomans for protection. While all of this was going on, Afghanistan threw off Safavid rule and invaded Persia from the east, and while all of this was going on, Peter the Great spied an opportunity to push Russian influence eastwards and started what became known as the Persian Campaign of Peter the Great.

Cutting a long and complex story to its bare bones, there were massacres split on sectarian lines, sieges and rampaging armies and Safavid Sultan Husayn, who was a hopeless ruler in a hopeless situation. He was captured by the Afghans and the new ruler, Shah Ashraf Hotak (an Afghan, not a Safavid) executed him when he heard that an Ottoman army, led by Ahmed Pasha, the governor of Baghdad, was invading to put him back on the throne. Ashraf sent Sultan Husayn's head to the governor with a letter that said that he 'expected to give Ahmed Pasha a fuller reply with the points of his sword and his lance'. Ahmed Pasha was unable to reinstate what would have been an Ottoman puppet, but this did end the Safavid threat. It would take a decade for Persia to settle into normality again, and in the meantime the border between Persia and the Ottoman lands all but solidified along the present Iran/Iraq border.

Households
By now you've heard the word 'Ottoman' a lot, but there is another meaning to the word: a chair or sofa with no back. The

name is accurate in terms of its origins, as this was the common means of seating in Ottoman homes. Wealthy Ottomans could afford to have a kind of mini-palace arrangement, where there was a *haremlik*, the private quarters, reserved for the women and immediate male members of the family, as opposed to the *selamlik*, the reception rooms for the public or male visitors. In the average household there was one room for receiving guests (women would stay or withdraw, depending on who the visitors were), and this was the heart of the home, the place where people socialised. However, unlike their Western European counterparts, rather than gather around a table or sit in chairs, the Ottomans sat around the edges of the room, along the walls, on low seats or floor cushions, a seating arrangement that was popular throughout the empire and a sign that some elements of Ottoman culture cut across class and ethnicity. This particular Ottoman arrived in Europe as a piece of furniture towards the end of the eighteenth century and is still in use today. If you see one that is not positioned against a wall, it's in the wrong place.

If you're wondering what was on the floors of Ottoman homes (and I'm sure you are), you might well have guessed that it would be 'Turkish' carpets. Again, the word 'Turkish', in reality, means 'Ottoman' because these knotted rugs (and the woven version called a *kilim*) were made throughout the empire (and beyond – in Persia, for example) and reflected the various cultural and tribal traditions dating back centuries. The Ottomans wore slippers in the home, so the beautiful and intricate designs were not damaged by outdoor shoes.

Sultan Ahmed III worked hard at keeping a good supply of heirs and spares in the harem. It is estimated that he had seventy children, about thirty of them boys, and while many never made it to adulthood, two would later become sultans. Ahmed III had tried to change the court and had been in contact with foreign powers (including France and Britain as well as Sweden), but he overreached himself when he tried to westernise and modernise every sultan's perennial headache, the Janissary corps. This was a miscalculation that was to have grave consequences. Unusually, the Janissaries were not the cause of a revolt that sprung up against Ahmed III; that was a Turkish bath worker named Patrona Khalil. In 1730, there was news that Afghan-controlled Persia had thrown off its Russian/Turkish overlordship – the old enemy that Ahmed III had told everyone was vanquished. It wasn't. The people of the empire were furious, and Patrona Khalil whipped a protesting mob into a frenzy, while the Janissaries, fearing that they might be restructured to the point of irrelevance, stood aside and merely watched as the potential revolution unfolded. When the mob stormed Topkapı Palace, demanding that the sultan abdicate and that his grand vizier, Nevşehirli Damat Ibrahim Pasha, be executed, Ahmed III faced them alone. With no support or protection, the most effective and innovative sultan for generations agreed to the demands. The grand vizier was strangled in the palace grounds, and Ahmed III chose his nephew Mahmud to become the new sultan.

Mahmud came to the throne in dangerous circumstances. Patrona Khalil was ruling the capital through mob violence, a grand vizier had been murdered on his command and now, as Mahmud was girded with the sword of Osman, Khalil, a lowly commoner, took charge. Almost immediately Khalil demanded various positions for relatives and allies. Mahmud acquiesced and bided his time. Events in the first few months of his reign were beyond his control, but once he was ensconced and once deals had been brokered Mahmud turned to the one group that was far enough from the centre of power to be trusted (if they could be bothered to act): the Crimean Tatars. They obliged and moved on Khalil and his rebels in 1736, when thousands of Tatar cavalry descended on the capital. Patrona Khalil was strangled and thousands of his supporters were executed. It had taken a few months, and the situation had come close to total disaster, but Mahmud had emerged as the secure sultan of the Ottoman Empire – well, as secure as any sultan could be.

For the first six years of Mahmud's reign, his uncle Ahmed III lived quietly in the palace studying the Qur'an and working on his calligraphy until he died in 1736. He never once challenged Mahmud, even though he had been forced to abdicate in his favour. Mahmud, however, was not particularly interested in the affairs of state and withdrew to the harem to spend much of his time writing flowery poetry in Arabic.

> ## Windows
>
> There was an interesting architectural feature in play that made it hard for ministers to know whether the sultan was present and listening to their discussions. The ministerial meeting room of Topkapı Palace has a window-like opening high up on one wall, but it is ornately decorated, making it impossible to see if anyone is on the other side. This opening leads directly into the harem so that the sultan, and sometimes his mother, could monitor proceedings unobserved. When the ministers and viziers met to discuss the topics of the day, the sultan might – or might not – be observing. It was always best to assume that he was there, rather than say something that might displease him. This feature also enabled the *valide* sultan to wield power by keeping abreast of events in the empire.

Meanwhile, over in Persia, there was a new ruling family known as the Afsharid dynasty, which threw off Russian-Ottoman control and then attacked the Ottoman eastern lands. They even threatened Baghdad, but were pushed back and took a different tack. With Russia's assistance (yes, they'd just been enemies, but political alliances in the eighteenth century were changeable, complex and, most of all, confusing), they were able to capture Armenia and Georgia from the Ottomans – for a time. The war changed so that, just as things were wrapping up between the Ottomans and the Afsharids, the Russians and Habsburgs decided to declare war against Mahmud. It was a reminder of the problems facing an empire with three fronts, and by now the empire was well and truly boxed in. The best it could hope for was a strong defence of its borders rather than the capture of any new territory.

For the Russians, the target was the Crimean Tatars, the allies and affiliates of the Ottomans. As Mahmud owed his reign to their support, there was no question that he would go to their assistance even though they had proven less than reliable allies on the battlefield in recent years. The campaign in the Crimea showed the limitations of both sides. When the Russian army besieged a Crimean fort, they would invariably win. The improvements to equipment and tactics that Peter the Great had introduced were paying dividends (although by now the Tsar was Anna I). However, the Crimea was a long way from the centralised power of the Tsars, and poor logistics, corrupt administration and a general assumption that the army could surely live off the land led to starvation, desertion and a rapid deterioration of fighting potency. By the end of the campaigning season the Russian army retreated, having lost 30,000 men, but only some 2,000 of those had actually been casualties in battle. This would not be the only time the Ottomans would repel a Russian army by virtue of its own disintegration, but for now the Russian Tatars could breathe easy.

On the Habsburg front, meanwhile, morale among the Christian troops was high. The Ottomans had lurched from one defeat to another at Habsburg hands for fifty years. In the interim the Habsburgs had grown complacent about Ottoman military power, and, while there had been no revolution in Ottoman strategy, many of the earlier battles had been close-run affairs. If everything remained the same, it was only a matter of time before the Ottomans won.

In 1737, at the Battle of Banja Luka (in modern-day Bosnia), there was the rare sight of an Ottoman army outnumbered 2:1 (22,000 versus 10,000) by the Habsburgs. Despite the odds against them, it was an emphatic Ottoman victory. Two years later, two much larger armies met at the Battle of Grocka. Here about 100,000 Ottoman troops, with more than a hundred artillery pieces had the high ground. The Habsburg forces numbered around 40,000, and it was decided to attack the Ottomans, otherwise they would be under constant artillery fire. The result was little short of a massacre and a serious defeat for the Habsburgs, who now had no standing army left in the Balkans. As a result, the Ottomans recaptured the strategically vital city of Belgrade, and the conquest was recognised in the aptly named Treaty of Belgrade. The Ottoman Empire was clearly not to be underestimated, and Europe was forced to take note of the Sublime Porte once more.

In addition to writing Arabic poetry, Sultan Mahmud involved himself in trying to modernise the army. It was a case of baby steps, and some progress was made, but a much-needed complete overhaul did not happen. Mahmud's improvements were overseen by a French aristocrat by the name of Comte de Bonneval, but he converted to Islam and changed his name to Humbaraci Ahmed Pasha. The French military in the early eighteenth century was one of the best fighting forces in the world, and such an advisor would have been a great asset to the Ottomans, but, unsurprisingly, the Janissaries resisted any change. Seeking foreign advice on military and administrative matters became increasingly common on the part of the Ottomans in the eighteenth and nineteenth centuries – and even into the twentieth. The advisors' nationalities varied, but the idea of seeking outside help became the norm, a tacit admission that, in terms of knowledge and power, the Ottoman court was no longer leading the world as it had done two centuries earlier.

In the 1740s, there was yet another war between the Ottomans and Persia. This time the fighting was inconclusive. There were no decisive victories for either side, and, after three years of bloodshed, the peace terms showed no changes to the spheres of either empire's influence. This did mean, however, that in every decade in the eighteenth century so far the Ottomans had been forced to fight expensive wars. They had lost Armenia and Georgia and gained Belgrade, but this was scant reward for endless war. After this stalemate the Persians turned towards the Mughal lands to the east. The Mughals and the Ottomans had had good relations for centuries, and while the relationship rarely went beyond trade, the occasional exchange of learned men in their courts and some very cordial letters, it was a sign of the times that the Ottomans didn't even consider sending troops to aid their ally against their old enemy.

> *Museums*
>
> It was in this era that one of the great artefacts of the Ottoman treasury was created, an object which further connected the court to contemporary events in Persia. The Topkapı dagger is just one of the many treasures in the Topkapı Museum. The former home of the sultan and his court now displays everything from a jewel-encrusted cradle to an emerald as large as a fist. Every item of household use and décor is here, covered in gold and smothered with fabulous jewels. They may look gaudy, but these were the objects meant for the sultan of an enormous empire, and they were intended to impress everyone who visited the palace. In a section set aside for ceramics there are examples from as far afield as China as well as, closer to home, porcelain from Europe, but there are also world-famous Iznik tiles that

decorated most of the empire's finest buildings. If some of the simple designs were not thought impressive enough, they might be gilded in 22-carat gold and sprinkled with rubies and pearls, the way we would add toppings to ice cream. The famous dagger is sheathed in gold, with a row of emeralds the size of whole walnuts on the hilt; a tiny clock is hidden under another, hinged emerald. The irony is that the Topkapı dagger was never meant to reside in the palace. It seems that the weaker the Ottoman Empire became, the more lavish the gifts presented by its diplomats.

After the war, in 1747, the dagger was sent to Persia, which was in turn sending its own gift in a diplomatic exchange. As the gifts were en route, the *shahenshah* died and there was an unseemly rush for power. Despite the internal chaos, the Persian ambassadors got as far as Baghdad and handed over his gifts (a great way to stay out of the way of trouble in the process). But the Ottoman gifts to the Persians never got as far as Baghdad and were absorbed back into the sultan's personal possessions. The Persians had sent the famed Mughal Peacock Throne, a sign of their conquest of Indian lands, which explains why a Mughal throne is now in Istanbul. But the museum holds relics far more precious to the faithful than any jewels. One room is full of Islamic religious artefacts, a reminder that the sultan was the governor of the most holy places on earth for the three main monotheistic faiths. There are coverings and parts of the wooden frame (which needed renovation) from the Kaaba in Mecca. There is a suspiciously short staff said to have belonged to Moses, a hair from the Prophet Mohammed's beard (along with some of his possessions), the turban of Joseph (but not his coat of many colours) and – the author's favourite – the cooking pot of Abraham.

The provenance of many of these items is questionable, but their power is immeasurable for those who believe. The author was in this room when a small group of Muslims began praying in front of some of the holy relics, an act that is considered to be idolatrous in Islam and inappropriate in a museum. The guards became agitated and made it clear that the group must stop praying or risk being thrown out, but the excitement and fervour of people in the presence of such objects was palpable.

Meanwhile, the empire enjoyed a decade of relative peace. There were no major wars; trade continued throughout the empire, and there were no rebellions or attempted coups. Mahmud died in Topkapı Palace of natural causes, still sultan in 1754. It had been a long time since a sultan could boast of such an achievement. The next sultan was Osman III, brother of Mahmud I and another son of Mustafa II. He had spent all of his life in the palace and was now in his fifties. He was completely ill equipped to become the ruler of an empire, and it showed.

One of the unique areas of revenue for the empire was pilgrimages. Thousands of Muslims from outside the empire would travel on the haj pilgrimage to Mecca, and thousands of Christians and Jews wanted to visit Jerusalem. Since the high point of Suleiman the Magnificent's renovations of Jerusalem, religious tourism in Jerusalem had done brisk business. Jerusalem was never a major city compared to Cairo, Baghdad, Damascus and Istanbul, and, as such, it rarely got a governor of anything other than ordinary ability. Running Jerusalem was simply not a good job in the empire. Consequently the governor, who was usually based in Damascus, would make an annual appearance to extort revenues from the locals in what was essentially payment of their annual tax. With so little regular attention paid to the city's affairs, the local garrison became a byword for corruption and incompetence, while the aristocratic Muslim families all vied for power and generally pushed everyone else in the population (Christians, Jews and poor Muslims) to the bottom of the pile.

Osman III wasn't a lot of fun, and this situation was exacerbated when he introduced unusually draconian laws against Christians and Jews. He wasn't quite as mad as Ibrahim, but he clearly wasn't normal either. He hated music, so much so that he banned any form of it in the harem – giving the women even less to do. He didn't want to come across female servants, so he wore steel-capped boots which made a distinctive noise so the female servants would run away at the sound of his approach. He also decreed specific attire for Jews and Christians to make them instantly recognisable, a practice that had been colourful but innocuous earlier in the empire but which now caused further tensions in Jerusalem. None of this could be described as normal behaviour, and his measures ensured that the situation in Jerusalem became even more tense, particularly among Christian sects. The Church of the Holy Sepulchre was so fought over by the different Christian groups that the only thing everyone agreed was that a Muslim family should hold the keys to ensure no favouritism. In the meantime, to make certain no one sect could impinge on another's 'territory', around 300 Christian clerics were locked inside every night. The latrines were not up to the task of dealing with such numbers, and many contemporary accounts talk of the stench. But that was just for the lucky ones. By decree of the Roman Catholics and the Armenians, the Greek Orthodox Christians weren't allowed to use the latrines at all. Food had to be fed through a hole in the main door, but the Ethiopian Christian priests were so poor they could only afford food given to them by the Greek Orthodox priests in return for emptying their buckets of human waste.

Interestingly, no one pointed the finger at the Ottomans; instead, responsibility for this disastrous situation was heaped on competing Christian groups. Unbelievably, the state of the Church of the Holy Sepulchre, the site where Jesus was believed to have been resurrected, the single most holy Christian shrine in the world, was full of squabbling priests. Things really boiled over on Palm Sunday in 1757, when Greek Orthodox priests attacked the Franciscans as they processed through the church. This wasn't an unarmed punch-up; eyewitnesses say the Greeks had clubs, maces and even swords. Nobody appears to have died in the clash, but that's mainly because the Franciscans fled and barricaded themselves in the nearby Church of St Saviours. So much for 'love thy neighbour'. Jerusalem was teetering on the edge of anarchy, and across the empire there was a general loosening of central control. It hadn't begun in Osman III's reign, but he certainly did nothing to help it. Ottoman policy seemed to consist of playing off one interest against another. This worked for a time, but people were beginning to feel more loyalty to their group than to the empire. This was fertile ground in which to sow the seeds of nationalism in the nineteenth century. And what was Osman III's solution to all these woes (apart from banning music)? He fired his grand vizier – and did it again and again. He had seven in his three-year reign. The effect of this parade of constantly changing prime ministers meant that not only was there little leadership, but also the day-to-day administration of the empire lacked consistency.

12

A Barrel of Schnapps

Fortunately for everyone except Osman III, he died in 1757, lamented by almost no one. The next sultan was the first son of Ahmed III to come to power. This was Mustafa III, the exact opposite of Osman III. This sultan was energetic in his actions as ruler and one who chose to embrace the West, while attempting to modernise the army and the administration, both of which were badly needed but enormous tasks. Once again experts from the West were brought to the Ottoman court.

It will not have escaped the reader's notice that there have now been several times when a new sultan has attempted to implement much-needed changes. For those that were implemented, the question is: why did none of them last? The reasons are threefold. Firstly, there is always a resistance to change. 'If it ain't broke don't fix it' is a well-known saying, and it makes sense. Nothing in the Ottoman system was fundamentally broken. Trade still flourished, crops still grew, armies still marched. Many of the territorial losses had stabilised and the borders were relatively quiet. Certainly there was no threat of collapse or imminent danger from an enemy empire in the mid-eighteenth century. But to start restructuring the fundamentals meant confronting a lot of natural inertia, and that would take an enormous amount of energy and initiative, which brings us to the two other reasons for the lack of change.

The bureaucratic system of the empire was largely self-sustaining. Christian children were still recruited under the *devşirme* system, still in existence more than 400 years after it was first introduced. Virtually all of the decision makers in court had been through a system that had given them wealth and power, a system that had benefits for the communities of the empire. To change it would have meant undermining the very structure of the court, the government and the empire itself. Therefore any proposals for change from a new sultan would be agreed, then delayed or watered down and, finally, abandoned or introduced in name only. An example of a tradition that had lost its original purpose could be seen when a new sultan came to power and showered the Janissaries with gifts to ensure their loyalty. This gesture of goodwill over the centuries had become little more than extortion. It had made sense when someone like Bayezid II had to fight a civil war, or when a brother came to power after a palace coup, but by the 1700s the question had to be, what did the sultans get out of the deal? The Janissaries were not as effective as they had once been on the battlefield; their reliability and loyalty were often in doubt. The sultans were not without justification in thinking that they were more trouble than they were worth – but what could be done about them under the present system?

Finally there was the issue of the sultan himself. In the heyday of Ottoman power, when a sultan gave an order, it was obeyed and obeyed without question. On the face of things he was still as powerful as his predecessors had been in earlier times, but the courtly intrigues, the dynastic infighting and the number of genuinely insane sultans could not disguise the fact that the sultan, while always respected, did not have the power, let alone the drive and ambition, to see these changes through. Too often they were distracted by genuine concerns such as war with the Habsburgs or an outbreak of plague, to the extent that all other considerations were put on hold; or they didn't last long enough to oversee long-term change; or they lacked sufficient interest, preferring instead to write poetry and spend time in the harem. All of these factors combined explain why the Ottoman Empire, once at the cutting edge of power in Europe, had by now become of secondary importance. The reality was in contrast to the explanations offered by European contemporaries, who arrogantly ascribed the empire's decline either to the 'backward' nature of Islam or to the sultans who indulged themselves in the pleasures of the harem.

> *Delight*
>
> In the 1770s, a man called Bekir Efendi was returning to
> Istanbul from the haj pilgrimage when he had an idea for a
> new kind of confection. His creation was so popular he set up
> a shop selling *lokum*, known in the West as 'Turkish delight'.
> The traditional recipe produces a gel from starch and sugar,
> but after this, the variations are endless. Chopped pistachios or
> walnuts are often added and rosewater is a favourite flavour.
> The finished product is commonly dusted either with icing
> sugar (the author approves) or coconut (the author thinks
> this should be forbidden). The irony is that in Turkey these
> are sweets with no particular historic associations. In the rest
> of Europe, however, they are very much associated with the
> Ottoman past (except for 'Cyprus delight' and 'Greek delight'
> which, let's be honest, are just former areas of the empire
> jumping on the bandwagon). For generations Turkish delight
> has been seen in the West as a taste of the exotic. In the famous
> children's book *The Lion the Witch and the Wardrobe*, the
> ice queen offers up some Turkish delight to lure one of the
> children. I guess C. S. Lewis thought that beans on toast didn't
> have quite the same appeal.
>
> The shop that Bekir Efendi founded in 1777 is still in
> operation in Istanbul, and many other *lokum* producers have
> subsequently opened shops almost everywhere in Turkey, echoes
> of the Ottoman Empire in a new republic. There is speculation
> which says that something as popular as Turkish delight cannot
> be traced back to one named individual (for example, we do
> not know who invented ice cream or spaghetti), but certainly
> there's no evidence of this confection existing any time before
> Bekir Efendi. The gifts the Ottomans gave to the West are
> either beautiful or delicious (sometimes both): the tulip, Turkish
> carpets, baklava, coffee, Turkish delight – and virtually the
> only word in the English language that comes from Turkish –
> 'yoghurt' (pronounced yo'urt in the original).

Back in the Ottoman court, the foreign advisers who were called
in (on many occasions) to help the ailing empire had every reason
to enjoy their postings. Not only were their reputations positively
enhanced back in the West, but they were well paid for their time

and attentions. Fast-forwarding a generation from the period of Mustafa III, it is interesting that a young second lieutenant in the French army, Napoleon Bonaparte, seriously considered going to Istanbul to teach new techniques in the use of artillery. For a poor boy forced to support his family after his father's death, the opportunity must have been a tempting one, and the history of nineteenth-century Europe would have been very different had he taken the sultan's payment for his services.

Mustafa III began his reign with the empire's longest period of peace with Europe in its history (1747–68). This was shattered in 1768 when Russian fighting with Polish rebels drew the Ottoman lands that bordered these areas into the fray. When Cossacks attacked the border town of Balta and massacred the population, Mustafa III demanded an explanation. When Empress Catherine replied that they weren't *her* Cossacks, it was time for war. Peter the Great had long since died, and Russia was now led by a new Tsar with the same epithet; this was the era of Catherine the Great. To start off, however, Catherine and her Russian forces didn't appear to be all that great. Mustafa III had brought in British officers from the Royal Navy to train and observe the Ottoman navy. It had always been Russia's goal to dominate the Black Sea with its own fleet, but this Anglo-Ottoman led navy acquitted itself so well that the Russians got nowhere in terms of naval superiority in the Sea of Azov, let alone in the whole of the Black Sea.

This war was to rumble on for more than six years and ended in the reign of another sultan. The critical (and most audacious) moment came in 1770 when, for the first time in history, a Russian fleet entered the Mediterranean Sea. It had not come from the Black Sea but, instead, took the long way around, from the Baltic Sea, down past Britain and France, then into the Mediterranean, where it could spy on North Africa and Spain. The fleet, led by Admiral Orlov, landed in Greece and whipped the local Greek rebels into an uprising against Ottoman rule. It was yet another sign of the close connections between the Russian Orthodox Church and the Greek Orthodox Church. Spiritually, they were brother faiths, and Russia wanted to give succour to their brothers living under the yoke of Muslim rule. While it all sounded great, this ideology was spiked by the practicalities of opening up another front with the Ottomans in the form of a rebellion in Greece, which would lead to further fires for Mustafa III to put out. However, the Russians were isolated from both supplies and allied regular forces and were compelled to leave Greece, which allowed Ottoman authorities to put down the uprising, something that the powers in Istanbul had become quite adept at doing.

Orlov also met the Ottoman navy just off the coast of Anatolia, where twelve Russian ships engaged twenty-two Turkish vessels and destroyed most of them with the use of fire ships. This daring voyage of Orlov was used by Catherine the Great to consolidate her reign over Russia, and, while the original plan of breaking into the Black Sea – or, better yet, attacking Istanbul – failed, Orlov's journey signalled to the rest of Europe just how far Russian power had come since the time of Peter the Great. Russian forces did better in capturing territory in Ukraine and Romania, including the city of Bucharest. The fighting was bitter, with no quarter given by either side. Russian tactics in the land battles were simple, and, yet again, thousands of Russian troops never made it to the front lines because they got lost, deserted or died on the way. If either side had had better logistics or tactics, more could have been made of the war; instead it was akin to two men swinging clubs at each other until one finally gave up.

Perhaps the best example of this occurred at the massive Battle of Kagul, also in 1770, in southern Moldova. Here some 40,000 Russians met a huge Ottoman force of around 60,000 (with another army of Crimean Tatars just as large, if not larger, nearby but too far away to affect the course of the battle). The battle had no grand plan or clever tactics; the Russians just charged at the Ottoman centre. Either through surprise or through the ferocity of the Russian attack, the Ottoman forces did a poor job of stopping them even though they had 130 cannons to do just that. The initial clash turned into an Ottoman rout, and it's estimated that between 20,000 and 30,000 Ottoman soldiers drowned trying to cross a nearby river to get away from the oncoming Russians. This was a great victory for Russia, but when Frederick the Great of Prussia compared it to the Roman victories of the past it felt like something of an exaggeration.

The unimaginatively named Russo-Turkish War of 1768–74 had an unusual element to it when, at first, Britain backed Russia (despite some ex-British officers working for the Ottoman navy). Britain wanted to keep the supply of raw materials flowing from Russia into their country, which was then on the cusp of the Industrial

Revolution. However, as the war progressed, Britain realised that Russia was winning too comfortably and the balance of power in the East could tip irrevocably in favour of Russia – which could start expanding its fleet into the North Atlantic and push eastwards in Asia towards India. Over this six-year period Russia went from being just a provider of raw materials to being a competitor, in which case Britain couldn't allow a complete collapse of Ottoman power. The war culminated in the 1774 Treaty of Küçük Kaynarca. It was enormously embarrassing for the Ottomans, but it could have been so much worse. Most of Moldova was returned to the sultan, but areas of Ukraine and the northern Caucasus were relinquished to Russian rule. The key area was Azov and the Crimean Khanate of the Tatars. Azov became a permanent Russian port, and the land of the Tatars became an independent state. It was the first time the Ottomans had lost control over Muslim lands, and while the Tatars were now theoretically independent, they were really a vassal state to Russia. One other concession that would come back to haunt the whole of Europe as well as future sultans was an agreement concerning Russian 'protection'. It was agreed that Russia now had the right to protect Christians in the Ottoman Empire and could even intercede if Christians in Moldova were mistreated. This created the perfect pretext for any war that Russia wanted to start, and, less than a century later, it was to lead to one of the most tortuous reasons for war in history.

The sultan who ratified the treaty back in Istanbul was not Osman III but his brother Abdul Hamid. Osman III had died in January 1774 and was replaced without any social unrest. With the same system in place to raise the sons of the sultan, Abdul Hamid was another ruler who was smart and gentle but spent more time praying than ruling. Significantly, Abdul Hamid was the first sultan in centuries not to pay off the Janissaries on his accession to the throne, saying, 'There are no longer gratuities in our treasury, as all of our soldier sons should learn.' This one statement shows that Abdul Hamid was an honest if naïve man. Not paying the perennially rebellious Janissaries was a very high-risk strategy, but not only did they not deserve the payoff (certainly not after their poor performance in the recent war with Russia), but the war had been ruinously expensive, meaning that Abdul Hamid was telling the truth when he said that there was no treasure to dish out. After a century of reversals, the sultan's treasury was bare. Amazingly, the honesty paid off and Abdul Hamid remained in power, a greatly admired ruler although perhaps for the wrong reasons. Everyone agreed that he was courteous, intelligent and very religious. Not a bad word was said about the man by anyone either in or out of the empire, but that's not the same thing as being an effective ruler. After signing off on a treaty that cost the empire a substantial amount of territory and influence, Abdul Hamid spent the rest of his reign trying to re-impose central control on unruly outlying regions such as Syria.

Schnapps

The strangest story from Abdul Hamid's reign comes towards its end during yet another war with the Habsburgs. The fighting had produced only minor gains along the borders between both powers. The result, in essence, was a stalemate, a sign that if the Ottomans were not a spent force then the Holy Roman Empire wasn't what it had been a century earlier either. The Treaty of Sistova was brokered by Great Britain, Prussia and the Netherlands. A few minor towns were ceded to the Habsburgs, but it was very little reward for a lot of effort, and the true significance of the treaty was that it ended any further clashes between these two struggling empires. After this the Holy Roman Empire became distracted by the French Revolution and, later, Napoleon, who dissolved the title in 1806, which ended a thousand-year history. So far so normal – but it's what happened on 17 September 1788, in Karánsebes in Romania, that is strange and also highly contested.

A massive Habsburg army was setting up camp on the night in question when a group of Hussars was sent out to scout the area for any signs of 'Turkish' forces. They crossed the Timiş River and found no evidence of any Ottoman troops in the area. The Hussars did, however, run into a group of Romani Gypsies, who offered to sell them a barrel of schnapps. Tired and thirsty (and what soldier would say no to such an opportunity), the Hussar cavalrymen bought the barrel and began enjoying their purchase. However, when infantry reinforcements caught up with the Hussars and saw the men enjoying their schnapps, they demanded some for themselves. The now drunk Hussars refused, and the subsequent argument got so heated that the

Hussars set up a makeshift defence around the schnapps. Angry words turned into actual shooting. In all the confusion, some men started to shout, 'Turci!' ('Turks!')

Chaos engulfed the scene as Habsburg infantry and cavalrymen began running around looking for the attacking Turks. The returning Hussars were mistaken for Sipahis, and someone ordered cannon fire. The whole army began shooting at itself or the shadows, and casualties mounted in the ensuing maelstrom of friendly fire. It was even said that the Emperor Joseph II was pushed off his horse into a nearby river. Eventually the entire army retreated from the supposed ambush. The Ottomans, of course, were in no way involved in the engagement and were more than a little bewildered when they arrived in the area several days later to find 10,000 dead and wounded soldiers. The Ottoman army moved on and took Karánsebes without a fuss.

One problem with this story is that the source is a military magazine written about fifty years after the event. No Austrian officers make mention of it in their journals, but then how likely is it that anyone would ever admit to such a disaster? The other problem is that the Emperor Joseph II was not on campaign in Romania in September of 1788, so maybe someone thought to add a bit of colour to an exaggerated incident of poor discipline in the ranks. In any case, it all sounds too fantastical and is, therefore, likely to be made up.

It is recounted here for two reasons. Firstly, what is not in any doubt is that Karánsebes was easily captured by the Ottomans in 1788, so in that respect the story could be true. The second and main reason that it's worthy of discussion at all is that the story is a candid metaphor for how low the Habsburgs had sunk since the heyday of their great victories in the 1680s. In other words, by the 1780s it wasn't just the Ottomans who were displaying diminished grandeur.

13

A New Enemy and a New Ally

By now the city of Istanbul had grown to about the same size as it had been in its prime under Byzantine rule, and life was falling into a regular pattern. But whether Constantinople or Istanbul, the city had a history of disasters; it seemed that every decade had a major fire, earthquake or outbreak of plague. Sometimes the city got really unlucky and had all three at the same time. In 1782, yet another great conflagration erupted in Istanbul's narrow lanes. The tightly packed wooden houses were easily set alight and the inferno spread across whole districts of the city at breathtaking speed. Given the frequency with which the fires erupted, an effective response to these disasters and to matters of public health was desperately needed, and it was thought wise to set up some kind of firefighting service. That job fell to the Janissaries, who were to become the city's firemen (when they weren't at war). Galata Tower, which had been temporarily converted into a mosque for the Muslims who had fled Spain, was now used as a watchtower to look for outbreaks of fire, and the city even had a rudimentary fire service. But all of this came too late for the fire of 1782, which resulted in the loss of 7,000 buildings and came perilously close to the Blue Mosque. At the forefront of the efforts to contain the blaze was Abdul Hamid, who was seen in the streets of the city organising the response. His efforts showed him to be a ruler who was concerned about his people – although that didn't stop the destruction of 7,000 homes and shops.

Meanwhile, just as Abdul Hamid was fighting the Habsburgs to a stalemate, Russia and the Sublime Porte clashed once more. As previously mentioned, the Treaty of Küçük Kaynarca created more problems than it solved. The provision concerning the Russian protection of Christians had turned into constant meddling and demands from Catherine the Great's court. In 1787, any pretence that the Crimea was an independent state was dropped when Empress Catherine journeyed through the area in a triumphal procession. Enough was enough, and Abdul Hamid, who was known to be a pacifist at heart, had no option but to declare war on Russia. It is interesting that on this occasion the Ottoman declaration of war was backed by both France and Britain.

This war ran simultaneously with the one against the Habsburgs, but in this war there was no good news (or barrels of schnapps) for the Ottomans. Virtually every time the two sides met in battle, the Russians won. On a number of occasions the Russian Prince Potemkin ordered the population to be massacred. The fighting was brutal but efficient, and Western powers grew uneasy over Russian successes at the cost of Ottoman power. This time Prussia warned Russia that it was time to end the war. Russia had every reason to respect Prussia's martial abilities, so a ceasefire was agreed in 1791. In January 1792, the Treaty of Jassy was agreed and, quite frankly, couldn't come soon enough as the Ottomans relinquished Yedisan, another Ottoman territory, to the Russians. This one bordered the Black Sea, which meant that now the entire northern coastline of the Black Sea was Russian. These capitulations to the Russian Tsars were becoming alarmingly and dangerously regular.

Abdul Hamid may have been austere and religious, but one of his favourite wives was Nakşidil Sultan. Legend says (and by now you know how much the Turks love a good story) that she was the cousin of the woman who would become the Empress Josephine (Napoleon's wife). There is no hard evidence of this, but there were multiple rumours that some of the women in the harem were French. It is possible that they were introduced as a way of connecting the Ottomans to the rulers of France and binding the two through progeny as well as the political alliances that regularly existed between the two states. What isn't in doubt is that Nakşidil Sultan was a very Western influence in the harem and may only have reflected an increasing desire on the part of the sultans to look to the West, whether or not she was related to the French throne. She was primarily a sign of the times.

Once more a war started by one sultan was ended by another. In 1789 Abdul Hamid died peacefully in his palace in Istanbul, just like his brother. This time a son of Mustafa III came to power, and he was known as Selim III. He agreed to the terms of the Treaty of Jassy, and at the time it looked as if there would be more clashes between Russia and the Ottoman Empire, but then came something nobody in Europe was expecting. If the French Revolution, culminating in the execution of Louis XVI, sent shockwaves across Europe, that was nothing compared to the impact of a young Corsican general capturing the whole of Italy in just one campaign (in 1797). It was in this campaign that the Venetian Republic was dissolved. By the 1790s, its time as a trading empire was long gone. Now it was just one of the exotic stops on the 'Grand Tour' that was then the fashion among young aristocratic men. The Venice of this era was better known for its brothels and casinos than for anything its shipyards in the Arsenal could produce. Napoleon's rise meant that he had neutralised two of the Ottomans' ancient enemies (Venice and Genoa); a third, the Holy Roman Empire, was defeated later. Now the whole of Europe had a new nemesis.

A year after Napoleon shocked Europe with his conquest of Italy he was planning something even more audacious: an amphibious invasion of Egypt, which would then be used as a base to attack British imperial India. In many ways it was an insanely ambitious idea that was always doomed to fail. Even in the twentieth century, with all the benefits of later technology, it would be a campaign fraught with difficulties; in the late eighteenth century, in the age of sail and gunpowder, it would take a demigod to pull off – which is pretty much how Napoleon regarded himself. On the way to Egypt, Napoleon stopped off in Malta and forced the knights (who had been there ever since the time of Suleiman the Magnificent) to surrender to him. They did so with no resistance, and the end of this once fierce group of holy warriors came with a whimper and not a bang. This was yet another reminder of how impressive it was that the Ottoman Empire was still a going concern, when many of its old enemies were quietly shuffling off into the history books.

By 1798, Egypt was only technically part of the Ottoman Empire. As long as it paid lip service to the sultan, its people, like others far away from Istanbul, lived largely autonomous lives. However, an attack from a Western power galvanised the Muslim Middle East. There may have been big differences between Murad Bey of the Mamelukes in Egypt and Selim III in Istanbul, but neither wanted Egypt to fall to French domination. The French revolutionary wars, which are often referred to as the Napoleonic Wars, were a (roughly) twenty-five-year period of conflict in Europe and beyond. Over the years a total of seven coalitions were created to fight France. Napoleon's invasion of Egypt provided the impetus to form the second coalition; this was the only one that involved the Ottomans, but, with so much of the action of this era happening in Ottoman lands, it's hardly surprising that the sultan would want to protect his interests. This was the only time in history that the Ottoman sultan and virtually the whole of Europe were fighting on the same side – and all of them were fighting against France.

The British didn't want the French fleet to get to Egypt, so Nelson was sent to intercept it; but the Mediterranean is a big sea, and this was the era of semaphore and dispatch riders. Trying to find an enemy fleet that didn't want to be found was a difficult business, and it was a rare failure on Nelson's part that Napoleon landed unopposed in Alexandria. The Alexandria of 1798 was a small town of no strategic significance, but that wasn't the point. Napoleon was ahead of his time in the then non-existent field of public relations, and he understood that this success would make a good story back in Europe. He knew that when the newspapers reported that he had landed in Alexandria, the educated classes would recognise the name as a place where pharaohs and Roman emperors had once walked, and he knew they would be impressed. Napoleon was a great general, politician – and PR guru!

Napoleon also attempted some remarkably progressive (if politically expedient) views on Islam. At the time Islam in Western Europe was synonymous with decades of violence (a taint that lingers in some quarters to this day). To have Napoleon state that the Prophet Muhammed was 'a great man who changed the face of the earth' would therefore have gone down well with the local population. His proclamation to the Egyptians was remarkably conciliatory in tone and begins,

People of Egypt: You will be told by our enemies that I am come to destroy your religion. Believe them not. Tell them that I am come to restore your rights, punish your usurpers, and raise the true worship of Mahomet (*sic*). Tell them that I venerate, more than do the Mamelukes, God, His prophet, and the Qur'an.

On one occasion he even dressed as a local by putting on a turban, much to the acclaim of the crowd. However, Napoleon's secretary, Bourienne, puts things in a more realistic context:

> It has been alleged that Bonaparte, when in Egypt, took part in the religious ceremonies and worship of the Mussulmans (*sic*); but it cannot be said that he celebrated the festivals of the overflowing of the Nile and the anniversary of the Prophet. The Turks (note the lack of understanding about the difference between an Egyptian Muslim and an Anatolian one) invited him to these merely as a spectator, and the presence of their new master was gratifying to the people. But he never committed the folly of ordering any solemnity. He neither learned nor repeated any prayer of the Qur'an, as many persons have asserted.

This was another PR stunt to get the locals on board. However, he first had to humble the local army, which meant fighting the Mamelukes. The cavalry that faced Napoleon at the legendary Battle of the Pyramids was, much like the backdrop of the ancient pyramids, a splendid relic of the past. Apart from their carbines and muskets the Mameluke cavalry that fought on that day would have been familiar to Osman 500 years earlier. The Mamelukes were resplendent in their brightly coloured silks and plumed helmets. Their weapons were inlaid with mother-of-pearl or ivory. History was in the air, something Napoleon emphasised when he spoke to his troops, saying, 'From the heights of these pyramids, forty centuries look down on us.' It was East versus West; it was the new tactics of France against the traditional bravery of the Mamelukes, but the one thing Napoleon took great pains to emphasise was that this was *not* Christian versus Muslim. Even though his forces were in Egypt, and later Syria, this was – most emphatically – *not* a new crusade!

At this time in the West there was a standard tactic to deal with the dangerously mobile cavalry of the enemy forces. Napoleon ordered each of the five divisions of his army into hollow rectangles with cavalry and baggage at the centre and cannon at the corners.

The men stood in multiple rows. All had fixed bayonets and as one line of men reloaded, they were covered by another line that could fire. The square shape of the divisions meant that the Mameluke cavalry had no way to flank the French. Murad Bey had split his forces. He was with the thousands of cavalry on the French side of the Nile, next to the town of Embabeh, where he had thousands more infantry behind its not inconsiderable walls. However, another 10,000 of his infantry watched uselessly from the other side of the Nile during the course of the day. Although they were in the wrong place at the wrong time, it was unlikely they would have tipped the battle to the Mameluke advantage.

Murad Bey let the French sweat under a scorching sun and didn't attack until 3.30 in the afternoon. When the attack came it was instantaneous, ferocious and a sharp lesson to the French about what the skilled Mameluke horsemen could do. However, despite the bravery and the exquisite costumes, they were no match for superior tactics mixed with cold steel and hot gunfire. The cream of the Mameluke forces was gunned down. Men screamed and horses whinnied as the sand of the desert turned red, with one pointless charge leading to another ineffectual attack by Murad Bey's men. By the end of the day Napoleon's force of 20,000 had suffered just twenty-nine deaths. The French surveyed the carnage of the battlefield as thousands of brave Mamelukes lay dead or dying on the sands of Egypt or in the streets of Embabeh. For both Murad Bey and Selim III, 21 July 1798 had been an unmitigated disaster. Napoleon was now in charge of Egypt – and he was still only twenty-eight.

However, less than two weeks later, the British finally caught up with the French fleet. The French had, of course, disembarked and were already the lords of Cairo, but Napoleon needed the fleet to keep supplies and communications flowing back to France. On seeing the French fleet anchored in Aboukir Bay, Nelson ordered an immediate attack. It should be noted that it wasn't just the French who could spot a good bit of PR because this battle, in the shallows of Aboukir Bay, became known as the Battle of the Nile – again because the people back home had heard of the Nile even though the battle wasn't fought on or near the Nile.

Vice-Admiral François-Paul Brueys d'Aigalliers was the French commander in charge of the fleet, and he had anchored his ships close to the shore near a hidden reef, where he believed his flanks were protected. But he hadn't counted on the sheer naval brilliance of Admiral Nelson, who managed to get half a dozen warships behind the French line and then proceeded to blow them to bits from both sides. The battle started in the early evening and raged on into the night. Brueys was on his flagship, the aptly named *L'Orient*, during the battle and fought like a man possessed. He was shot twice but was still standing on the deck giving orders when he was cut almost in half by a cannon ball. By now he was certain to die, but insisted that he should be propped up in a barrel so he could stay on deck to give orders until he bled out.

An hour later, at roughly 10.00 p.m., *L'Orient*'s gunpowder store ignited and tons of gunpowder exploded, ripping the flagship to pieces and killing about 800 men in an instant. The explosion was so deafening it was heard miles away in towns along the coast. The fighting actually stopped for about thirty minutes while both sides helped to fish survivors out of the water. With their commander dead, their flagship in ruins and attacks on both sides, there was no option for the French but surrender. Nelson was gravely wounded during the fierce fighting, and his officers feared he would die. Divers were sent into the bay to retrieve some of *L'Orient*'s mast so that it could be used for his coffin. As it turned out, Nelson recovered; nevertheless, when he did die (at the Battle of Trafalgar), he was buried in the coffin made from the mast of *L'Orient*.

The important point about this battle is that it isolated Napoleon. He was the ruler of Egypt, but he was also a very long way from his power base in France, with the British Royal Navy between him and his reinforcements. The Battle of the Nile ended any hope (no matter how crazy it was to begin with) of using Egypt as a launch pad for attacks on British interests in India. What Napoleon began to realise was that just wanting to rule Egypt and being sensitive to local religious customs and culture wasn't enough. In a way, Napoleon's failure to stop the uprisings that would occur in Egypt against his rule was a microcosm of the problems the sultans had been facing for generations. Selim III continued the policy of playing one group off against another, but that ultimately led only to political unrest. While Napoleon liked to be seen as a liberator, he didn't actually do much liberating. Instead, his soldiers were seen as new occupiers, and it didn't help that Napoleon made a number of missteps by having his name mentioned in the same sentences as that of the Prophet Mohammed. This was dangerously close to idolatry and gave common ground for rebellion among the disparate groups of Egypt.

As the uprisings became more serious, so did Napoleon's responses. When some rebels hid in a mosque, Napoleon showed a measure of sensitivity by ensuring the imams were left unharmed (a message to the locals that he respected their holy men and holy places), but the rebels themselves were beheaded. This was an unnecessarily cruel form of execution, and one that was becoming more frequent. Despite this, the revolt continued to grow throughout September and October. Whenever the French met an enemy army on the field of battle (Murad Bey was still skulking around in the Egyptian hinterland) or an opposition force attacked, the French destroyed it without breaking a sweat, but suppressing dissent in a large city was a messier affair. On 22 October, French garrisons were attacked throughout Cairo. French soldiers, administrators and even scientists (Napoleon had brought 200 with him) were hacked to pieces or shot by angry mobs. Napoleon himself couldn't get back into the city as it had been barricaded by armed men. Eventually he pushed the rebels back to the grand mosque, where any previous restraint evaporated, and he fired his artillery at this Muslim holy place of worship. The rebellion was silenced (for a time) but at a terrible cost to his reputation in Egypt.

Selim III, like his predecessors, had started to modernise the army by the time Napoleon attacked. Unlike his predecessors, however, Selim III had actually made progress, to the detriment of the Janissaries and the ancient *devşirme* system. A new elite corps called the Nizam-i Cedid (the new order) had been trained and drilled by Western officers. They were equipped with the latest muskets and, a little ironically, wore new uniforms based on those worn by the French. Most importantly, the soldiers were not Christian youths who had been brought into the corps, but Muslim youths from Anatolia. In 1799 this new unit was not big enough to replace the army, but it could be part of the force sent to fight Napoleon. Selim III came up with a grand but sensible strategy: he would attempt to corner Napoleon in a giant pincer movement. One army would march through Syria and the Sinai peninsula and attack him from the east, while another army of European soldiers would muster in Rhodes and land at Damietta at the mouth of the Nile Delta and attack him from the north. It was a good plan, and had Selim III been fighting anybody other than Napoleon it might have worked.

Napoleon's scouts reported that the army from Syria had recaptured a fort on the frontier, so Napoleon, showing his usual flair and aggression, decided to muster an army of 13,000 and meet it head-on in battle before it could cross the Sinai. He raced through the key town of Gaza and then arrived at the walled port of Jaffa, defended by Ahmad Pasha al-Jazzar, a name that reeks of the Middle East, except that he was the Ottoman governor of the area and was of Bosnian stock. The French still had some ships, and the fleet bombarded Jaffa from the sea, while Napoleon attacked from the land with thirteen field guns ranged at the city. When Napoleon sent in a local to discuss terms of surrender, al-Jazzar had him beheaded. When a French messenger was sent in, he was said to have been tortured, castrated and then beheaded, all of which sent Napoleon into a fury. Al-Jazzar tried to sally forth and meet Napoleon in battle but was beaten back. On the fifth day of the siege, the French guns had been so effective that Napoleon ordered an attack of the breached defences, and the city fell.

Al-Jazzar escaped but his actions, while normal in the context of Ottoman conduct in war (remember how many of the wars with Russia at this time were followed up by massacre and counter-massacre), had clearly enraged and sickened Napoleon. He ordered a general execution of all prisoners (2,000–4,000) and demanded that they be bayoneted to save on gunpowder. Whatever you may think of Napoleon, his name is not synonymous with massacres or atrocities; the longer he stayed in the Middle East, though, the more savage his actions seem to have become. Apologists point out that he would have lost a considerable amount of his manpower guarding the prisoners (rather like one of the arguments for Henry V massacring his prisoners at the Battle of Agincourt), but there seems to have been an unnecessary and uncharacteristic level of brutality about Napoleon at this time.

Plague was sweeping the area and some of his men became too sick to march. Apparently Napoleon seriously considered having them poisoned to put them out of their misery. This is the only campaign when he suggested such drastic measures, further indicating his desperation. Napoleon allowed some of the locals to leave Jaffa in order to spread the word of his atrocities, expecting that, as a result, local leaders would fling open their doors to him. In fact, the opposite happened. While central Ottoman authority was regarded with suspicion, at least the people of Syria were dealing with a known quantity when it came to the Sublime Porte – as opposed to the barbarous acts of this foreign invader. Napoleon was, in an unexpected way, a unifying factor in the Ottoman Empire; the different factions may have hated each other, but they all agreed they hated Napoleon more.

The siege of Jaffa had been short, sharp and brutal, and Napoleon still had an intact army and a desire to advance. But where to go? What next? The original plan had been to attack India, but he was now, quite understandably, heading away from the subcontinent. We will never know exactly what his plan was, but his actions show that he wasn't thinking clearly or, at least, not as clearly as he did in every other campaign. At this point he seemed to be making up the campaign objectives as he went along. This was a dangerous way to conduct war.

The next major city along the coast (so he could be resupplied from the sea by his fleet) was Acre. In the first chapter it was mentioned in passing that the city had suffered a great siege at the time of the Middle Eastern crusades. The siege of Acre by the Muslim Mamelukes was epic and ended Christian rule in the Holy Land back in 1291. Now, more than 500 years later, there was another siege, but this time it was Western Christians doing the besieging – and it wasn't just Muslims being besieged. This is the one occasion in the Wars of the Second Coalition that Britain and the Ottomans actively worked together in the same struggle. The defence of Acre was in the hands of al-Jazzar for the Ottomans and Sidney Smith for the British. Smith had been sent to the Ottomans not only to open up diplomatic connections in Istanbul, but to carry out practical assistance to Ottoman defences in the Middle East in order to stop Napoleon. Smith certainly had no love for the French – less than two years earlier, he had been languishing in a French jail after being captured by French forces. Smith had two ships of the line, *Tigre* and *Theseus*, and a full complement of marines to contribute to the defence of Acre. He arrived there just before Napoleon and took some of the ships' cannons to help reinforce the formidable (if medieval) double walls of the city. Having done what he could on the outer defences, Smith sailed to intercept Napoleon's ships and successfully captured them before making sure that Acre's garrison was bolstered with his marines. After that he anchored his two warships parallel to the coast, ready to fire broadsides on the approach to the city. Napoleon was finally up against an innovative opponent in the Middle East.

On 20 May, Napoleon laid siege to the port, firing the few cannons he had at these mighty defences, while the defenders sought refuge behind the city's walls. As Napoleon was now committed to the siege, Ottoman forces were able to gather a relief force and march to the aid of the city.

Napoleon had always picked competent generals and, even though his force was small, Jean-Baptiste Kléber was a battle-hardened and highly capable general. His force of around 2,000 men (later joined by 2,000 of Napoleon's men) met the relief force at Mount Tabor in Palestine. By comparison, Abdullah Pasha al-Azm, the governor of Damascus, had gathered an army of over 30,000. The French were outnumbered about 9:1 but, as we have seen, numbers don't count for everything, and the Battle of Mount Tabor was possibly the greatest (often forgotten) humiliation of Ottoman martial power.

The Ottoman forces were made up of Sipahis, Mamelukes and other outdated but brave warrior classes. From dawn to late afternoon, Kléber sat in the hollow anti-cavalry squares, resisting every attack by Pasha al-Azm's men. The Ottoman governor's losses were mounting, but his army so dwarfed the French force that he could afford them. Meanwhile, after ten hours of fighting under the sweltering Palestine sun, Kléber's men were tired, thirsty and dangerously low on gunpowder and ammunition. It was then that Napoleon arrived with about 2,000 men, not enough to match the numbers in the Ottoman army but enough to distract them by sending a few hundred men to attack and loot the Ottoman camp. Abdullah Pasha al-Azm thought Napoleon's tiny force was the vanguard of a larger army and panicked, thinking he was about to be attacked from the rear and flanks. He ordered a general retreat, at which point the two French forces charged the disengaging Ottomans, and the orderly Ottoman retreat turned into a messy rout.

Total losses of Ottoman soldiers were around 6,000 killed and another 500 captured, versus two dead French soldiers. An army of around 4,500 had fought an army of over 30,000 and not only won but sustained just two fatalities. It was a devastating humiliation for Selim III and a spectacular triumph that allowed Napoleon to continue his siege of Acre. The reason why the Battle of Mount Tabor is forgotten is that it achieved nothing in the long term. Every time Napoleon attacked Acre's walls, his men were beaten back by the muskets and cannons of the defenders and the ships of the Royal Navy. A month after his victory at Mount Tabor, Napoleon had lost nearly half of his army trying to take a city that had no meaning in his grand plans. Smith and al-Jazzar resisted everything that Napoleon could throw at them, from artillery barrages to direct assaults and attempts to undermine the walls. Napoleon stood outside the walls for two months and was frustrated at every turn.

On 21 May, Napoleon admitted defeat. There was no formal proclamation, no treaty, just an about-face of his army and a long, arduous and sweaty march back to Egypt. Selim III and George III could claim a first victory over the living legend that was Napoleon. Later, in 1805, the great general declared, '(Had I) been able to take Acre I would have finished the war against the Turks with Arabic, Greek, and Armenian troops. Instead of a battle in Moravia, I would have won a Battle of Issus, I would have made myself emperor of the East, and I would have returned to Paris by way of Constantinople.'

It's a great quote, and if Napoleon had had the troops to spare he might well have crossed through Anatolia and taken the Ottoman capital (later he did, against the odds, capture most European capitals, including Moscow). But the key word in the first sentence is 'if'. According to the quote, Napoleon assumed the locals would rally to him. He had tried that in Egypt and, after the siege of Jaffa, it failed every time. Also, as both Jaffa and Acre had shown, there were a lot of nasty diseases in the Ottoman realm, and they did a better job of destroying his forces than Selim III's armies. Putting it bluntly, the chances of Napoleon's successful capture of Istanbul was about as likely as an invasion of India using Egypt as his base of operations.

Napoleon returned to Egypt to find out he was dead – at least that's what the British and Ottoman authorities had been telling the locals and the French garrison. His return temporarily quelled the growing rebellion against French rule, as it seemed that Napoleon had come back triumphantly and had even cheated death. However, just a few weeks after his return, the second Ottoman army arrived at Aboukir Bay (the same one that had been the site of the so-called Battle of the Nile), transported by the Royal Navy. The vanguard of the force stormed the French defences, and within hours 300 French soldiers had been killed, captured or forced to retreat.

The leader of the Ottoman forces, Mustafa Pasha, was sufficiently well drilled in European tactics to know that if he unleashed Murad Bey and his Mamelukes, Napoleon would simply form the hollow squares and kill his cavalry. Instead, the pasha created a fortified camp on the coast of Aboukir Bay so that he could be supplied by sea and protected from any flanking attack. It was a sensible plan, and one he hoped would make the camp a formidable nut for Napoleon to crack. Under normal conditions Royal Navy ships anchored in the bay would have been able to attack the coastal defences with their cannons (as they had done at Acre), but at the time of this battle the bay was so shallow that the ships were forced to anchor too far out to be of any use as artillery platforms. When Napoleon heard the news, he responded with relish. A fight on a field of battle was one he could understand and probably control, so he drew together as many troops as he could; he had a total of 7,700 men and 1,000 cavalry, a force even smaller than the one he had at Acre.

Napoleon was able to position his artillery on high ground and fire into the Ottoman encampment. When some of his soldiers broke ranks and began to attack the Ottoman defensive line, Murad realised that he could either watch the attack falter or commit his cavalrymen. He chose to engage. The fighting was a bitter hand-to-hand affair, but as the French pushed the Ottomans back, the huge flaw in Mustafa Pasha's plan was revealed. Trapped as they were on the edge of a bay, there was nowhere to retreat. Of the approximately 6,000 Ottoman casualties on that day (about a third of the Ottoman force), 4,000 drowned. Aboukir Bay would have been littered with bobbing corpses. About 3,000 Ottoman soldiers fled to the local fort, but they were leaderless and without supplies, so Napoleon surrounded it and allowed thirst and hunger to go to work for him. They quickly surrendered. It was

Napoleon's final victory on Ottoman territory, and it showed that, while his original plan to use Egypt as a base for attacking India was strategically flawed and that his wild goose chase up the coast of Palestine had been a costly mistake, he was a peerless tactician and battlefield leader.

After all of this Napoleon did something ignominious: he left his army in Egypt. Kléber was put in charge, and the capable general did a good job with regard to the military, but something more was needed to suppress an uprising. Kléber recognised his limitations and negotiated the extraction of his army with Sidney Smith and the Ottoman court in an agreement known as the Convention of El Arich. However, the rebellion made it difficult for Kléber to disengage his troops, and Selim III was dithering over the terms of the accord. This delay may have been due to genuine incompetence on the part of the Ottoman court, but it also bought them time. In 1800, Selim III sent another army to attack the now entrenched French. This one, numbering around 40,000, marched across the Sinai Desert and into Egypt, where Kléber met them at Heliopolis, just a few miles outside of Cairo. Kléber only had about 10,000 troops, but he had superior tactics and strong motivation: the desire to avoid being killed or captured by the 'Turkish barbarians' meant that the French fought harder and better. Once again a French army sustained minimal casualties against a much larger Ottoman army that was forced to retreat. The result was an atmosphere in Cairo that was surreal. The French wanted to leave but couldn't, and the Egyptians yearned for them to go but made it difficult for them to do so. Egypt could expect no more help from the sultan. Three Ottoman armies had been bested by French forces, and these emphatic defeats proved to Selim III's court that military modernisation was desperately needed. Since nothing else was working as it used to, the Nizam-i-Cedid seemed to be a step in the right direction.

Then, in June 1800, as Kléber was walking in the garden, a man who seemed only to be a harmless vagrant suddenly produced a knife and stabbed Kléber in the heart. The already fatal blow was followed by a frenzied knife attack on the body of the fallen general. The assassin was Soleyman el-Halaby, a Kurdish Syrian student, who tried to escape but was soon captured. The assassin's right arm was burned off, and he was impaled in a public square in Cairo, where he was left to die a slow and agonising death. The French took extra revenge by sending his skull to France where it was use to teach the pseudoscience of phrenology, which supposedly revealed character type. It was said that el-Halaby's pronounced bump was a sure sign of 'fanaticism'.

With Kléber dead and Napoleon having forgotten Egypt altogether, leadership passed to General Menou, but the reality was that the French *armee d'orient* had been abandoned in North Africa. The end of the French operations in Ottoman territory didn't occur as the result of Egyptian revolt or Ottoman military success, but when a British expeditionary force arrived in 1801. This was led by Sir Ralph Abercrombie, who would die of his wounds on this campaign. Most of the fighting was centred on Alexandria, where the British, with superior numbers and volley fire, were able to overwhelm the French and force a general surrender, so it was a battle between two armies from another continent that sealed the fate of Egypt. This led to the Capitulation of Alexandria (1801), when various French spoils were split between Selim III and the British Empire (and is how Britain came to be in possession of the Rosetta Stone). After a string of the most humiliating defeats in Ottoman history, it could be reasonably argued that Selim III was now on the winning side in the Wars of the Second Coalition, except that most of the hard work had been done by British forces. The Eternal State remained, but its star had dimmed to a dangerous low.

Selim III was unlucky enough to be the sultan at the time of Napoleon. While Ottoman defeats at the hands of the French were humiliating, the same can largely be said for the rest of Europe's powers. It was the war with France that proved how badly the Ottoman administrative and military systems had fallen behind Western Europe. The two saving graces of Napoleon's campaigns were that they had created a practical military exchange with Britain, the new rising power in the world, while France/Napoleon distracted the rest of Europe for a quarter of a century. One of the main reasons why Russia didn't follow up its overwhelming victories against the Ottoman Empire in the early 1800s was because Napoleon was rampaging all over northern Europe and, later, Russia itself. Napoleon would, of course, become famously unstuck with his 1812 invasion of Russia, but it was some time before Russia looked south again.

The Elgin Marbles
The improvement in relations between the Ottomans and Britain led to one of the most contentious issues in artefact preservation, one that rumbles on today. In 1801, Thomas Bruce, the 7th Earl of Elgin, contacted the Ottoman authorities to purchase the remaining statues on the Parthenon in Athens. They were boxed up and sent to his estate, where they remained until his death, when they were bequeathed to the British Museum. No one objected to Elgin's purchase at the time, but fast-forward a couple of centuries and Greece, not unnaturally, now wants the statues back. Claims that they were stolen aren't true, and if something was purchased from the proper authorities of the day (Greek independence didn't come until about a generation after this deal) and the legal owner doesn't want to return them, then the situation is tricky. It's an emotive issue today, but it wasn't at the time.

The most recent attempt to modernise the military at the expense of the Janissaries held, but it came at a high cost. While the Nizam-i-Cedid has been described here as specifically a transformation of certain troops, the truth was broader than that. Selim III was an accomplished musician and composer, and he was determined to make the empire more harmonious. To that end he was responsible for the creation of a new treasury and revenue collection system. Education was broadened and courtiers were sent to Europe to attend the best (Christian) universities (the madrassas had their limitations given their emphasis on religious education). But to achieve all of this, he had first to get past the Janissaries – and they had, in the past, rebelled against less. It was a classic example of special interests getting in the way of what needed to be done, and in 1807 everything came to a head.

By 1806, the Nizam-i Cedid military corps was over 20,000 strong. They were the centre of a new army that didn't require Janissaries. As we know, the core of the Janissaries had been traditionally recruited from the Balkans, the closest and most reliable source of young Christians. After centuries, this was the centre of opposition to change, the place where people felt they had the most to lose. Edirne rose in revolt. Janissary bands marched on the capital, and Selim III watched as support in his court melted away. The Janissaries demanded he disband the new army. But who would blink first? Would it be the perennially disgruntled Janissaries? Or would the great sultan demur? In the end, Selim III backed down. He acted in the way that circumstances demanded, and his decade-long plans for progress were dismantled. Things soon got worse for Selim III, who was overthrown and strangled in his own palace. His crime? It was said that he failed to respect the religion of Islam and the traditions of the Ottomans. This was a fig leaf to cover the ugly face of a coup; he was guilty of nothing more than trying to drag the Ottoman Empire into the modern world. His punishment for this set an ominous precedent, and Selim III's brother became Sultan Mustafa IV.

14

When Is a Turk Not a Turk?

Mustafa IV's brief reign was plagued by continuing insurrection from both the Balkans and the Janissaries. It seemed that the overthrow and death of Selim III had done little to cool hotter heads. It is not unfair to speculate that Mustafa might have been responsible for the death of his brother, as he apparently wanted both Selim III and his other brother, Mahmud, killed so that he would be the only heir to the throne and would therefore have to remain as sultan. This was well-founded lethal logic because, less than a year into his reign, there was yet another coup, and this time Mahmud became Sultan Mahmud II. He turned the tables on Mustafa IV by having him murdered, which meant that Mahmud II was now the only adult male heir to the House of Osman.

A portrait of someone like Ahmed III reveals a very Western style of dress and portraiture even though his clothes were clearly of Eastern origin. What is most striking about Mahmud II's portraits is that they begin with him wearing the usual garb of a sultan but, after reforms in the 1820s, he's seen wearing a Western-style military uniform. The portraits alone reveal this sultan's agenda. The reforms of Selim III were not dead, and modernisation was happening whether the Janissaries liked it or not. The cause of Westernisation was eagerly taken up by Nakşidil Sultan, one of the wives of Abdul Hamid I, who was now in the position of adopted mother to Mahmud II, when she was seen taking girls out of the harem for picnics (in *very* secluded areas, closely guarded by the sultan's bodyguards). This was a sign not only of further

Westernisation, but also that things were stable enough to allow the defenceless core of the palace out into the capital.

To the south, though, there were the problems that inevitably arise when there is a power vacuum. The French had tried to rule Egypt for three years, only to leave a mess behind when they finally departed. The Ottoman court saw this as an opportunity to reinstate more direct control, and Muhammad Ali Pasha was seen as the man for the job. The pasha was of Albanian origin but was every inch the Ottoman lord. What he did in Egypt was to play the Ottoman and Mameluke forces off against each other so that he looked like the main conciliator and gained popular backing. Once he was sure of firm local support, he declared himself to be the new ruler of Egypt while also expressing his loyalty to the court in Istanbul. About the same time as he was carving out his fiefdom in Egypt, the Saudi Arabs captured the sacred cities of Mecca and Medina. What happened next reveals the pragmatic side of Mahmud II. Rather than pushing for more direct control of Egypt, he got his subjects to fight a war he couldn't afford to fight. Mahmud II ordered Muhammed Ali Pasha to retake the Hejaz region of the Arabian peninsula from the Arabs, and, after two campaigns (and some bitter fighting), that's exactly what he did.

So there was now an Albanian Muslim convert ruling Egypt and fighting Arabs for the Muslim holy cities because the sultan in Istanbul asked him to do so. This all makes sense, right? Muhammad Ali Pasha was an example of the old system, where borders didn't matter. If you prospered under Ottoman rule, why not be an Ottoman? But in the nineteenth century something new was happening, and it was happening first in Greece. Ironically, for centuries, about a third of all Ottoman ministers and administrators had been Greek. Many of the *valide* sultans had been Greek, which meant Greek blood flowed through the veins of the sultans. As the first section of this book showed, the late Byzantine Empire was rotten to the core and was superseded by an empire that, even in the nineteenth century, was still relevant and still covered a greater area than the Byzantine Empire had for its last few centuries. But all of that was being ignored, and a new narrative of the past was being created by scholars like Neophytos Doukas, who printed (and modernised) many of the Ancient Greek classics to emphasise Greek contributions to the wider culture. Pamphlets such as *Logios Ermis* were written in Greek for Greek consumption but produced outside of the empire. They all had the same message: the Greeks were oppressed; the Greeks owed the 'Turks' nothing; Greece had been great and would be great again.

There have been a number of revolutionary and seminal trends in history, and in the nineteenth century the idea of the 'manifest destiny' was intertwined with nationalism. Many European writers of that period framed history to show the rise of the West as the inevitable pinnacle of civilisation. Great emphasis was put on the superiority of the European powers, which at the time was felt to be logical. Over the rest of the world there were only two large and ancient non-European empires in existence at this time – China and the Ottoman Empire – and both had clearly fallen behind the West in terms of knowledge, expertise, industrialisation and virtually any other significant measure. The West was surging forwards; the East was decaying and moving backwards. It was in the later nineteenth century that the Ottoman Empire became known as the 'sick man of Europe', an epithet that was then well founded.

Of course, this kind of thinking also led to racism. 'My civilisation is more advanced than yours' easily turned into 'my people are better than yours'. It was a heady brew that would have many implications across the globe. Some of the conclusions reached as a result of this seminal thinking were 'interesting', to say the least. The political philosopher Georg Hegel concluded that the pinnacle of culture was Prussia, which was never the largest empire in Europe and would later be associated with militarism and Nazism. Hegel's view can be explained by the fact that he was, of course, German.

Nationalism

If a grand narrative of European culture was being created, it needed to have come from somewhere. The start point was generally agreed to be ancient Greece. This was because that civilisation influenced Rome, and the Roman Empire had been regarded as the cultural zenith across Europe since its fall about 1,500 years earlier. All of this fed into propaganda about a Greek 'renaissance', and like all nationalist propaganda it ignored any

---

inconvenient historical facts. Ancient Greece produced some truly astonishing art, science, history and philosophy, but what is forgotten is how much the individual city states hated each other. Technically speaking, there was no such place as 'ancient Greece'. The rival city states had a language and the pantheon of gods in common, but they spent much of their time attacking each other; this was not a paradise of Greek brotherhood, nor was there much evidence of brotherly love during the Peloponnesian War. Everyone remembers that democracy was invented in Athens, but what most people don't know is that it didn't last that long and was altered and suppressed multiple times. If this is news to you, it is an indication of how this nineteenth-century Greek propaganda still echoes in the West today.

While the Greeks had a difficult relationship with the Ottoman court, this was not the first time there was friction with an empire. By AD 1400, there wasn't a lot in common between the ailing Byzantine Empire (which considered itself to be the Eastern Roman Empire) and the Athenian democracy from the Hellenic era; the lines had blurred between what was 'Greek' and what was 'Roman'. During this period Constantine XI was resurrected as the marble emperor and unofficial saint of the Orthodox Church. He may have lost Constantinople to Mehmed II, but he would rise again to lead Greece to victory over the Turks. This may be an inspiring legend about a national messiah, but it is based on the myth that Greece had previously been some kind of nirvana.

To put all of this in another context, let's move to fifteenth-century England, where peasants associated themselves with their local town. They might live in an area of Cambridgeshire, only a few days' travel from London, but any idea that they were somehow connected to London would have been as remarkable to them as being connected to Constantinople. London was just too distant, too far beyond their limited horizons. Nationalism couldn't – and didn't – exist in such circumstances, but with improved transportation, more of the world could be seen and more of history could be understood. So, by the nineteenth century, the descendants of those

Cambridgeshire peasants were proud Englishmen and subjects of the British Empire. Of course, when parts of the British Empire began to realise that they had more in common with their neighbours than with a place called London on the other side of the world, the empire began to unravel. Nationalism is the single greatest threat to an empire. It's more unstoppable than Napoleon.

In Istanbul, Mahmud II was facing this spreading threat of nationalism. When an empire was as diverse in cultures, languages and religions as the Ottoman Empire it was only ever going to shatter, but the Ottomans were in an even trickier situation than most other empires. If ancient Greece was the starting point of Western culture, why was it not under the control of one of the great Western powers? Why was it in the hands of decadent and corrupt Muslim sultans? This was an idea that grew in the West even as the idea of independence began to take hold in Greek-speaking areas of the empire.

In 1814, *Filiki Eteria*, the Society of Friends, was founded in Odessa (Russian territory at this time) along the same lines as the Freemasons, but this secret society was dedicated to the overthrow of Ottoman rule. Within five years its message had spread like wildfire until there was an extensive secret network of associated organisations not only in Greece itself but in virtually every Greek community in Europe, both in and outside of the Ottoman Empire. When there had been rebellions by Greeks in the past, the Ottomans simply allowed bandits from Albania to descend on their towns and cause enough chaos for the rebels to put down their arms. The Ottomans didn't have to raise a formal army to suppress the unrest, and the Albanians could return home with carts groaning under the weight of their plunder. To this day tensions remain between Greeks and Albanians.

Albania wasn't a very powerful country, and if a few bands of outlaws could keep the Greek rebels in check, it shows how badly Greek freedom fighters needed outside assistance to stand any chance of achieving independence. As in the case of the American Revolutionary War, during the Greek War of Independence there was a remarkable number of foreign troops (and, critically, equipment and weapons) floating around to help the cause. All of this was a little ironic as Mahmud II was the great reformer, the first sultan in centuries to make radical changes that lasted.

In 1821, Persia made a move against Ottoman-held areas of Armenia in the Caucasus. This culminated in the Battle of Erzurum in 1821, with Crown Prince Abbas Mirza of Persia at the head of a column of 30,000 troops. However, by the time the 50,000-strong Ottoman force met up with them, the Persian forces were suffering from dysentery. It should have been an easy victory for the Sublime Porte, but with the help of superior tactics and modern weapons, Abba Mirza inflicted a serious defeat. This was the main battle of the war, and while nothing changed in terms of territorial borders, the Ottoman armies were shown to be painfully far behind. The need for reform was greater than ever. Once again, the main issue was the Janissaries. In the past their insolence and intrigues had been tolerated because of their martial prowess. Now, though, they were nothing but trouble; they couldn't even win battles. So what was the point of the Janissary corps in the nineteenth century?

In 1826, Mahmud II forced the issue in the biggest gamble of his long reign. He had continued to build and develop the Nizam-i Cedid, Selim III's new elite, Western-style army of Muslim youths from Anatolia. They wore Western-style uniforms and borrowed tactics from the recently concluded Napoleonic Wars in Europe. Meanwhile, the Janissaries had 500 years of history and a vested interest in the empire; they were not going down without a fight. When 135,000 of them rose up against the sultan, the Sipahis, the Istanbul mobs and the new troops overwhelmed the Janissaries in one of the most widespread popular uprisings ever to take place in Ottoman history. The events around this coup are called Sekban-ı Cedit, which in Turkish means 'the fortunate event'. It was seen at the time as a necessity by everyone except, of course, the Janissaries, whose leaders were executed. Thousands more died in the uprising and in later, minor rebellions, while the vast majority tried to blend into the fabric of the empire. Some of the Janissaries returned to their original homes, but these Muslim converts were regarded with suspicion (and sometimes with violent hostility) by their old Balkan, Christian neighbours.

The Fez

At this point it is worth mentioning what was, perhaps, the most famous fashion item in the empire: the fez. This simple brimless cap (brimless so as not to interfere in prayer), with a tassel worn to the side, was first seen centuries before Mahmud II, but for most of the empire's duration the average male Ottoman was likely to wear a turban, even though there was a multitude of different hats that showed status or even profession. The Janissaries, with their plumed hats, instantly stood out over the centuries in Ottoman society, whereas the fez was not common until Mahmud II's drive to modernise. To differentiate his new troops from the Janissaries, it was decided that they should wear Westernised uniforms but also that, to give them an 'Ottoman' identity, they should wear the fez with a cloth band wrapped around it like a mini turban. At roughly the same time, ministers were told to stop wearing turbans and start wearing the fez, but without the cloth band. So the image of the fez as ubiquitous in the Ottoman Empire is really only true for the last century of its history.

Meanwhile, back at the uprising, what was even more striking about the events with Persia and the Janissaries was that they ran concurrently with the Greek War of Independence. It was remarkable that Mahmud II was able to deal effectively with so many different challenges during his reign, especially considering that most of the sultans from the previous century would simply have crumbled under the pressure (and the Janissaries would have either overthrown or murdered them). That's not to say that Mahmud II was able to overcome all of the problems he faced, but he did the best that almost any leader could have done under the circumstances.

That last point is important because there have been a number of mentions of the dangers inherent in fighting simultaneous wars on three fronts (and two continents). It's a minor miracle that due to a myriad of influences – and a lot of luck – this didn't happen prior to the 1820s. But it is in this context that we have to place the Greek War of Independence. When the Russians started to back the Greek rebels covertly, their role evolved into not-so-covert backing with their navy, which led to a separate but simultaneous war with

Mahmud II – on top of his war with Persia and the increasingly serious uprising in Greece. To put all of this into perspective, the rulers of semi-autonomous areas of North Africa, including Muhammad Ali of Egypt, fought for Mahmud II. The Greeks, by comparison, had formal help from France, Britain and Russia, plus volunteers and funds from various groups in other countries as well. Mahmud II had less of everything, and his allies were minnows by comparison to the mighty empires that backed Greece. It was a miracle that the whole empire didn't collapse in the 1820s; instead, it would last for another century.

Alexander Ypsilantis is seen as one of the key Greek revolutionary leaders (there are a lot of them). He is an example of the complexities behind the supposedly simple idea of 'Greece for the Greeks'. While there is no doubt that he had Greek ancestry, he also had Wallachian aristocratic blood, had spent most of his life in Russia and had started his military career in Russia fighting for the Russians against Napoleon. The ancient Spartans certainly wouldn't have recognised him as a fellow Greek. What Ypsilantis illustrated was the cosmopolitan nature of the Ottoman Empire, but that didn't matter. He felt 100 per cent Greek, had important political connections with the Russian court, was one of the founders of *Filiki Eteria* and, of course, was a battle-hardened veteran. He was exactly the person needed to spark the tinderbox. Interestingly, in what was a Greek war of independence, Ypsilantis started things in 1821 in Moldova. He realised quite quickly that while ethnic Greeks wanted to support the cause, they were not the majority in the area; there wasn't enough of a groundswell of local support to embed the insurrection, and the uprising in Moldova came to nothing.

These uprisings were brutally suppressed by the Ottomans under Mahmud II in the early years. Areas where there was rebellion could expect Ottoman troops and irregular forces of loyal Albanians and Kurds to arrive and massacre local populations. Churches were also desecrated, and while this may have been an acceptable tactic in the fifteenth century, it wasn't in the nineteenth century; indeed, it only served to confirm to the West how barbaric the 'Turks' were. (The Albanians and Kurds were simply lumped together with anything else not Greek or Western.) Putting it in modern parlance, such actions made the Ottoman Empire a pariah state. One of the most infamous (and earliest) massacres happened in 1821 in Istanbul. It's unknown exactly how many Greeks were killed but it certainly would have been in the thousands, and when an angry mob hangs the Patriarch of the Greek Orthodox Church, you know a line has been crossed. The massacres spread to other major cities in the empire: Adrianople, Smyrna, Nicosia and more. By the end of this frenzy of violence, tens of thousands of innocent Greeks lay dead. While it is likely that some of the dead supported the uprising, not all did. This was not 'justice for traitors', as I have heard some Turks suggest, but ugly sectarian violence.

Later in the war the forces of other Muslim powers (such as Egypt) carried out similar massacres on some of the Aegean islands, notably Crete. (As a brief aside, the Greek leader of the resistance in Crete was Hatzimichalis Dalianis. There can be no doubt that he was a loyal supporter of the cause, and to this day he's seen as a revolutionary martyr in Greece. But here's the thing: he's always pictured wearing a turban and looking suspiciously like an Ottoman general. His clothing is neither Western nor a throwback to the Greece of the Byzantine Empire or the Hellenic era. It's an inadvertent reminder of how generally cosmopolitan the Ottoman Empire was. This shows that even some Greeks fighting for independence didn't really know what it meant to be 'Greek' – apart from language, religion and not being 'Turkish'.) The massacre on Crete stopped the uprisings in their tracks, and Crete was to remain an Ottoman territory until 1913, which again has led to apologists arguing that the ends justify the means. But there is no justification for the sickening and dehumanising actions of the Ottoman soldiers who went on 'Greek Hunts', running down Greek peasants and rounding them up, hunting them like wild animals. Had this happened in the Middle Ages it would have been seen as normal behaviour, but by the nineteenth century armies in the West didn't carry out the random slaughters that their ancestors had carried out in the past.

Perhaps the most appalling event took place a year into the war on the island of Chios when, in 1822, the Ottoman garrison killed at least 50,000 of the island's population. It is estimated that three-quarters of the 120,000 people on the island either died or were taken into slavery. By any measure, this was a war crime. However, before the reader assumes that the Ottomans were playing to type as the callous Muslim despots, the response from the Greek rebels was hardly any better. Morea, an area that had been fought over on many occasions, was the first area of Greek territory to rebel. By now the events of 1821 were playing out in a kind of reversal of the final Ottoman conflict with Venice; the locals sided with the Greek cause, meaning that the Ottoman forces rapidly lost the countryside and had to retreat to their forts. The forts leading up to the capital of Tripolitsa (also called 'Greek Tripoli'), where most of the Muslims and the main Ottoman garrison had found refuge, were attacked in turn. When that fell, the Greeks poured in, plundered the city and carried out their own massacre. Although most Western sources refer to this as 'mob violence' or say that the Greeks 'ran riot', this reduces the seriousness of what took place. The numbers killed in this massacre were fewer than in Chios, but the fact remains that such atrocities were being carried out by both sides in the conflict, and to conjure images of a David-and-Goliath struggle would be dishonest. It should also be noted that the Jews in the so-called 'liberated' areas were either exiled or massacred; this could be because they tended to live in areas where there were Muslims and were thus caught up in the frenzy, but Judaism played no part in the reforming of a Christian Greek society so it could have been straightforward anti-Semitism.

Even without the massacres, events in the Peloponnese were a disaster for Mahmud II. Other territories had been lost in the past, but this was a central part of the empire, with access to the Aegean Sea – and the situation was to get a whole lot worse when central Greece exploded in revolution. Athens was captured and the Ottoman garrison at the Acropolis was surrounded. The people of Athens were at the mercy of rebels, and as about a half of them were Muslims, including Muslim Greeks, that was a new concern. An Ottoman army, headed by the capable but psychotic Albanian general Omer Virion, met the main Greek rebel force at Thermopylae. This was, of course, the site of the famous Greek resistance to the Persians in 480 BC, but it was such a strategically important location that it was the site of eight different battles, the last in the Second World War. This particular confrontation was the seventh Battle of Thermopylae, referred to as the Battle of Alamana.

The leader of the Greeks was the now legendary freedom fighter Athanasios Diakos. He is largely famous for what happed after the battle, because during this fight he made the fundamental error of splitting his forces. This fails ten times for every occasion on which it works, and only a general of Napoleon or Julius Caesar's calibre can carry it off. Diakos was no such general, and Virioni used his overwhelming force to keep the other parts of the Diakos army pinned down while he attacked each of the three sections of Greek rebels in turn. The Greeks routed and left Diakos with about fifty men to defend a strategic bridge. Diakos refused to retreat, intending to fight to the last man and die in battle. As his line was overwhelmed in fierce hand-to-hand fighting, his sword broke and he was captured alive. Virioni (unusually) offered clemency and made him an offer to join his forces as an officer. Diakos's response has become virtually a Greek motto: 'I was born a Greek and I will die a Greek.'

Virion had him impaled, a horrific form of medieval execution that was completely inappropriate for 1821. Diakos was still slowly dying the next day when a comrade-in-arms arrived and shot him to put him out of his misery. Diakos is, understandably, considered to be one of the great martyrs of the Greek independence movement, and the Greek flag echoes the impassioned rhetoric of the era. The number of stripes on the flag is the same as the syllables (in Greek) of the phrase 'Freedom or Death', so the national flag of Greece is a literal declaration of independence.

One of the strangest heroes of the war was the very English Lord Byron, the greatest romantic poet of the early nineteenth century, who was usually regarded as a lover, not a fighter. Like many romantic poets of his day, he felt drawn to the hallowed ground of Socrates and Plato. The Greek rebels didn't need more poets but they were perennially short of cash, and Lord Byron spent more than £10,000 (about £1 million today) financing Greek ships. He even managed to evade the Ottoman fleet on his journey to Missolonghi (in western Greece), where he died of fever. Byron was one of the most famous men in Europe, so his support for Greek independence and his eventual death in Greece brought wider attention and further support to the cause.

As territory was taken from the Ottomans, the rebels had to create their own systems of government in what was the first period of self-rule since the fourteenth century. It's unsurprising that the road to freedom wasn't exactly smooth, but, unbelievably, in the middle of fighting for freedom from the 'Turks', the various rebel groups began fighting a civil war. The sides could be roughly split between the Continental Greeks and islanders against the Peloponnesians. The war rumbled on for about a year, and the central government secured more than it conceded, but it shows the power of old rivalries and petty politics that while the new Greek government was still fighting a war with the old enemy, it was also fighting with other Greeks (a dynamic not exclusive to the Greeks and examples of which the world has seen very recently).

Even a cursory glance at a map of Greece shows the importance of the islands and the waters around them. Like the Americans in the 1770s, the Greek rebels weren't in a position to build their own navy. What they really needed was help from outside, and, as with the Americans, France came to the rescue. The fight for control of the waters around Greece culminated in the 1827 Battle of Navarino, and, as it was a naval battle, it did not end with the massacre of a local population. Navarino is a bay on the Peloponnesian coast, and it was here that an Ottoman-Egyptian fleet, anchored in a defensive crescent shape and covered by friendly shore batteries, met an allied navy of France, Britain and Russia. The Muslim navy had more ships and cannons, but their ships were outdated, and the Royal Navy was at its martial zenith against a failing Ottoman state. The British fleet was led by Admiral Codrington, a man of vast experience, who had fought in the American Revolutionary War and who had been at Trafalgar.

It was customary for the sides to get into position before battle commenced, but on this occasion the Ottoman-Egyptian fleet began its assault and released a fire ship aimed at the allies while the British were still manoeuvring (most ungentlemanly behaviour). By naval standards the two fleets were very close, and the damage to both sides was therefore considerable. HMS *Asia* and the French flagship *Sirène*, as well as another of their ships, the *Scipion*, were all heavily damaged in the furious broadsides. The French, Russian and British navies worked effectively together (a rare sentence in any history book), and while the Muslim crews fought valiantly and were by no means a soft target, their lack of modernisation and experience meant they were simply outclassed.

By the late afternoon, all of the large warships from the Muslim side had been either neutralised or captured. This left a mass of smaller ships that, while numerous, were hopelessly vulnerable to the large ships of the line of the allied fleet. Codrington twice ordered a ceasefire, but his signals were either invisible because of smoke or ignored. By 6.00 p.m. there was nothing left of the fleet of smaller ships except shattered hulls and a mass of bodies floating in the bay. The news spread like wildfire across the Peloponnese and beyond, where crowds of Greeks cheered and celebrated everywhere now under Greek control. Meanwhile, Mahmud II managed to keep an army of 40,000 Egyptian troops in the Peloponnese (the army was led by Muhammad Ali's own son), and it was then that Mahmud II played a card rarely used by the Ottoman sultans: he declared a jihad.

Jihad

Today the word 'jihad' groans under a ton of baggage because it is a term used by Muslim extremists. The word literally means 'struggle', not 'holy war'. The Qur'an states that the greatest struggle for any Muslim is to be pure in and of themselves. Therefore, every Muslim every day faces a jihad with himself to remain pure and true to the faith. The term is sometimes compared to 'crusade', but the idea of jihad is not necessarily associated with violence or a specific moment in history, which the crusades are. A jihad of war, where Muslims are duty bound to fight against non-believers, can only be conducted by the caliph, the leader of Islam. At this particular time, the Ottoman sultan was the caliph and, therefore, the correct authority to call for a jihad of war. (Today, terrorist leaders like to give themselves the title of caliph and pretend they have the authority to declare a military jihad, but that title and authority now reside in Mecca, the location of the Islamic supreme authority).

In the past, when a Muslim leader declared a jihad against various Western armies, it was almost always for political, not religious reasons. Therefore, Mahmud II was invoking a time-honoured tradition of cloaking a political decision in a veil of pious belief. As the great reformer and the man who clearly looked to the West this was a sign of desperation, but despite the fact that the sultan was also the caliph and that Muslims

---

> of the world should rally to the cause, nothing much happened outside the empire. India, Afghanistan, Indonesia and Malaya all had millions of Muslims, but there was absolutely no appetite to fight for Mahmud II or to overthrow their (largely) British imperial rulers. Mahmud II's jihad was something of a damp squib.

If you can believe it, the situation got worse. When the Russians, with a 100,000 strong army, invaded along the Black Sea coast, they took the major port of Varna and continued to advance further south. Following the Battle of Navarino, peace terms stated that the 40,000-strong army should go back to Egypt, which left Muhammad Ali in a bind: should he follow the agreement and succumb to the realities of the situation? If he did so, it would mean that he was a Muslim ruler ignoring the caliph's call to jihad and, at the same time, that he was leaving his son with no choice but an ignominious retreat. I trust that the reader now has a strong sense of the violence and chaos that erupted across the empire during the 1820s. Neighbour turned on neighbour, and rampaging armies (Russian, Greek, Egyptian and Ottoman) stalked through the Balkans, bringing misery with them. The Ottoman Empire was surrounded; it was an empire on the brink of collapse.

When those involved had exhausted themselves with blood and battle, many were ready to sign treaties. Under the Treaty of Adrianople (1829), parts of Armenia and Serbia achieved autonomy. It gave Russia most of the eastern and western shores of the Black Sea, including the strategically important mouth of the Danube. Russia continued to occupy Moldavia and Wallachia and to spread its influence ever closer to the Ottoman capital, in essence holding these territories to ransom until the Ottomans paid a huge indemnity to free them. This was all agreed in 1829, and took some of the pressure from Mahmud II, but any official agreement with Greece had yet to be ratified.

While the fighting ended in 1829, Greece did not become a newfound paradise just because the 'Turks' had been ejected. The first head of state, Count Ioannis Kapodistrias, lasted roughly a year before being assassinated – not by Turks, but by disgruntled Greeks. The fate of the new nation did not lie in Athens or Istanbul, but in London. The 1832 Convention of London formalised the independence of the nation and showed how big a part the major powers played in forging the new Greece. The good news was that they got a new king, and the not-at-all Greek Prince Otto of Bavaria became King Otto of Greece. It was also decided that there should be a formal treaty to end the war and recognise the new state, so the Treaty of Constantinople was drawn up and signed in Istanbul. The new country of Greece was not the country that exists today. It covered the Peloponnese, central Greece (including Athens) and the island of Euboea as well as most of the islands in the Aegean. The Ionian Islands, Crete, Cyprus and northern Greece (areas such as Macedonia) were still Ottoman. A great chunk had been torn out of the Ottoman Empire, but it could have been a lot worse for Mahmud II.

15

The Church Ornament That Started a War

Mahmud II started his reign with Janissaries, a unified Balkans and an empty treasury. By the end of his reign, he had finally been able to carry out the much-needed reforms of his army and navy (the empire got its first steamship under his rule). For over a century the sultan had been the figurehead for a system that was controlled from behind the scenes. The eighteenth-century Ottoman Empire can be summarised by saying that the sultans lost their authority to the Janissaries, the grand viziers and various court intrigues. Mahmud II had successfully retrieved much of the imperial authority, but he had been brought to his knees by wars on all frontiers. To make matters worse, he now had a new nation within a few days' march of his capital, a nation that was itching to invade and conquer. It's hard to see Mahmud II as anything but a failure, but he did the best he could in an impossible situation and certainly acquitted himself better than a number of his recent predecessors.

Mahmud II died peacefully in 1839, and the sultanate passed without incident to his son, Abdülmecid, who inherited a war between Egypt and the Ottomans, showing that there were limits to Muhammad Ali's loyalty. Backing the Ottomans were Britain, Austria, Russia and Prussia, some of whom had been at war with Mahmud II barely a decade earlier. The reason for the change of sides was the age-old problem of too much power vested in any one place. It was a sign that the Ottoman Empire's days were numbered, but also that no one nation would allow its overnight collapse either. While the empire was greatly diminished, it was still significant in size. The North African fiefdoms, which had always been loosely associated with the empire, were now all but independent (North Africa, while out of direct control, still paid tribute annually), and other losses have already been discussed. However, looking at the areas that remained in the empire and using the names of modern countries, the empire still consisted of most of Bulgaria, parts of Romania, Albania, Cyprus, roughly half of modern Greece's territory and islands, Turkey, Western Armenia, Syria, Iraq, Kuwait, Jordan, the coastal area and religious sites of Saudi Arabia, Qatar and Palestine/Israel. Compared to the size of the Byzantine Empire in its last century, the difference is startling. Also, most of this territory remained in Ottoman hands right up to the last days of the empire.

It was at this point that Prussia became involved for the first time in the affairs of the Sublime Porte. Their chief representative was General Helmuth Karl Bernhard Graf von Moltke, who was Chief of Staff for the Prussian Army for thirty years and uncle to Helmuth Johann Ludwig von Moltke, a German commander in the First World War. This was the start of a military alliance that would last for generations to come. However, unlike the Greeks, the Ottomans still did not achieve victory with all this international support, showing that their army still had a long way to go. Although Muhammad Ali had to renounce claims to Syria, he and his descendants were recognised as the legitimate rulers of Egypt, meaning any pretence that Egypt was part of Ottoman territory was over.

The grand alliance mentioned above was a sign of the political realities of the time and something that Abdülmecid embraced. He had gone to university in Europe (a first for a sultan) and could speak fluent French (another first and, as it was the international language of diplomacy, very useful too), so he was eager to continue, as his father would have wished, to modernise, Westernise and adapt to the political realities of the nineteenth century. The sultans had always been rather remote figures, sitting behind palace walls, talking only to officials or being even more introverted and remaining in the harem. The most contact a sultan would have had with the common people was in going on campaign, and a sultan hadn't done that in a very long time. Therefore it was a breath of fresh air and a sign of how seriously

Abdülmecid took his role (and the situation in the empire) that he now had regular meetings with petitioners on Fridays. This was a major change of protocol for a sultan. These attempts to connect with his subjects evolved into a number of tours to the Balkans, some of the islands and a number of towns and cities. At last the people of the empire could see their sultan, and some even had meetings to express their grievances and concerns. Abdülmecid had seen what nationalism and popular uprisings could do, even in the Ottoman heartlands, and he understood that his actions were for the good of the empire. Some of the northern areas of the Balkans were still technically Ottoman, but in reality they were all but ruled by Russia, which continued to interfere on matters regarding the rights of Orthodox Christians in the empire and attempted to undermine the sultan's authority at pretty much every possible opportunity. The war in Egypt and the continued minor rebellions across the empire showed the need for a unifying glue to hold the empire together. Sultan Abdülmecid tried to make himself that glue.

Had the empire not had a huge meltdown in the 1820s, it is likely that Mahmud II would have had more success with his reforms. However, it was on Abdülmecid's watch that the Ottoman Empire really began transforming for the first time in centuries. This was a reminder that real power was once again wielded by the sultans. The Ottoman Empire had diminished under insane or distracted rulers, with too many coups and plots to keep a consistently reliable government in place. With the reigns of Mahmud II and Abdülmecid, the empire enjoyed a fifty-year period of capable rule.

Early on in his reign, in 1856, Abdülmecid announced the Islahat Fermani. This was an enhancement of the 1839 edict called the Tanzimât Fermânı (Imperial Edict of Reorganisation), although its other title, which translates as the Supreme Edict of the Rosehouse, sounds wonderfully poetic. This was the core of the modernisation and introduced the new concept of 'Ottomanism'. It was spearheaded by the highly capable Grand Vizier Mustafa Reşid Pasha. The edict had three main objectives. The first was the overhaul of the tax system, which was vital – dull, but vital. The level of detail showed that the sultan was serious about reform and that rather than changing the dressing and pretending everything was fine, the whole financial system was completely transformed.

One very sensible idea was to levy tax proportionate to wealth rather than to levy one flat rate for all. This made the tax liability on poor farmers less of a burden.

The second objective tackled the issue of conscription. After the Janissaries were disbanded, an army was still needed, and great care was taken to include European Christians in the system. But now they had a choice. They could join if they wanted to, or pay the traditional *cizye*, the tax for non-believers. These innovations meant that the third objective, under the heading of Ottomanism, which guaranteed the rights of all Ottoman subjects regardless of religion or ethnicity, would be easier to implement and that greater stability and security would follow. After the Greek War of Independence, Abdülmecid was painfully aware that what had happened in Greece could happen in Cyprus or Bulgaria or further afield in Baghdad. Ottomanism was a rather shrewd counter to local nationalism. Great emphasis was put on how all peoples of the empire were equal under the law and had equal opportunities. In essence it was screaming, 'There's no need to break away from the mother empire; you've never had it so good.' This was a vital response to the fact that at the start of the nineteenth century about 40 per cent of the population of this Islamic empire was Christian. While there was a genuine argument for staying together, it was becoming harder to ignore more clearly defined ethnic and religious identities.

In the meantime, Greece was hardly going from strength to strength. Mobs, government officials and courtiers argued about the constitution. There was widespread corruption, and government bonds became worthless through gross economic incompetence, making it harder for the fledgling state to finance much-needed infrastructure projects. It seemed that no one was happy with King Otto, and when he attempted to become an absolute ruler within the first few years of his rule, the uprising against him forced his abdication in 1862. It took about a year to find a replacement, and again a man with no Greek blood was chosen: Prince Wilhelm of Denmark became the Greek George I. George was able to expand the borders of Greece by bringing the Ionian Islands as a coronation gift from Britain. At a time when Abdülmecid was trying to promote the concept of Ottomanism, instability in Greece probably helped his argument.

On the front line of the reforms, observers of the empire liked to say that they were too little, too late. It's a great line, but the situation was far more complicated than that. There can be no doubt that the results of the reforms were patchy. The reorganisation of the government and army worked well, but broader reforms had varying success. Some of the laws that were implemented were progressive even by today's standards. Homosexuality was legalised in an era when it was still a crime in Western Europe. Also, there was a wonderfully pragmatic religious ruling on contraception. The argument was simple: birth control does not interfere with Allah's plans because the creator of the universe cannot be thwarted by man's interventions. This undeniably logical statement put an end to any opposing views (and is an argument that the Catholic Church might want to consider).

By the end of his reign, Abdülmecid had an early version of parliament, banknotes in a new currency of Ottoman Lira (rather than coins), a reformed military and a ministry for education. Slave markets were abolished and there was talk of a railway to Mecca to help pilgrims make the haj. Despite all this, it is fair to say that the empire still had a long way to go. It is also fair to say that the empire was constantly short of money to fund these changes. Putting it simply, in one generation Ottoman society had moved on from its medieval malaise, but it still lagged behind Western Europe.

The empire was still poor at the end of Abdülmecid's reign, and divisions defined by religion and ethnicity still flared up. The massacre of Christian communities happened all too frequently and showed a general ambivalence on the part of local Ottoman authorities to protect all peoples of the empire – which is what Abdülmecid had desired and decreed. But, despite its shortcomings, the Tanzimât (reorganisation) era was a definable period in late Ottoman history that proved the Ottomans were capable of implementing reforms that were more than window dressing.

Palaces

Despite his desire to drag the empire forward and the lack of funds that dogged the total fulfilment of his objectives, Abdülmecid felt no need to curb his personal spending. The man loved luxury, and the symbol of his extravagant spending (and his desire to modernise) can be seen in Dolmabahçe Palace. For the vast majority of the empire's sultans, home had been Topkapı, but that had been constructed in the fifteenth century (and continually modified and extended over the centuries). It was beautiful, but Eastern in its design and medieval in its comforts. There was an argument for a more modern palace to reflect the sultan's more modern outlook, but with a general shortage of funds and, specifically, with a shortage of funds for reforms, could the empire afford a new palace? Of course it could. Adjusting the figures for inflation, more than £1 billion was spent in the construction of this Baroque/Rococo monstrosity. Dolmabahçe Palace was said to have been built to prove that the Ottomans still had the resources to undertake such a grand enterprise – and bankrupted the empire in the process. It isn't quite as neat as that, but, as a result of this profligate spending, the currency was partly debased and some of the loans from Britain and France, designed to help with modernisation (and fighting the Crimean War), were spent on a double-horseshoe crystal staircase and the world's largest collection of Baccarat crystal chandeliers, including a ridiculously enormous one that weighs 4.5 tons.

Whereas the architecture of Sinan is rightly lauded around the globe, this late display of imperial power by the sultans is not highly regarded (or even regarded) by any architectural historians. The building is a lavish take on the sultan's concept of what constituted a grand European palace, but the detailing is a nightmare combination of the Islamic, the neoclassical and the ephemeral. The result can be summarised with the phrase 'more is more'– and it didn't fool anyone. No foreign ambassador saw it as a sign that the empire had returned to its glory days. The Ottoman subjects needed good governance and a healthy economy, not crystal chandeliers.

After thirteen years of construction, the palace was finished in 1856, the same year the Crimean War ended. It became the new seat of imperial power and would remain so (with only a few breaks) until the end of the empire. Today the queues for Topkapı Palace are always much longer than those for Dolmabahçe, still the unloved palace of the Ottomans. For such a seemingly modern palace, electricity was added only after

> Abdülmecid's reign, but the lights are never switched on because
> no insurance company will cover the building in the event of an
> electrical fire. It seems the only person who was happy with this
> white elephant was Abdülmecid.

Meanwhile, it's worth looking at the sultan's intended reforms
in a wider context. At this time, there were only two global
powers outside of Europe: the Ottomans and the Qing dynasty
in China. Both had come to realise that the Western powers had
enormous technological advantages over their civilisations, so
deeply rooted in the past. China decided that it had won the
moral argument and did nothing to modernise as it watched
its empire shatter under the hammer of change. The Ottoman
Empire, on the other hand, decided to act, and the changes were
wide-ranging. One other contemporary parallel is with Russia,
which vacillated wildly between tradition and reform, meaning
that any progress was usually turned back by the next tsar. Even
though Russia's zenith had been more recent, by 1900 both
Russia and the Ottoman Empire were notably past their prime –
and Abdülmecid still hadn't dealt effectively with the rising tide
of nationalism.

Nor was Ottomanism having much success in overcoming
religious identities, as was being demonstrated all too readily by
the Christians of the empire. The levels of animosity among the
Christian sects in Jerusalem have already been highlighted, but they
weren't any better in Bethlehem at the Church of the Nativity, the
site of the cave (let's not go into the how-a-stable-became-a-cave
argument) where Jesus was said to have been born. This is one of
the holiest places on earth for Christians, but by the late 1840s,
after having been hit by two earthquakes in recent years, it had
fallen into disrepair. That didn't stop it being a hotbed of religious
power politics. The Roman Catholic powers wanted to share the
keys to the doors of the church, but the Armenian and Orthodox
churches would not agree.

In order to please Napoleon III of France (nephew of the
original Napoleon), the Ottomans allowed the French to present
a silver star ornament to the Church of the Nativity, a sign,
said the French, of their intention to protect the Catholics of
the Middle East. Although it was true that the Roman Catholic
power had been a recent ally, more Ottoman subjects were

Orthodox or Armenian Christian, so when Russia objected to the placement of the star as a symbol of Catholic supremacy, the Ottomans removed it – an act which insulted the French. Abdülmecid's attempts to remain neutral in this Christian dispute were overtaken by the pettiness of those involved, so, with no resolution in sight, the sultan did what any politician in a similarly tricky situation would do: he set up a commission. This group of Christians argued bitterly on multiple subjects for five years, and still they couldn't agree on anything. At some point in the proceedings, the silver star 'disappeared' from the church. The Catholics blamed the Orthodox Christians (who were probably responsible), and it was the turn of the Orthodox Christians to be insulted.

If you are wondering why this ridiculously petty scenario is given space in this book, it's because the disappearance of the ornament was the trigger for the Crimean War. Of course, the war itself was less about church ornaments and more about vying political interests between the great powers of Europe. Unfortunately, when France, Russia and Britain flexed their muscles, the Russian army and navy sent an invading force to Ottoman territory.

The Crimean War of 1853–56 was the first major European war since the Napoleonic era. It took many powers by surprise, with Austria and Prussia thinking a diplomatic solution could be found while real fighting was going on. Indeed, the confusion around the war has led its misnomer. It's called the 'Crimean War' because the Crimea is where most of the land battles took place, but there were naval engagements in the Baltic Sea, the Balkans, the Black Sea and the Pacific (against eastern Russian territory), and there was fighting in the Caucasus too. At the time it was referred to by most combatant nations as the 'Russian War', which is probably a better name for it.

Field Marshal Ivan Paskevich and General Mikhail Gorchakov marched an 80,000-strong Russian army into the Danubian Principalities (Moldavia and Wallachia). These had been under Russian 'protection' for decades, and now the dithering around Christian rights gave Russia the excuse it had been seeking to invade these areas and seize real control. But Russian logistics were still behind the times, and within months the army was less than half its original size as men deserted or died of disease. Omar Pasha led a small column of Ottoman troops towards the Russians and managed to push them back, but the victories were minor ones. The best that could be said for the Ottoman forces was that they didn't collapse.

In Russia there are sixteen days of Military Honour (some are national holidays), days set aside every year to commemorate multiple victories over many centuries against many enemies. The Battle of Sinop is one so commemorated, although when compared to other great clashes (such as that against the Mongols in their prime, or the siege of Stalingrad) it does seem to be an overreaction to a fairly forgettable naval engagement, remembered, if at all, for the fact that it was the last battle involving fleets of sailing ships. However, that's not to take away from a comprehensive Russian victory. The Ottoman fleet was anchored in Sinop Bay (on the northern coast of Anatolia, so the first battle of the 'Crimean War' was hundreds of miles away from the Crimean peninsula) and was protected by shoreline forts. Russian Admiral Pavel Nakhimov led his ships into the bay under fire, and his crews skilfully lined up to engage the Ottoman vessels. Nakhimov was so precise in his orders that his warships covered the entire harbour with interlocking fields of fire. While the ships on both sides dated from the old era of sail, the artillery on board the Russian ships were the new Paixhans guns, and they were not like the usual cannons. The cannon had, for centuries, fired solid projectiles: cannon balls, canisters of ball bearings or chain shot. These new guns were the first naval cannons to fire shells, explosive rounds that did damage not just from the projectiles but from violent chemical reactions leading to explosions. The Russian guns simply blasted the opposition wooden ships to splinters or set them on fire. All but one Ottoman ship was sunk or run aground.

It was a comprehensive victory, showing Nakhimov's skill, but it isn't considered one of the great naval battles of history. Regardless, one of Abdülmecid's fleets now lay at the bottom of Sinop Bay. This meant that a Russian fleet could sail into the Ottoman capital unopposed, and from there could link up with the Russian army in Wallachia. The defeat was so emphatic that the French and British press claimed that the Russians had ambushed the Ottoman fleet, which was not true.

The events of October and November of 1853 showed that Abdülmecid's attempts to modernise the navy had not paid off with the dividends both he and his allies had expected. France and Britain could stand by and watch Russia's (likely) capture of the Ottoman capital, or they could engage. The Russian intervention in the Danubian Principalities was a clear violation of earlier treaties and gave a credible reason to go to war – and then the Greeks joined the Russians. This was technically a revolt against their Ottoman overlords rather than a declaration of war, but it was the right thing for the fledgling Greek state to do. Russia was their ally, the Ottoman Empire was their enemy, and there were still millions of ethnic Greeks under Ottoman rule. This was seen as a chance for Greece to expand her borders. The bizarre reality was that all of the major powers (bar Russia) that had allowed Greece to create an independent state now needed to help the Ottomans avoid fighting a war on two fronts. It was a remarkable and genuine reversal. Napoleon III told Otto of Greece that an attack on Ottoman territory would be considered an attack on France, and while Prussia and Austria remained neutral in the shooting war, they backed France and Britain's threat to call in the international loan used to fund the creation of the Greek state. The pressure was unbearable, and Greece had no option but to back down – but that didn't stop more than a thousand Greeks joining their Russian 'cousins' in the fight against the Ottomans on the Danubian frontier. After the war, the survivors of these two Greek battalions were banned from returning home and had to resettle in Russia. A crisis had been averted, and now the Western powers changed their strategy from one of political pressure to one of military power.

The Crimean War is remembered in Britain as a mainly British affair. It is acknowledged that the French were also fighting and that there were some Ottoman troops acting as stretcher-bearers or something like that, but it was largely about 'the thin red line' and the historic clashes, such as the Battle of Balaclava. This was not the case. While British efforts were considerable and British forces fought bravely and suffered through horrific conditions, some 200,000 British servicemen fought in the war compared to 300,000 Ottoman troops and 400,000 Frenchmen (Sardinia also joined in as they wanted to keep France happy; their small contingent acquitted themselves well). This meant that nearly a million allied troops were moved around a continent (with some naval assets in the Pacific) against more than 700,000 Russians. It was the clashes in the Baltic that were the most worrisome for Russia. Saint Petersburg was then the capital (not Moscow), and was as vulnerable as Istanbul to a potential maritime invasion. Also, most of Russia's exports and imports flowed through the Baltic shipping lanes, and a blockade greatly reduced the much-needed income from exports. Russia could still move goods overland, but that took considerable time and effort.

The siege of Kars was the most important engagement in the campaign in the Caucasus. When General William Fenwick Williams arrived in the ancient city, he was not impressed with what he found. The garrison was much smaller than had been reported, poorly equipped and populated by raw, demoralised recruits whose pay was in arrears. Williams put all his efforts in turning the situation around, and by the time the Russians made their anticipated move he had a force of 17,000 Anglo-Ottoman soldiers ready to defend the city. The initial Russian attack, which was meant to sweep away all resistance, was easily fought off, and the Russians were so taken aback by the stout opposition that an invading army morphed into a besieging force. This had never been the plan. The idea had been to mop up Ottoman cities and towns in the Caucasus and then invade Anatolia, forcing Ottoman troops in the Crimea to redirect to defend their heartland. Instead, the siege of Kars lasted five months into the winter of 1855.

The besieged forces repelled a number of concerted attacks by the Russians. Food became scarce, and medical facilities were worse than rudimentary. Some Ottoman troops were found dead at their posts – sometimes from snipers, other times from exposure. Once snow began to fall there was no chance of a relief force coming to save the day, but the Russian attack had also bogged down. The desperation felt towards the end of the siege can be seen in Williams's diary: 'We divide our bread with the starving townspeople ... I kill horses in my stable secretly and send the meat to the hospital, which is now very crowded.'

A few weeks later Kars surrendered, and the Russians were horrified to see the state of the townsfolk and the defenders when they entered the city on 28 November. They might have won the siege, but the prize had not been worth the effort; the delaying action had stopped the threat of an Anatolian invasion by a now exhausted and freezing Russian army.

Meanwhile, the allies had their own epic siege to worry about with the Siege of Sevastopol. So far this strategically important Russian port had successfully resisted all attempts to capture it and its Black Sea fleet. The Russians knew they had to keep it as no other port under their control would be a viable substitute. For the allies, capturing Sevastopol would neuter Russian naval dominance in the Black Sea. This was the siege neither side could afford to lose. The Russians attacked the allied forces positioned to shield the ongoing siege. This led to the Battle of Balaclava (a Black Sea port). As part of their defences the allies had built a number of earthworks (redoubts), most of which were manned by Ottoman troops. Lord Raglan (the geriatric allied leader who had a habit of calling the enemy 'the French', much to the disgust of their French allies) arrived two hours late to this battle and claimed that the Ottoman troops panicked and fled. This is not what happened.

The main thrust of the Russian attack centred on a redoubt almost exclusively manned by 500 Ottoman troops who had been under fierce cannon fire for hours, with no support. Eventually, after losing a third of their men, they were overwhelmed. The British fared little better as this was the clash that led to the legendary (and legendarily pointless) Charge of the Light Brigade. However, this was also the battle that produced the term 'the thin red line'. Thanks to the professional and highly effective volley fire of the Scottish 93rd Highland Regiment, a small force of men routed a Russian cavalry charge (the figure of speech now refers to any thinly spread military unit holding firm against attack). This battle is a classic example of the fact that many mistakes are made in war and that victory comes from making fewer than the enemy. The result of the battle was inconclusive. While the allied redoubts had been captured, and the allies had seen the British Light Cavalry charge into the 'Valley of Death', the Russian losses had been as heavy as those of the allies, yet no breakthrough was made on either side. At the time Tsar Nicholas I portrayed it as a great Russian victory, but two weeks later, at the Battle of Inkerman, the result was indisputable. British and French forces were outnumbered almost 4:1, but it was the allies who won an emphatic victory when the Russians attacked in fog and lost more than 10,000 men.

The Siege of Sevastopol rumbled on for a whole year. The port was able to receive regular supplies and at one point had more than 400 cannons on the walls, ready to make life hell for the besiegers. Like the Crimean War itself, the siege is remembered in Britain as a largely Anglo-French affair, but the Ottomans were there with a force of 60,000 – twice the British numbers. The defence of the port was led by Vladimir Kornilov and Pavel Nakhimov (the hero of Sinop). Kornilov was to die during battle, but the two navy men proved to be as talented on land as they were at sea. Most of the well-known battles of the war concerned the defence of allied supply lines as they besieged the port.

The Battle of Chernaya was another battle linked to the siege and is much less well remembered in Britain, primarily because the allies doing the fighting were the French, the Ottomans and the Sardinians. This allied force of 47,000 men met a Russian army of 58,000, which again chose to attack during foggy conditions. The Russian forces were mainly militia rather than regular army, and the allies showed them what happens when trained soldiers meet a poorly organised mob. Effective artillery and musket fire brought down waves of Russians. The Russian forces broke and fled, having achieved nothing – which proved that the Ottoman soldiers were more than stretcher-bearers.

The Crimean War shows how far the Ottoman forces had come in a couple of generations. The Battle of Mount Tabor had happened just over fifty years earlier, when an archaic Ottoman army met modern French forces and the tiny French force had annihilated the massive Ottoman army for the loss of just two men. Much had changed since then, and although the Ottomans were still second-rate compared to the French and the British soldiers of the time, they were now regarded as a serious fighting force once more. It was a sign that Abdülmecid's and Mahmud II's drives for change were having tangible results, although the state of the garrison in Kars prior to British intervention showed the transformation was by no means complete.

Letters Home

An area that isn't given much attention in this war is the letters sent home by the Ottoman troops. They were a positive sign of a general increase in literacy. The foot soldiers of any power weren't doing much in the way of letter writing in the 1600s, but by the time of the Crimean War enough people could read and write to make correspondence the norm. However, the letters and the reading of them highlighted a problem with written Ottoman Turkish. The troops were writing about the grim conditions on the frontlines (something that every nation acknowledged), but the prose and style of Ottoman Turkish in the nineteenth century had become so florid and so complex that the recipients understood them to say that conditions at the front were good and the men were doing well. When the intention of what is being written is completely lost on the reader, the language is no longer fit for purpose. It would take the end of the empire to change the written language, so, for the time being, written Ottoman Turkish remained imprecise and unwieldy.

On 7 September 1855, allied guns pounded Sevastopol with a colossal bombardment. The next day two sectors of the city were attacked: Malakoff by the French, and the Great Redan by the British. The Ottomans were not involved in these final, breathtakingly bloody assaults. The British threw some amazingly brave men into the hell that was the Great Redan. The city's series of gun emplacements had repelled all before them, but it was with renewed vigour that the British attacked one last time. The fighting was insanely fierce. Major Augusta Welsford had his head torn off when a single cannon fired on him at point-blank range. The Russians clung on, but their losses had been heavier than those of the British.

At Malakoff the French similarly assaulted a staunchly defended Russian redoubt. This one also had a thick tower with five cannons that could fire down on the attackers. The French charged and captured the Russian defences but were thrown out of the trenches by a ferocious counter-attack. The fate of the battle hung in the balance as Russians and Frenchmen fought with knives, bayonets and swords because the men were too close and the action too fast for them to have time to reload their muskets. Eventually the French held their gains, and while the Russians had been triumphant at the Great Redan, the defeat at Malakoff meant their defensive ring was shattered. After nearly a year of brutal fighting in terrible conditions, Sevastopol fell to the allies the next day. The wounded of these numerous battles in and around Sevastopol were sometimes treated in field hospitals near the front lines, but others were treated at Mary Seacole's 'hotel' (which was actually on the Crimean peninsula), or at Florence Nightingale's hospital in Scutari (in Ottoman territory on the shores of the Bosphorus).

Sevastopol is more than 1,300 miles south of Saint Petersburg, so the new tsar, Alexander II (who was crowned the day the final bombardment of Sevastopol started), needn't have worried unduly. Russia could absorb the losses, and the chance of an allied march to other cities was unlikely as the Russian winter was lurking. In theory, Russia could have fought on, but there were other considerations. Russia had lost 500,000 men in the war, including most of its trained troops. It had millions more men, but they were poorly trained and equipped militia. The trade embargo was shrinking the Russian economy, and while Russia had fought bravely, it was doing most of the fighting on its own territory and gaining nothing in return. Even the men in Wallachia had been pushed back (but not by much), showing that any hope of a lightning-fast strike on the Ottoman capital was nothing but fantasy. Alexander II was (by the standards of a tsar) a peaceful man who did not want the war. The fall of Sevastopol therefore marked the end of major conflict in the Crimean War.

'Firsts'

While not directly related to Ottoman history, this war saw a number of firsts. William Howard Russell became the first war correspondent, sending dispatches back to *The Times*. It was also the first time a war had been documented with photographs, and as the soldiers had been ordered to stop shaving (to reduce infections) they had, unusually for soldiers of the day, bushy beards, which became the fashion for all men (and is why there is so much facial hair in the American Civil War, which took place a few years later). The Victoria Cross was created to honour the bravery of soldiers of any rank (in the past only officers received medals), and every Victoria Cross is forged from one of the Russian brass cannons captured at the siege of Sevastopol. It was also the first war to use a steam engine, not in battle, but to take supplies from the fleet to the front lines. Thanks to the freezing temperatures, balaclavas (from the Battle of Balaclava), the protective helmet-like headgear, were widely used for the first time by British soldiers.

In addition to these 'firsts', the Ottomans invented something during the war that would go on to have widespread usage. The fighting in the trenches and the poor supply lines meant that soldiers' clay tobacco pipes were being broken faster than they could be replaced. While cigars and forms of cigarettes that involved wrapping a tobacco leaf around loose tobacco existed at this time, pipes were still the main way most people smoked tobacco. It was some enterprising Ottoman soldiers who decided to roll the tobacco in newspaper or the cartridge paper used to fire their muskets – and so gave birth to the modern cigarette.

The result of the Crimean War was the Treaty of Paris in 1856, and this can be seen as the agreement that re-established Ottoman power. The empire had been on the slide for 200 years, and in the last fifty to sixty years had become an embarrassment. The treaty was a humiliation for Russia, which lost its political influence over the Danubian Principalities as well as the areas around the mouth of the Danube that had once been Ottoman territory. The Black Sea became a demilitarised zone, neutralising the Russian fleet, and islands in the Baltics were also demilitarised. The city of Kars was returned to the Ottomans. Britain recognised the importance of the Ottoman contribution to the war and made Abdülmecid a Knight of the Order of the Garter, the highest honour Britain could confer. In contrast to a stance that had prevailed over centuries, the West was now trying to make the Ottoman Empire feel like part of the Western powers (which it was). While by no means an equal partner or even a key power, it had much to offer the West: a counter-balance to Russia, access to the eastern Mediterranean and the Black Sea trade routes as well as influence on two continents. The sultans, for so long seen as 'other' and leaders to be ignored, were now players at the table of global diplomacy.

The strategic gains for the Ottomans were at the expense of the Russians, but it was the loss of internal influence within the Ottoman Empire that Russia felt most keenly. Russia could no longer claim to be the guardian of Christians and Christian shrines. That honour (and power) now lay with France. Going all the way back to the missing silver star in the Church of the Nativity, at the end of the war in which half a million had died, the star miraculously reappeared in the church. So all the bloodshed had been worth it ...

16

Changing Tides

In 1859, riots and unrest began to break out across Lebanon and spread into Syria, and in 1860 this civil disorder turned into a full-scale war. The fighting was split between Muslims, Druze (a separate ethnicity and religion in the area) and Christians, but the alliances, such as they were, varied. The Ottoman central government had always depended on local leaders to resolve local issues, something they had failed to do when the fighting turned into multiple massacres. Approximately 20,000 Christians were killed by the Druze (showing that violence in the Middle East wasn't always Muslim *versus* Christian), and hundreds of Christian churches and villages were destroyed. Abdülmecid allowed a French-led coalition of Austrian, British, French, Prussian and Russian forces into the area. The result was good news for Lebanon, which became semi-independent, and good news/bad news for Abdülmecid. The great powers were willing to engage the Ottomans rather than simply blame them, which was good news, but the bad news was that an empire in need of external help was signalling weakness.

Abdülmecid died peacefully in 1861, and the title of sultan passed to his half-brother, Abdülaziz (another son of Mahmud II), who had grown up in Dolmabahçe Palace and wasn't interested in building any more palaces. His passion was classical music (he was an accomplished composer in his own right), but he was also a skilled archer and an excellent wrestler too. However, and more importantly, once again there was a sultan who recognised a pressing need for reforms and modernisation. Under Abdülaziz the Ottoman navy was restructured and developed to the extent that by time he died it was the third-largest fleet in the world, surpassing the likes of Russia, the United States and Prussia. The ships were modern steamers, a sign that with naval advancements there was no chance of another Battle of Sinop. Abdülaziz was an ambitious sultan and his greatest achievements were those in the field of diplomacy. It was fortunate that at the time the Russian tsar was Alexander II, who was similarly minded to talk first and attack second. Abdülaziz managed to patch up relations with Egypt, and, while it remained autonomous, Egypt now paid a most welcome annual tribute to the Ottoman tax coffers.

Abdülmecid may have been the first sultan to tour the empire and meet the people, but it was Abdülaziz who was the first to travel outside the empire to meet with other leaders. This included a meeting with Queen Victoria, who was not too eager to meet him but, in her own words, would endure it as 'the Sultan was not likely to come again'. The meeting was a political success, and another sultan became a Knight of the Order of the Garter. Christian societies in England were quick to point out the Muslim massacres that the sultan had done little or nothing to stop, but the general population was more interested in seeing the exotic sultan from the East – and he was reminder of the victories of the Crimean War. At the time Britain was far richer than the Ottoman Empire, but Britain has never done ostentation in quite the same way as Eastern monarchs, so while the family silver was on display there were also things that money (almost) couldn't buy, such as the latest in Industrial Revolution technology. Abdülaziz and his entourage were whisked around on fast trains, the marvel of the era, and were shown various Royal Navy ships, all the best in their class and, of course, part of the world's largest fleet. The sultan's tour also took in the courts of France, Prussia and Austria-Hungary. Abdülaziz was sending out the message that he was 'one of them', another imperial power of Europe. Accompanying him was his young nephew, Abdul Hamid, later Abdul Hamid II, who always had fond memories of the way he was treated by the court in Vienna, which was quite remarkable considering that his ancestors had twice planted their lances of war on the walls of that city, a fact not forgotten in Austria.

Insults

That's not to say every diplomatic meeting went well. When Napoleon III's wife, Empress Eugénie, visited the sultan at Dolmabahçe, she (no doubt unintentionally) offended his mother, Pertevniyal Sultan, who slapped the empress in the face. The incident caused quite a stir and could have had serious political repercussions, but things were quickly smoothed over.

Meanwhile, Abdülaziz was so impressed with the technology he had seen during his travels that he returned home to further modernise not only the Ottoman military, but general communications as well. It was under his rule that the empire's postal system was updated to use stamps. While a few local railways had existed prior to his reign, Abdülaziz had seen the value of an integrated rail network and invested in a rail system that greatly reduced the time required to travel across the western reaches of the empire. Although the cost was enormous, the railway became a symbol of Ottoman practicality and progressiveness, unlike Dolmabahçe Palace, which was expensive and without benefit to the people of the empire who had paid for it.

By 1870, however, a key figure in the reform movement, Mehmed Fuad Pasha, had died. Fuad Pasha had been foreign minister, and was therefore part of the government body tasked, among other things, with finding an international response to the massacres in Lebanon. Not only that, he had been the driving force behind the Tanzimât reforms. Abdülaziz had lost a powerful ally, and progressive reforms slowed noticeably after the pasha's death. A year later and Prussia and France were at war with each other (which would end Napoleon III's rule). The gears of power were changing, and Ottoman efforts to build influence and assistance over a generation seemed now to be on the wrong side of that change.

Things got worse. In 1873, there was a drought in Anatolia and the crops failed. Then, in 1875, due to the expense of the new navy, plus his own spending on top of a healthy dose of financial mismanagement, Abdülaziz's government had to declare a sovereign default. The problem had been growing for decades. From 1855 to 1875, the Ottoman debt increased twenty-eight fold! The international bond market might not be sexy, but it was as important then as it is now. Government bonds are, essentially, the way any nation gets a loan. The quicker governments pay off their debts, the more likely others are to back future projects financed by government bond issues. Sovereign default by the Ottomans meant that finding any future funding would be very difficult at a time when the economy most needed an injection of cash. The result was an increase in taxes on farmland, but farmers were only just recovering from the famine, so it was the worst possible time to demand higher taxes. The result was a terrible mess, which emboldened rebellious groups looking for any excuse to break away, to try their luck.

The financial crisis, the rebellions in the Balkans, the famine in Anatolia – it's not surprising that Abdülaziz's health started to fail. Had he found it all too much? For the first time in generations there was a palace coup, and Abdülaziz was quietly sidelined to make room for his nephew Murad V. It was reported that Abdülaziz committed suicide a few days later – but did he? The details are murky, and no autopsy was carried out. It could be that he had seen his considerable efforts thwarted and recognised that the work of thirty years and three sultans had shattered on his watch and found it too much to bear. If this was true, he was the first sultan to commit suicide. Or he may have been just another of the long list of sultans murdered by their own courtiers. However, if the latter is the case, he was the first not to be ritually strangled but, instead, killed in secret (he was found with both wrists slashed by scissors) and the details covered up.

Murad V gets just one paragraph. He was installed as part of a coup, but, as nobody heard much from him, it's entirely likely that he was another insane sultan who needed a miracle to survive in the role. If so, the miracle never arrived. We do know that Murad V vomited on hearing of the death of Abdülaziz and seems to have been crying just before the ceremony to gird him with Osman's sword. Throughout the ritual he was shaking with nerves and could barely mutter his oath of office. He was a disaster and was replaced after three months by the far more capable Abdul Hamid II, a son of Adülmecid.

Sultan Abdul Hamid II came to power after a coup and inherited the ongoing problems with Balkan rebels. Herzegovina and Bulgaria continued to raise their voices for independence, and this time they were backed by Russia, which led to full-scale war.

The Russo-Turkish War of 1877–78 didn't last a year and was triggered by the instability of Ottoman rule in Bulgaria. Things quickly escalated. When a Russian column crossed the Danube in the summer of 1877, one of the divisions was led by the future Tsar Alexander III. Ottoman troops in the area were pushed back but fought well, particularly compared to the last time the two sides had met without allies. The Russians pressed on and gained assistance from Bulgarian freedom fighters, but the advance of the Russians was starting to falter.

The key to the whole war turned out to be the city of Plevna, where 130,000 Russians, Bulgarians and Romanians besieged an Ottoman force (including militia) of about 65,000. The fighting was bitter, with four pitched battles around the town over the four and a half months of the siege. Russia eventually won in December of 1877, but, along with her allies, suffered casualties of nearly 15 per cent in this one siege alone. The fall of Plevna allowed the Russian forces to push on, but they were now fighting their way through snowy mountain passes. Plevna was an Ottoman defeat, but it was a vital delaying action. Had it fallen quickly there was little standing in the way of this large allied force intent on marching to Edirne or even Istanbul. However, Ottoman resistance, tactics and training were such that the Ottoman capital was now out of reach, greatly limiting the scope of what Russia could hope to achieve in this war.

For the first time in centuries, the Ottomans had a technological advantage. Even if the advantage wasn't home-made, it was an advantage nonetheless. This was one of the first wars where muzzle-loading muskets and rifles were a thing of the past. Both sides had (mainly) single-shot cartridge rifles, and it had been Abdülaziz, impressed as he had been with British technology, who had bought Martini–Henry rifles for his army. As a result the Ottoman forces were able to put down withering fire not only with these rifles, but also with some of the famous American Winchester lever rifles (think of the classic rifle that had to be hand cranked to reload in almost every 'Western' film). The Ottomans might ultimately have lost the war, but they had made the point that they were not to be underestimated in their military capabilities.

It's a miserable and brutal fact that massacres had been carried out by both sides. The Russian and the Bulgarian militias took particular pleasure in rounding up Muslims and killing them as well as burning down mosques. Similarly, Ottoman soldiers didn't think twice about slaughtering an entire village if it was thought that just some of the occupants were resistance fighters. As such, when the war ended, about half the Muslim population of Bulgaria left for Ottoman territory. As for the Jews, they recognised the Ottomans as their protectors, so virtually the entire Jewish population of the area left with the Ottoman troops. All too often, when Christian powers regained Ottoman territory, Muslim families were either massacred or forcibly removed from their homes (today we would call this ethnic cleansing, and it would be considered a war crime). This pattern did not go unnoticed at the Ottoman court, where a feeling was developing that the empire was the only safe haven for Muslims because the neighbouring Christian territories were just waiting for an excuse to inflict devastation on bordering Muslim populations.

Family (Part 2)

My own family was caught up in this swirl of politics and violence, but allow me to backtrack. The Duducu clan was based in Shumen in eastern Bulgaria, where they had been for generations (as stated earlier, the DNA of the family is Bulgarian and not Turkic). In earlier times, the clan had probably been Christian and Bulgarian, but now it was Muslim and owed everything to the empire; the Duducus represented the epitome of Ottomanism. We know that over time the family moved (centuries earlier) from Jerusalem and then to Konya (middle Turkey), where it rose to prominence. Putting the pieces together, it seems that after the Ottomans conquered Bulgaria (in 1396), at least part of the clan moved there to protect the sultan's interests, and it was there that they acquired the Duducu name, which means 'the keeper of the (sultan's) hunting birds' in old Turkish. It was a measure of their status that they had a family name at a time when most people did not. Accounts of the earlier mentioned Duducu Hasan Pasha mean either that his branch of the family remained in Konya while another branch went to Bulgaria, or that he was sent from Shumen to Konya (in the early 1600s) to serve the sultan, first as governor of the province and then in a military capacity. Presumably the remaining family members made their way to Bulgaria after his death in the mid-1630s.

The fall of Duducu Hasan Pasha marked the lowest point in the clan's fortunes. It would have lost everything not only materially, but also in terms of status and prestige. However, my ancestors seem to have been a resourceful lot and, over time, slowly recovered. By the late 1800s, they had become one of the foremost families in Shumen. The patriarch of the time, Hayri Bey, financed the building of a mosque complex in what is now the old town. Part of the complex included a clock tower, which also served as a minaret for the call to prayer. The mosque itself is surrounded by some thirty small shops whose rent paid for the upkeep of the mosque, a very practical arrangement which met all needs. In this period of history, the Duducu clan made its money as traders and seems to have gone as far as Samarkand in pursuit of a good deal. On one occasion they were caught short on the payment of a tax so, instead of settling the debt in coin, Hayri Bey negotiated a payment in carpets. These rugs still hang the Black Church in Transylvania, a piece of Ottoman history which decorates a Christian church.

Hayri Bey had his fingers in many pies, but he had a particularly ingenious side-line in buying up obsolete cannons and melting them down to make cooking pots and other kitchenware (I have his very impressive solid brass pestle and mortar). From these titbits of information it is easy to see that any family so entrenched would leave their roots with heavy hearts, although some clan members did leave when Bulgaria became independent. But despite Shumen being an epicentre of Bulgarian nationalism, my immediate family stayed on. When the war was over there was no persecution, and the Duducus, once again, were just part of the fabric of the town. While the violence against Muslim populations was very real, it was by no means constant and absolute. My family history is a microcosm of the times. No matter how much Greece or Bulgaria felt they were now their own independent state, with their own destiny, they could not avoid the ties of the past. Trade, intermarriage and travel all continued in places that were still Ottoman.

At the conclusion of the war, the Treaty of San Stefano recognised the independence of Romania, Serbia, Montenegro and the autonomy of Bulgaria. It also made Ottoman Armenia a Russian territory. However, Britain was concerned that so much territory had been ceded from the Ottoman Empire, and the follow-up Treaty of Berlin revoked the Armenian territory transfer. The Ottomans were allowed to keep it after all, much to the dismay of the local Christian Armenians.

Abdul Hamid II started his reign with a bankrupt state, the outlying regions in open rebellion and the loss of large amounts of territory in the Balkans. For a few months he must have worried that he might share the same fate as Murad V, but, instead, he endured for decades. He did this by means of the kind of brutality that would have been recognised by the tsars – which brings us to the Armenians. They and other ethnic minorities were the victims of the massacres that took place when they tried to overthrow the sultanate and achieve independence. The Ottoman Empire was well aware that it encompassed many different ethnic and religious groups that could easily fracture and break off. The Russian tsars faced many of the same problems and used the secret police and the military to fight their own people. Abdul Hamid II did the same.

Empires often faced insurrection in the late nineteenth and early twentieth centuries. The evolution of sometimes seemingly minor events into atrocities occurred according to how desperate the powers were to retain control, and the Ottomans were willing to stamp out violent opposition, usually at any cost. Armenia had powerful allies, and the Ottomans were on the losing end of history, with powerful enemies. While all of this explains the political reality, it does not excuse the fact that massacres of local minorities were an all too common occurrence in the late Ottoman Empire. Some of these were against Muslims, and some were perpetrated by Muslims. Regardless of the political nuances, Abdul Hamid II became known as the 'Red Sultan' because he was an absolute ruler, and his policies meant he had blood on his hands.

The massacres in the 1890s took place when the Armenian insurrection was backed by a Russia eager to seize on any perceived Ottoman weakness. In 1896, the Ottoman national bank in Istanbul was attacked and taken over by ten Armenian revolutionaries. A gun battle ensued, and while all ten Armenians died, so did Ottoman soldiers. The Armenian uprising and its attempted destruction of the national bank could only lead to a forceful response. For more than a century the standard Ottoman reaction to any rebellion had been to send troops and irregular forces into the area to attack indiscriminately. The policy was barbaric, and in the resulting Istanbul pogroms many innocent Armenians died, far more than rebel fighters. Had the Armenians fought and won their independence, it would have been seen as a price worth paying. But, as Armenia failed to break free, the blood was on the hands of their oppressors – not 'Turks', but Ottoman soldiers who, as we have seen, came from all parts of the empire, so Anatolians, yes, but also ethnic Greeks and Arabs. The militias in many of the Armenian areas were Kurds, who also joined in with the killing, and yet today all of the blame is laid at the feet of the Turks in the Republic of Turkey. This nation is not the same thing as the Ottoman Empire and cannot justifiably be held to account for something that happened on someone else's watch.

A key moment from very early on in Abdul Hamid II's reign was the creation of the Ottoman constitution. It had been drafted by reformists known as the Young Ottomans, a group of intellectuals who wanted to change the framework of power as well as the empire's finances, military and social structure. The constitution called for a multi-house democratic parliament, which guaranteed the sultan's power but was clearly based on Western democratic ideals, incompatible with the autocratic rule of a sultan. Unsurprisingly, Abdul Hamid II did not like it, and it lasted only two years before it was abolished in 1878.

In 1881, France claimed that Tunisian troops had crossed the border into Algeria (a French colony), which led to the French annexation of Tunisia (a bloodless move). Suddenly the pretence of Ottoman control over the already largely independent Tunisia was removed. The next year Britain landed in Egypt, where the situation was the same as it had been in Tunisia, and the British, for all intents and purposes, seized control of Ottoman territory. Despite the loose reins of power, both countries had been paying taxes to the empire, and the money was much missed. More importantly, nations once allied to the empire now seemed to be enemies – polite enemies, with no intention of seeing the absolute end to the empire, but enemies nonetheless. Abdul Hamid II desperately needed a powerful European ally himself, and if the enemy of my enemy is my friend, then that made Germany the obvious choice.

Germany/Prussia had been seen for decades as a key provider of military advice, so it was on this basis that a strong relationship with the Ottomans developed at the very end of the nineteenth century. German financiers restructured the debt obligations of the empire, and German engineers helped to build the Berlin–Baghdad railway. Later still there was a tram system for the capital and a railway from Damascus to Medina for haj pilgrims (although paid for by German money, this was the only train line at the time built by Muslims for Muslims, which created a sense of tremendous pride in the empire). The Germans continued to be involved in military training and tactics, with German officers regularly rotating in and out of the Ottoman army, now supplied with the latest weapons from Krupp. The importance of the relationship for both sides was underscored when Kaiser Wilhelm II paid two state visits to the empire during Abdul Hamid's reign.

As Abdul Hamid II cast around for other allies, an unusual situation arose on the other side of the planet. America was building its own empire but had come late to the game. It had been fighting a war in the Philippines, which had a large Muslim population governed by the Sulu Sultanate, and asked Abdul Hamid II, as a Muslim leader, to help negotiate the peace treaty. As ridiculous as the idea sounds, it actually worked. The Americans later broke the treaty, but Abdul Hamid II had proven his worth to another potential ally. Like his fellow sultans of the nineteenth century, Abdul Hamid II was open to new ideas, innovations and advancements. Perhaps the only area that was non-negotiable (as the matter of the constitution showed) was the idea of a constitutional monarchy, with the sultan's powers second to a parliament.

In 1897, Greece tried to increase its territory by declaring war on the Ottoman state. This war is now known in Greece as 'The Unfortunate War' or by the cooler name of 'Black '97'. By now you will have guessed that the plan didn't work. Thanks to the Germans, the Ottoman soldiers were able to show that they were now comparable to Western troops, and as the Greek forces were still few in number, the best Ottoman forces outdid them. However, the European powers stepped in, once again, to dictate terms. A token amount of land near Thessaly was given to the Ottomans (well, they had won the war) but Crete, which had been rebelling for decades, was given its independence, in effect making it Greek again. Greece had to pay war reparations, which meant that the Greek economy was being overseen by foreign economists and bankers. This humiliation showed that it had not yet grown into a fully fledged state and was still in obvious need of outside help.

In 1905, as Abdul Hamid II was on his way to the mosque, a group of Armenian nationalists tried to assassinate him with a delayed-fuse bomb. The bomb missed its mark but killed several of the Armenian assassins and dozens of innocent bystanders, so yet more innocent civilians were victims of the violence coming from both sides, violence that was to continue until the end of the empire. A number of historians have commented on Abdul Hamid II's perceived paranoia. Throughout his reign he had faced rebellions, watched the European powers break off parts of the empire, survived a serious assassination attempt and seen off an attempt to curb his power with a constitution. It's entirely possible he had good reasons to be paranoid. The fact is that, while he may have been worried about palace intrigues and potential coups, he didn't react within his own court as, say, Murad IV had done, killing virtually everyone. His wrath was aimed only at blatantly disloyal or rebellious regions. While he was a vain man, he was also one of frugal tastes. He was not a poet or a musician but a carpenter, and the profits from the furniture he made were given to the poor. While he does not fit the decadent Eastern tyrant mould, no amount of donations to the poor could compensate for the vicious massacres and pogroms he unleashed.

In the 1870s, Abdul Hamid had faced the Young Ottomans; in the early 1900s, he faced the Young Turks, a group of nationalist democratic idealists. Revolutions had been simmering against all three of the remaining great imperial autocrats of the world (China, the Ottoman Empire and Russia) for years. France had earlier seen a revolution and now vacillated between monarchy and republic, but the idea of political accountability to the masses was a genie out of the bottle. Abdul Hamid II had been able to reject the constitution in the 1870s, but by the 1900s his power and health were waning, and the clamour for power to the people was becoming an irresistible force. In 1908, the Young Turks got the backing of some military units and forced Abdul Hamid II into discussions. When the sultan heard that troops were on the way to the capital from Thessalonica, he immediately capitulated.

Along with an amended constitution, the parliament was resurrected. Abdul Hamid II's speech at the opening of the parliament can be seen as one of the greatest pieces of spin in history, when he said that parliament had been 'temporarily dissolved until the education of the people had been brought to a sufficiently high level by the extension of instruction throughout the empire'. This was an outright lie, but it was one that everyone swallowed because they had what they wanted. The makeup of the new political landscape was composed of a couple of liberal-leaning major parties and a whole patchwork of parties defined by ethnicity: the Bulgarian party, the Jewish party and the Armenian party, the largest of all the ethnic groups represented. This is worth mentioning to show that, despite the recent attacks by Armenian nationalists in the Ottoman capital, the Armenians were allowed to participate in the new political process.

In the winter of 1908, there was a general election and a unionist party won a majority. Within a few months the Ottoman Empire seemed to have leapt forward by generations in terms of progressive politics. Could it really be that easy? Well, no. The politicians were suspicious of the old sultan, who seemed to be biding his time, which he was; in 1909, there was an attempted counter-coup known as the 31 March Incident. One of the officers involved in trying to stop this return of autocratic powers to the sultan was a young captain called Mustafa Kemal, who became known as Atatürk, the founding father of the Republic of Turkey. The outcome of the coup was complex, but essentially the secularisation of the political and legal framework wasn't as popular as might be expected, and the sultan's promise to bring back a legal system based on Sharia law gained considerable approval from the masses. However, in the course of the coup, Abdul Hamid II had outmanoeuvred himself. His views were clearly from the past, so he was deposed in favour of a son of Abdülmecid, who became Mehmed V.

While they still had a few more decades to go, in a way, the story of the sultans ends with Abdul Hamid II. All the rulers of the empire had not just blood in common, but theoretical power as well. Of course some were actually more powerful than others, but they were all 'the government', the head of state and the ultimate authority. While there had been the occasional lie to cover up a palace coup, there had never been any challenge to the theory of absolute power – not until the reign of Abdul Hamid II. He saw the dangers to his authority in the first constitution, which is why he quashed it after only a couple of years, but the return of the idea in 1908 was unstoppable. Mehmed V was put in place by the government, not the other way around. Mehmed V was the first constitutional monarch of the empire, a figurehead on which to hang allegiance and little else. The real flow of power now went through the cabinet and the ministers in the capital city.

17

Ashes and Blood

Mehmed V was a quiet man, a poet who had spent his first thirty years isolated in the harem; nine of those years were spent in the cage, which was, essentially, solitary confinement. He was neither a great statesman nor a great warrior, and yet his reign would cover three devastating industrial wars that would ultimately tear the 600-year-old empire apart. In the background of his reign was Abdul Hamid II, who had retired to palace life.

Mehmed V was in his sixties when he was girded with the sword of Osman. He was old, low on energy and uninterested in the day-to-day affairs of state, which is exactly what the fledgling parliament needed. However, just because the reins of power had finally been taken from the sultan didn't mean that the empire was only going to improve. In September 1911, Italy invaded Libya, the last Ottoman territory in North Africa. King Victor Emmanuel III was keen to expand his Italian imperial possessions and looked back, misty eyed, to the days of Roman imperial dominance. Italy was completely outclassed by the other main European powers, but with all the political turmoil in the already weakened Ottoman state, an attack on their most distant possession seemed a clever move. No expense was spared, and more than 130,000 Italians were shipped to Libya. They brought with them hydraulic field guns, spotter balloons, machine guns and even rudimentary airplanes. One of these aircraft was flown by Lieutenant Giulio Gavotti, who threw some grenades from his aircraft, which meant that it was in this war that Lieutenant Gavotti invented the air raid (for more on this, see my book on *Forgotten History*).

Up against this large and modern army were 8,000 regular Ottoman soldiers and 20,000–30,000 irregulars, including Arab militia, Saharan nomads and others who knew the territory but were equipped only with muzzle-loading muskets. Some of the Young Turks' leading military figures were sent to Libya to push back this massive invasion force; among them was Mustafa Kemal. The war quickly devolved into an insurgency, with the Ottoman/Arab forces carrying out hit-and-run tactics and disappearing into the vast expanses of the Sahara before the Italians could bring down the might of their army. Early on in the war, 500 Italian soldiers were ambushed in one of these raids, and all 500 Italian soldiers were killed – no prisoners. Some of the men had been nailed to crosses in mock crucifixions and others (allegedly) had had their genitals hacked off, possibly because the Italian soldiers were rumoured to have been raping local women. Italian troops responded by scouring the countryside around Tripoli, where they rounded up thousands of innocent civilians, including women and children, and shot them. The willingness to commit atrocities was far from exclusive to the Ottomans.

The war extended to fighting between the two fleets. For the first time since the clashes with Venice, an Ottoman fleet met an Italian one at the Battle of Kunfuda Bay (on the Red Sea). When eight small Ottoman naval vessels were attacked by one cruiser and two destroyers, most of the Ottoman ships were blown out of the water. There was a more serious clash off the coast of Beirut, when two Italian armoured cruisers attacked one corvette and a torpedo boat. The Ottoman fleet was hopelessly outclassed at every turn, and the Italians scored another victory.

In December 1911, the Italians sent a small column of 1,000 men to reconnoitre the area around Ottoman-controlled Tobruk. Mustafa Kemal was the officer in charge, and he ordered an attack as the Italians were preparing their position. The fight took just two hours, but the Italians were routed after sustaining casualties. They even left three machine guns with ammunition for the Ottomans to use later in the war. The Italians captured the Aegean island of Rhodes far more easily, even though that was never an intended target. The war was meant to have been over by the end of 1911, but by the summer of 1912, while the Italians had naval superiority, their troops in Libya could not travel any further inland than the cover they had from their naval guns. Quite simply, the Italians couldn't leave the coastal areas of Libya, and so the war reached deadlock on the ground. It was the great powers that got the Ottoman authorities and Italy to sit down and talk peace.The result was the First Treaty of Lausanne, which required the Italians to return all of their Aegean conquests (including Rhodes) to the Ottoman state; however, they got to keep Libya even though they hadn't successfully conquered it.

Strangely, both sides saw the treaty as a victory for their side. The Italians had 'won' Libya; the Ottoman coalition of Muslim fighters had held off a large, modern Western European army. Both messages played well back home. This rather forgotten war showed what Europe could expect from future wars. Aircraft were used as spotting planes and as machines to attack ground troops. The hydraulic artillery proved to be far more devastating and accurate than old-fashioned cannons. Machine guns broke up infantry advances, and both sides dug trenches to keep their soldiers safe from the now lethal long-range weapons of the enemy. All of this was going to become horrifically familiar in the not-too-distant future.

No sooner had this war ended than Russia backed the Balkan states for an attack on the remaining Ottoman lands in Europe. The First and Second Balkan Wars (1912–13) are horribly complicated, so here is a simple summary: Bulgaria, Greece, Montenegro and Serbia (all politically and financially supported by Russia, which also supplied them with weapons) sought to free their 'brothers' still under Ottoman rule. While the various countries in the coalition were not necessarily natural allies, they agreed that if they combined their forces they could probably defeat the Ottomans in the field. Montenegro was the first to declare war and marched towards Shkodra (Albania). The other three nations all went to war a week later. The Serbs took Skopje and Kosovo and then moved west to capture Albania. Greece advanced towards Thessalonica, and Bulgaria aimed to take Istanbul. While this can be seen as an ambitious undertaking, Bulgaria was counting on a weak defence of the capital, knowing that Ottoman forces would find it difficult to push back attacks from four separate directions. Fighting a war on multiple fronts is dangerous for any country, and while the

Ottoman Empire had vastly more resources than even these four countries combined, they were all at the end of relatively long supply lines and would take months to respond. The Balkan powers had been planning and building resources for months in advance of their declaration of war, and in this respect they had the advantage.

At the battles of Elli and Lemnos, the Greek navy defeated the Ottoman navy, and ancient victories were dusted down and compared to these new ones. This First Balkan War was the point at which Greece felt it could draw a line under the disastrous conflict of 1897. They won a major victory at Bizani and even had six aircraft to help in the battle. Meanwhile, the Ottoman war was going so badly that the Young Turks faced a coup after the naval minister and the brains behind the defence of Ottoman lands in the First Balkan War was assassinated. The grand vizier was then forced to resign and a new grand vizier was put in place; he was also assassinated. The result was the era of the so-called 'Three Pashas', who became the *de facto* rulers of the Ottoman Empire (Sultan Mehmed V was still in place but a mere figurehead). Power was now exercised by Mehmed Talaat Pasha, essentially the prime minister; Ismail Enver Pasha was the Minister of War, and Ahmed Çemal Pasha became the Minister of the Navy.

Bulgaria made the least headway in the conflict, although it did capture Edirne (the old Ottoman capital), and while the other nations on the same side could claim significant expansion of their territories, Bulgaria had bogged down in the fight with Ottomans at the so-called Çatalca Line, to the east of which lay Istanbul, the greatest prize of all. But it remained out of reach. With the fall of Bizani and Shkodra, it was time to get an internationally ratified agreement to conclude the war. The Treaty of London came into effect as Albania was declared an independent state, something the treaty recognised. With the exception of Albania, the treaty ceded all Ottoman lands west of the Çatalca Line to the Balkan League. The Three Pashas also ceded Crete, but the status of all the other Aegean islands was left undecided and remained so until after the First World War, when it fell to the great powers to determine their fate. Austria-Hungary recognised a dangerous situation as Serbia (once an ally but now a proxy power of their enemy Russia) had grown substantially because of this war; it realised that ethnic Serbs in Austro-Hungarian lands might well fight to join Serbia.

The Three Pashas weren't happy, but the defeat had been a comprehensive one and, as such, there was nothing to do but accept that almost all of their European lands were forever lost. Bulgaria was not happy with the outcome either. The other allies had all gained considerable territories from this war, and Bulgaria believed it hadn't been properly compensated for its efforts – so it declared war against everyone. This remarkable piece of stupidity started the Second Balkan War, in which Bulgaria fought Serbia, Romania, Greece, Montenegro and the Ottoman Empire. During this time, one of my ancestors, Osman Pasha, was a senior officer in the Bulgarian army. We don't know in which of the two wars he died, but, as well as gaining a medal for his bravery and effectiveness on the field of battle, he made the ultimate sacrifice. My Ottoman ancestors spoke Turkish as their first language, and there were units in the Bulgarian army where nothing but Turkish was spoken, but now Ottomans were fighting the mother country. However, family bravery aside, for Bulgaria to go up against every neighbouring power on its own was madness. It took a lot for Greece and Serbia to ally themselves with the Ottomans, but Bulgaria's declaration of war managed it.

The Second Balkan War lasted just over a month. Assaulted on all sides, Bulgaria stood no chance at all. The staggering petulance of 'Tsar' Ferdinand I of Bulgaria led to over 150,000 casualties. The notable battle of Kilkis–Lachanas saw nearly 200,000 men clash and resulted in a resounding Greek victory. Again the fighting saw the use of heavy artillery and trench works. The Serbs' main clashes were at the Battle of Bregalnica, which they won, and the Battle of Kalimanci, where they failed to break through, leading to a surprising Bulgarian victory. In the meantime the Ottomans poured their resources into recapturing Edirne, succeeding when Bulgarian resistance crumbled. Tsar Ferdinand watched in horror as a Romanian army advanced on Sofia, his capital, and frantically contacted the Russians to broker a cessation of hostilities. A ceasefire was quickly put in place. Bulgaria signed the 1913 Treaty of Bucharest with their erstwhile allies, and a separate 1913 Treaty of Constantinople with the Ottomans in which Edirne was returned to the empire.

The Ottoman Empire had now fought three different wars in as many years, but 1914 would bring one more. This would be the empire's last.

This is the only chapter in this book where the House of Osman isn't central to everything. The power of the sultan may have been usurped before, but there had always been a certain acknowledgement that, at least in principle, he was in charge. With the Three Pashas, however, things had changed when they were openly acknowledged to be the ones in control. For the first time in history, the 'Ottoman' Empire wasn't, technically, 'Ottoman'. The new democratic policies had been born under the rule of a sultan, but now that democracy had a triumvirate of dictators. The Ottoman people had swapped one sultan for three.

The nominal sultan did, however, have another role to play: that of caliph, the spiritual leader of the Islamic world. This was similar to the role of the British monarch as the head of the Anglican Church. Islam was not popular in the ex-Ottoman territories. In places like Serbia it was a reminder of an embarrassing past, and in Greece, 'Islam' and 'Ottoman' were so entwined that today, in the twenty-first century, Athens is the only capital in Europe not to have a mosque (although there are plans to build one). The Ottoman Empire may have been weak and failing, but it was seen as a safe haven for Muslims, and it was this alleged influence in the Islamic world that was one of the reasons Germany allied itself with the Ottomans. According to a secret treaty with Germany, agreed on 2 August 1914, the Ottomans would enter the war on the side of the central powers one day after the German Empire declared war on Russia. But there was a problem with this agreement: Mehmed V thought it would be best to remain neutral in the brewing war between the great European powers, and, as the constitution stated that the sultan was the commander-in-chief of the army, this made the legitimacy of the treaty questionable.

Meanwhile, tensions were growing between the Ottoman navy and the shipbuilders in Newcastle, England. The Ottoman government had ordered two new warships from Britain, the master builder of navies. The two ships were to be called the *Sultan Osman* (which was fully paid for) and the *Reşadiye* (which had a few instalments to go). By the summer of that year, both ships were ready, but the engineers claimed they needed more time to run tests and check for faults. This was a delaying tactic. It wasn't clear to the Brits (or anyone else) whether the Ottomans would join in the approaching war and, while Britain didn't want to antagonise the Ottomans, neither did it want to deliver two state-of-the-art battleships to a potential enemy. The delay was ordered by none other than Winston Churchill, who knew that the Brits were walking a tightrope. The contract was legal and valid, but the political situation had changed dramatically in the years it had taken to build the warships. Less than a day before the Ottoman crescent-and-star flag was to be hoisted on *Sultan Osman*, a sign that the handover had officially taken place, the ship was confiscated, and the Ottoman crew was forced to evacuate. The day after that, Churchill declared that the British government had embargoed the two warships. When Britain declared war on Germany the next day, the two ships were taken over by Britain without compensation.

Some Turkish historians use this as an excuse to say that Britain declared war on the Ottomans first. They did not; they just didn't hand over two ships to a potential enemy (while the secret alliance between the Ottomans and Germany wasn't a known fact, the British government had guessed as much). It was wrong of Britain not to compensate the Ottomans, something that, under normal circumstances, would spark a diplomatic row, but Britain was willing to take a chance on the consequences of these actions as less severe than if they handed over weapons of war to the enemy. At the same time, two German warships, the *Goeben* and the *Breslau*, were being pursued by the Royal Navy in the Dardanelles. When these two German ships docked in Istanbul, they were confiscated by the Three Pashas, who announced that the ships had been 'bought' by the empire to replace the two ships they had not received from the British. The ships were renamed *Yavuz* and *Midilli*. The German crews remained, but they were issued with fez hats and raised the Ottoman flag. The Royal Navy was forced to break off the pursuit because, technically, the Ottoman Empire was still neutral even though the shooting had already started in Europe.

In October the *Yavuz* and *Midilli* sailed into the Black Sea and shelled Odessa and Sevastopol. The attacks caused minor damage but were completely unexpected and, of course, the entire crew of both vessels was German. This led to total confusion. Had the Ottoman attack been an accident? France, Britain and Russia were being pushed back on all fronts and couldn't afford to bring in another enemy by accident. At the same time the Three Pashas could have been duped by their German partners. Mehmed Talaat Pasha wrote, 'None of us knew about this ... so, we entered the war as the result of a *fait accompli*.' Then again this could be hindsight speaking after getting involved in a disastrous war and a later attempt to distance themselves from an arrogant mistake. It took a few days to unpick the rumours from the facts, at which point the Allied powers declared war on the Ottoman Empire. And this was the convoluted way in which the Ottoman Empire became involved in its last war, a wider war known to the world as the First World War.

A clever plan was immediately hatched which, for Germany, was always about cutting Britain off from its limitless resources in Asia. As the Ottoman Empire bordered Egypt, it was thought possible that an Ottoman-German force could spring a surprise attack and capture the Suez Canal. Initial probes led to the fabulously exotic image of the British Imperial Bikaner Camel Corps (the soldiers were largely Sikhs) fighting in the desert near El Qantara against a Bedouin militia. The ambush was successful, and the camel corps lost around half its men, but this was only the start of the fight for control of the canal.

The Ottoman main force was led by one of the Three Pashas, Ahmed Çemal, and General Friedrich von Kressenstein. They had prepared a number of supply depots, and engineers had gone ahead to drill wells to supply fresh water across the Sinai desert. All of the careful preparations were to allow the Ottoman force of about 20,000 to travel undetected right up to the edges of the canal. Von Kressenstein was also the designer of the pontoon bridge to get the Ottoman forces over the Suez Canal and on into Egypt. Had this raid been conducted just ten years earlier, it would have worked. The organisation was excellent, and the large force travelled across the desert without succumbing to any ambushes or logistical problems. But von Kressenstein had overlooked one development: the recently invented airplane. The British had a few aircraft circling the Sinai, looking for any potential Ottoman attacks. Although the force moved by night to avoid detection as well as the fierce daytime heat of the desert, even then it was impossible to hide 20,000 men from the prying eyes of observers in the aircraft, and the idea of a surprise attack failed before it had even started. The British were waiting for the raiders. Warships were anchored in the canal and used as mobile gun platforms. There was also an armoured train with artillery and heavy machine guns on board, which could travel parallel to the canal on a pre-existing rail line.

All this and the British imperial troops dug in on both sides of the canal. The British leader on the scene was the veteran General Sir John Maxwell. His forces were almost entirely Indian, including the famous Gurkhas (with some New Zealanders). Von Kressenstein and Ahmed Çemal Pasha had Kurds, Anatolian Turks, Circassians (from the Caucasus), Arabs and Bedouins in their army. Despite the multiple ethnicities fighting under the Ottoman banner, throughout the war all Ottoman forces were simply called 'Turks' by the Western powers. The ethnicity of the men on both sides and the location of this battle is a reminder that the First World War was a truly global conflict.

On the night of 3 February 1915, spotters saw the Ottomans position three pontoon boats on the canal. Firing between the two sides immediately began as the boats paddled furiously to the other side, but not enough men made it across to create a bridgehead; they were either killed in the battle or captured. As the sun rose, hundreds of Ottoman troops ran at the British front-line trenches on the eastern shore of the canal, where they came under fire not only from the trenches, but from the ships moored in the canal. Despite the heavy fire, they managed to get to the trenches and capture a portion of them. However, after a furious engagement that lasted much of the day, the counter-attack pushed the Ottomans out of the British trench works.

Ottoman artillery began targeting the two ships in the canal and, after hitting one of them several times, forced it to retreat out of range. The attack showed considerable skill by the Ottoman forces and proved they were able to fight on equal terms against one of the great powers. Only a couple of companies of men had managed to cross the canal, and the British forces were simply too well dug in to be dislodged with the troops Çemal Pasha and von Kressentein had at their disposal. They were left with no choice but an orderly retreat. Both sides had acquitted themselves well, and had the British not been forewarned it is entirely possible that the attack would have succeeded. As it was, General Sir John Maxwell was unable to get his troops across the Suez Canal quickly enough to chase after the enemy. Had he been able to do so he might also have taken the opportunity to attack Ottoman outposts in the Sinai as well as its large army in Gaza. These forces were later to hinder the British considerably in the war, and the opportunity to shatter them after the raid on Suez had been lost.

All of this happened a few months before the British launched their attack on Gallipoli. Entire books have been written on the Gallipoli campaign of 1915–16, so I will give only a brief overview. In some respects, the British attack on the Gallipoli peninsula had similarities to the Ottoman-German attack on the Suez Canal. Both plans were based on the undeniable logic that success would deal a major blow to the enemy. In the case of Suez, if Britain could be deprived of the support that came through the canal, it would find it much harder to wage long-term war in Europe. In the case of Gallipoli, if the allied forces could land and push on the few dozen miles to the Ottoman capital, then one of the central powers would be knocked out within a year of fighting.

Both attacks failed, but for different reasons. In the case of Suez, the troops were spotted well before the attack could take place. In the case of Gallipoli, the errors were multiple. There was poor mapping of the inland areas; the navy and army worked as rivals, not as comrades. After the landings, advances were too slow (due in part to the unforeseen high cliffs and rough terrain, but some units stopped for tea!). Had the different divisions pushed on as soon as they reached land, the Ottoman forces wouldn't have known where to send reinforcements. The momentum of the landings ebbed away in the critical hours of the first couple of days, leading to a deadlock just as onerous as the now fossilised trench warfare of the Western Front. What was inexcusable was the continuing underestimation of the ability and determination of the Ottoman forces. Suez proved that they could carry out highly technical operations and could fight effectively, and yet, only a short time later, it was assumed that the allies faced a 'Turkish' rabble. In fact, Otto Liman von Sanders and Mustafa Kemal created a highly effective resistance to the invasion, and when, months later, the allies tried further landings to break the deadlock, he neutralised these too. General von Sanders promoted Mustafa Kemal during the campaign because he demonstrated rare leadership skills, and this quality would increasingly come to the fore in the months and years ahead.

It is untrue that Gallipoli was largely an ANZAC campaign. The soldiers from Australia and New Zealand Army Corps fought bravely, but there were more French soldiers at Gallipoli than there were ANZACs, and both contingents were dwarfed by the other British imperial forces, with tens of thousands of Indian troops as well as those from the British Isles. In the end nearly 500,000 allied soldiers were sucked into this ill-fated campaign, which was repulsed by a little over 300,000 Ottoman troops. Britain suffered over 300,000 casualties, and the Ottomans lost a quarter of a million men – killed, wounded, captured or sick. It was an eight-month meat grinder. All the deprivations of the Western Front came to the edge of Asia, where they were made worse by a baking summer sun. The Ottomans, led by Mustafa Kemal, were fighting with almost no resources but a dogged resolve to save their state from a foreign invasion. Supplies, including food, were scarce and the story is told in Turkey of the starving Ottoman soldiers who, in full view of the enemy, dumped their meagre rations on the ground to show they had food to waste (they didn't, but Kemal inspired astonishing loyalty and determination). Had the siege gone on for much longer, the Ottomans might well have failed, and once again the Ottoman troops proved themselves equal to the abilities of their Western counterparts. This time their efforts led to a vital defensive victory, and the Allied forces were compelled to evacuate, sometimes slinking off under the cover of night.

During this epic battle, Talat Pasha (one of the Three Pashas) abolished the 'Capitulations', ending the special privileges the Ottomans had granted to foreign nationals, which meant that a significant part of the Ottoman national debt evaporated at a stroke. It was a shrewd move if the empire ended up on the winning side, but would have punishing repercussions if they lost the war. The measures also stipulated that some foreign assets were now to be placed under Ottoman/Muslim authority. It was an attempt to keep the Muslim majority of the empire happy, but further alienated other religious groups.

Mehmed V's only significant contribution to the war effort was his declaration of jihad against the Allied powers. Mahmud II had done the same thing almost a century earlier, and the response then had been muted, but the circumstances now were entirely different and threatened a 'worst-case scenario' for Britain. There were millions of Muslims in the British Empire, and if they heeded the call by their caliph, the empire could shatter through multiple rebellions. In the end, there was only one minor uprising declared in the name of jihad, and that occurred when there was a mutiny in the dockyards of Singapore by Muslims from India and Malaya. Non-Muslim troops were swiftly brought in and the resistance crumbled. Some 200 mutineers were court-martialled and forty-seven of those were shot by firing squad. This was not what Mehmed V had hoped for when he had called for the Muslim world to rise up.

As well as the start of the Gallipoli campaign, 1915 was also the year in which most of the atrocities against the Armenians occurred. According to the *Oxford Dictionary*, genocide is defined as 'the deliberate killing of a large group of people, especially those of a particular nation or ethnic group'. Some feel very strongly that the massacres meet the definition of genocide. Others feel just as strongly that they do not. Rather than dwell on labels, it is my intention to present the facts and put them in the context of the times.

Government Directive 8682 removed Armenians from the Ottoman armed forces and assigned them to work battalions instead. In Istanbul in April that year, 250 Armenian intellectuals were rounded up, imprisoned and killed. Meanwhile, the fighting between the Russians and the Ottomans in the Caucasus meant many of the battles took place in Armenian-populated areas, where Armenians were known to help the Russians. Later in the war, they formed and equipped their own army, which inflicted a notable defeat on Ottoman forces. It has already been mentioned that when areas on the fringes of the empire were captured by Christian powers, it invariably led to the exile or massacre of local Muslims. Talat Pasha's fear was that Armenia would become 'the Bulgaria of the East', which led to a pre-emptive series of murders and deportations in order to prevent this. It was a terrible decision, and Talat Pasha's fears were to be realised regardless.

Ottoman resources throughout the war were always scarce. The Three Pashas had difficulty getting supplies, men and materials to the right parts of the empire at the right time, and thousands of Ottoman subjects and soldiers starved and died through a combination of incompetence and the sheer poverty of resources. On one occasion a relief army to the Caucasus, consisting of 50,000 men, never made it to the front line. While some deserted, most of the men starved or died of frostbite and exposure or were invalided home due to illness. Towards the end of the war some units received only 15 percent of the rifles they needed, and by 1917 boots were becoming scarce throughout the empire. It's against this backdrop of dwindling resources and gross incompetence on the part of the Ottoman authorities that the atrocities against the' Armenian populations took place. Starving and desperate troops from a crumbling empire were fighting an insurgency with a brutal and disproportionate response.

The story of the Armenians in the Ottoman Empire is frequently compared to that of the Jews under the Nazis, so let's pause to consider that comparison. The treatment of the Armenian population (and other minority groups) in the time of the sultans was profoundly different to the systematic extermination of the Jews (and others) which took place in the Second World War. Although the Ottoman practice of allowing local massacres to cow the population was still being conducted into the twentieth century, these were predictable responses to insurrections rather than part of a cohesive government plan. Also, the Jews were part of German society whereas the Armenians fought a decades-long, low-intensity guerrilla war with the Ottoman state and, unlike the victims of the Nazis, the Armenian partisans and militias actively fought their Ottoman overlords, often with Russian help.

The month-long Battle of Sarikamish in the Caucasus was fought under the Russian flag by a volunteer Armenian army of 60,000 against an Ottoman army of twice that size. Enver Pasha (one of the Three Pashas) led the Ottomans, but it was a defensive Armenian/Russian victory. Unhappy with the outcome, the pasha blamed the duplicitous Armenians, and the Ottoman paranoia that Armenian communities might well be harbouring revolutionaries was well founded. Although the position of the

Armenians in the Ottoman Empire was not comparable to that of the Jews under the Nazis, this does not justify or excuse the massacres, forced marches and ethnic cleansing that took place. It doesn't help that Hitler is alleged to have asked, 'Who still talks nowadays of the extermination of the Armenians?' But the quote is false; there is no evidence he ever said this. It only serves to heap yet more fuel on an already inflamed issue. Further, what has been remembered as only 'Turks' killing Armenians is a distorted view. The country of Georgia actively fought with the Ottoman Empire in this region, as did the Kurds, Syrians and even Jews (who formed a key part of the Ottoman army officer corps; while no one is rushing to associate their ancestors with war crimes, it would be very strange if there were no Jewish officers in Armenian areas).

General Friedrich von Kressenstein, who was in the Middle East at the time, stated, 'The Turkish policy of causing starvation is an all too obvious proof (if proof was still needed as to who is responsible for the massacre) of the Turkish resolve to destroy the Armenians.' His comment shows that, by European standards, what was happening to Armenian civilians was beyond the conventions of acceptable tactics in warfare. In other words, these were war crimes. However, in his role as the overall (Ottoman-German) military leader in the region, he never once mentioned specific orders to exterminate the Armenians (or anyone else). While the fight against Armenian forces was happening on another, separate front, von Kressenstein's comments confirm that tens of thousands of deported Armenians were arriving in Syria. (It's likely the numbers were many times higher than that, but it's hard to be exact as records from the time are patchy.) So, while it would appear that he never received an order to exterminate these civilians, it is impossible to know if this was through incompetence or because there simply was no order. Despite von Kressenstein being surrounded by a varied ethnic mix of troops, he still regarded them all as 'Turks', thus perpetuating the mistaken view that atrocities were committed by only one ethnic group.

The only battle between an official Armenian Army Corps (rather than a volunteer force under the Russian flag, or a guerrilla insurgency strike) and the Ottomans took place in 1918, by which point Russia had gone home to tear itself to pieces in the Russian

Civil War. This left the Armenians to fight for their independence without any assistance from Russia, on which they had heavily relied. The Battle of Sadarabad has been forgotten by all but the Armenians, but it was a bitterly contested battle that the Armenians won, so the Armenians clearly had an army in the field. However, when the Russian/Armenian armies came into previously held Ottoman territories, the local Muslims were, in turn, subjected to violence and massacres for the very same reasons: they were regarded as a potential fifth column opposed to the new ruling power. In these instances a reversal of fortunes occurred, but the level of atrocities committed against Muslims by the Russian/Armenian forces was never on the same scale as that committed by the Ottomans. Nevertheless, this was a dark stain on the Armenian story that is often ignored when people speak of these events in the First World War.

It is estimated that some 1.5 million Armenians died during the war. While some died in combat, most died through starvation, massacre, forced marches and deportations. The modern country of Armenia has a population of just 3 million. Compare that with the approximately 6 million Jews living in Israel, a population that is well documented as having suffered widespread genocide, and there can be no question that the atrocities happened and that the Armenian population all but disappeared from Ottoman territories.

What happened to the Jews in Germany or to the Cambodians in the 1970s is not what happened to the Armenians in the First World War. The integrated communities of those countries were carved away from society as a whole and annihilated. The atrocities against the Armenians happened in the middle of an armed insurrection as a 600-year-old empire shattered under the weight of fighting a world war on multiple fronts. Any idea that the Ottoman state could organise an efficiently run genocide fails to take into account the mess that was the Ottoman Empire from 1914 onwards.

The Republic of Turkey should recognise the crimes of the Ottoman past but point out that the current republic is not guilty because it is not a continuation of the old empire. Further, all the heat is directed at Turkey when it is a matter of record that Kurds, Georgians and Arabs all had ancestors involved in these heinous crimes. Surely pointing the finger at the Turks alone is to single them out as scapegoats for the many others who were also complicit.

Some will read the previous passages about the crimes of the Ottomans against the Armenians and say that the account is biased in favour of the Armenians. Others, reading the same passages, will say it is a defence of the indefensible. This has been an attempt to discuss what is a matter of record. It is for the reader to determine what labels, if any, should be applied to the crimes against the Armenians.

In late 1915, while hundreds of thousands of British troops were committed to Gallipoli and fighting in the Caucasus, an expeditionary force of over 30,000 Indian troops landed at al-Faw in modern-day Iraq. There was a clash at Ctesiphon where the British faced heavy fighting against the Ottoman defences and suffered substantial casualties but won the day. They were now committed to marching along the rivers, making their route of advance predictable, and they ended up being intercepted and besieged at Kut. The siege lasted over four months as Ottoman reinforcements tightened the noose on a British army that, after receiving one relief column of nearly 20,000 men, was now cut off from any further chance of relief. The force suffered light casualties, but tens of thousands of British servicemen were now prisoners of war. It was a colossal humiliation for the British and yet another sign that the Ottomans were far from finished. The news of the capitulation at Kut was almost simultaneous with the retreat from the Gallipoli peninsula. The Ottoman Empire was not the easy victory Britain had expected.

In 1916, Britain sent T. E. Lawrence to the Arabian peninsula to see if he could galvanise the disparate Arab tribes into a concerted revolt against Ottoman rule. This British officer became known as 'Lawrence of Arabia', and the British promise to back Arab home rule worked wonders by opening up yet another front against the collapsing empire. This gave the Three Pashas a new strategic concern and stretched resources ever thinner. That's not to say that the Arabs swept to victory; Ottoman forces were still formidable in the field. For example, the Ottoman garrison defending Medina, the second-holiest city in Islam, was besieged for eighteen months before capitulating in January of 1919, almost two months after the war in Europe was over.

For the whole of 1916, Britain fought its way across the Sinai Desert in an attempt to push Ottoman forces back. The battles of Romani and Magdhaba are all but forgotten names, and, by comparison with Verdun or Gallipoli, the numbers involved were small. Trying to supply troops in remote desert locations was a logistical nightmare for both sides, but the British Empire (again using a majority of Indian and even ANZAC troops) finally pushed through the Sinai peninsula in January 1917 at the Battle of Rafa. It was this battle that showed there was still a use for cavalry as New Zealander and Australian cavalry brigades helped to outflank the Ottoman defenders. The other key event in 1916 was the secret agreement between the Allied powers outlining how the Ottoman state was to be carved up after the war. This was a breath-taking piece of arrogance since the reality on the ground showed the empire was doing rather well, particularly against the British.

The Sykes-Picot Agreement outlined many of the countries in the Middle East as they exist today and would go on to create a whole host of new problems. A look at the current map of countries in the Middle East shows that some seem to have *very* straight-line boundaries. This is because the borders were determined in the drawing rooms of Europe and simply failed to understand or consider the realities on the ground. Iraq, for example, has three distinct ethnic and religious groups: the Shi'a majority, the Sunni minority and the Kurds in the north. These three groups have been rivals for centuries, something that is apparent in the present day, and yet they were indiscriminately thrown together in one newly created country.

The Kurds were one of the big losers in the territorial carve up following the demise of the Ottoman Empire and are the largest ethnic group in the world not to have their own country. They are without a home state because no one at the time of Sykes-Picot thought they needed one. Today the Kurdish people are divided among Turkey, Syria, Iraq and Iran, where they are considered to be 'problem' minorities by their fellow citizens. A similarly uninformed decision was made about Palestine, which was secretly offered to both the Arabs and the Jews and yet, after the war, became a British territory for thirty years. This pleased no one and has created continual problems ever since.

At the time, no one in the Ottoman Empire knew about the Sykes-Picot Agreement. As the war was winding down, the Ottoman military, with some justification, must have felt it had acquitted itself as well as it had done in other wars where the empire had lost a few territories but remained intact. Certainly in 1917/18, it didn't look as if a 600-year-old empire and a way of life would evaporate in the space of five years. While it was true that the empire was living on borrowed time and that nationalism was, by then, an unstoppable force, the empire was deeply embedded in its heartlands and the dismantling of it would have lasting implications. The arbitrary redrawing of the map by European powers resulted in problems that would last for generations – and are still in the news today.

In March 1917, General Sir Archibald Murray amassed thousands of British imperial troops to break out into the Middle East proper through the town of Gaza. Murray led what was known as the Egyptian Expeditionary Force (EEF) and surrounded the key city, where he launched an all-out assault against von Kressenstein and the small defending garrison. There was poor communication among the allied units: some were ready to attack just after dawn, while others were only getting into position by midday. The fighting was patchy, but progress was being made on a number of fronts as the British artillery zeroed in on Ottoman machine gun nests. Once into the Ottoman trenches, furious hand-to-hand fighting broke out. Two captured German artillery pieces were used by the New Zealanders to blast through Ottoman-held houses being used as sniper positions. The fighting was fast and furious and went on after nightfall.

A relief column of Ottoman soldiers moved against the British but were pinned down by the fire from armoured cars with machine guns, supported by artillery and rapid rifle fire. However, the pressure from the Ottoman relief force to the east was enough to make the commanding officers worry about a potential flanking manoeuvre so, even though significant parts of Gaza and its defences had been captured, a general order for withdrawal went out. There were substantial casualties on both sides (although the Ottomans felt the losses more keenly) and, while it had been very close to a British imperial victory, by dawn the next day Gaza was still an Ottoman-held town. The British had suffered nearly 4,000 casualties, fired hundreds of artillery shells and about 150,000 rounds of rifle ammunition – and achieved nothing. After their string of victories in the Sinai, the British assumed they had the Ottomans on the run, but Gaza showed them that the Ottomans were not done yet.

About three weeks later General Murray tried again, but von Kressenstein knew this was the only target the British had in mind, so he had poured reinforcements into the city and greatly strengthened and enlarged the defences. The battle lasted two days as wave after wave of British imperial forces attacked, but the Ottomans had known they were coming and had excellent fields of fire over the approaches, while the artillery did an outstanding job of responding to various assaults. By the end of hostilities, Murray looked on in horror at nearly 6,500 British casualties. This time the Ottomans had come off much better, having lost fewer than 2,000 men. From now on Murray was far more cautious in his attacks and a stalemate developed. This mirrored a similar stalemate on the Western Front, but the conditions were very different: troops in Europe had to deal with mud and numbing cold, while those in the Middle East had to endure sand and blistering sun. Sand got into everything, making food unpalatable and weapon maintenance difficult.

Once the summer heat began to fade, the next significant battle was at Beersheba in October 1917. During the stalemate, the British regularly flew planes over enemy lines, sometimes to carry out reconnaissance, sometimes to bomb enemy positions. The bombing runs were almost always complete failures as they invariably missed their targets, in addition to which the aircraft had to fly relatively low in order to spy on the Ottoman troops or bomb them, so rudimentary anti-aircraft positions sprang up, and many of these aircraft were shot down with ominous efficiency. Pilots didn't then have parachutes, so they almost always died in the resulting crashes.

By this time Murray had been replaced by Sir Edmund Allenby, who had a significantly larger force of about 55,000 men. The British imperial forces at Beersheba outnumbered the Ottomans roughly 10:1, so the attack was an opportunity to simply overwhelm the enemy with sheer numbers. It worked. 90 per cent of the Ottoman force was killed, wounded or captured. The significance of this battle was that it was at the other end of the defensive line that Gaza anchored. By winning this battle British imperial forces could again manoeuvre to envelop the town. While victory was due largely to Allenby's overpowering numbers, there was a reason why von Kressenstein failed to reinforce Beersheba.

Allenby may have been determined to win, but he had some help in the form of an ingenious military intelligence officer by the name of Richard Meinertzhagen (who, despite the name, was not fighting for the Germans). Meinertzhagen wrapped some sandwiches in fake plans of attack and made sure the haversack with the sandwiches was found by the Ottomans. The so-called 'Haversack Ruse' convinced von Kressenstein that the attack on Beersheba was a feint for a larger attack on Gaza. As the reinforcements had made the difference in the First Battle of Gaza, it could well be that Meinertzhagen's plan won the day (and if this sounds familiar, it was the inspiration for much the same deception in the Second World War, called 'Operation Mincemeat').

In early November Gaza was again the target. This time Meinertzhagen came up with an inspired plan to help with the Third Battle of Gaza. British aircraft had been flying over the area for months. If they weren't spying or bombing, they were dropping cigarettes wrapped in propaganda to encourage the defenders to quit. The propaganda was largely ignored, but the cigarettes were gratefully received and, because Meinertzhagen knew the cigarettes were smoked, he ordered a special batch laced with opium to subdue the defenders. When he tried one, he was able to describe its mellowing effects. The opium cigarettes were dropped, and just a few hours later the British began their assault. It is not known exactly to what degree the drugged tobacco made a difference to the defence of Gaza (much like the fake plans at Beersheba), but what had been a tough nut to crack in the first two battles was won in a day of fighting in early November 1917. This victory enabled the British to break into the Middle East, albeit a year later than scheduled.

By mid-November British forces were on the outskirts of Jerusalem, where German generals Erich von Falkenhayn and von Kressenstein had around 25,000 Ottoman troops, and multiple battles were fought around the city. General Allenby's policy was one of doggedly chasing down the enemy so as to give little time or opportunity for Ottoman forces either to regroup or dig in. Gaza had demonstrated what Ottoman troops under German leadership could do if they were allowed to construct defensive positions. While Allenby tried to keep the fighting out of Jerusalem itself, he did allow several aerial bombardments, a new horror of war for a city that had seen dozens of attacks over the past millennia. The historical and religious importance of Jerusalem was not lost on the Egyptian Expeditionary Force. Many letters home and diaries of the time refer to hallowed ground and the almost mythical names of the towns they passed through. The weather was unusually harsh for the time of year, and the soldiers had to deal with fierce rain storms and quagmires of mud, so for a brief time the Middle Eastern front looked horribly like the European Western front. The British forces were not equipped for such extreme and unexpected conditions, and there was a real danger of losing thousands of men to the cold.

The British finally broke through the Ottoman lines at the small town of Nebi Samwil (the Tomb of Samuel). However, fierce Ottoman counter-attacks meant the army went no further and had to fight back regular assaults by the Ottoman soldiers. In December the British forces captured the port of Jaffa, but Ottoman forces were so close that it was useless as a disembarkation point for supplies as it was still within range of Ottoman artillery. The Scottish 52nd (Lowland) Division crossed the formidable barrier of the al-Auja River (known for its strong currents, which the recent rains had made more treacherous) during nightfall and carried out a close-quarters attack on the Ottoman positions on the far side of the river. The assault achieved complete surprise, and the Ottoman troops were forced to retreat (but not flee). Shortly after this von Kressenstein was relieved of his duties not because he was not an outstanding leader (his troops had been some of the most effective in the Ottoman Empire), but because he had now been in the Middle East for over three years. Ahmed Çemal Pasha (another one of the Three Pashas) filled the vacancy to work alongside von Falkenhayn.

While the newly arrived pasha took time to assess the situation, there was a lull in hostilities, giving the British a much-needed opportunity to resupply. They rotated their troops and used the pause to their advantage. On 27 November, Ottoman forces attacked and were repulsed only after heavy fighting. The British responded with a night attack on the 28th. For the next few weeks there were a number of vicious attacks from both sides, but there was no doubt that the overall momentum was with the British. Jerusalem eventually fell to the allied forces on 30 December 1917. By then the Ottoman frontlines were crumbling everywhere against the British, and Baghdad, too, fell in 1917.

A fresh British assault in early 1918 didn't materialise as the British were seriously caught out by the blunt-force shock of the final great German assault, known as the Kaiserschlacht, when more than 600,000 men were thrown at the Allied lines on the Western Front. Then, in April, enough forces had returned to the Egypt Expeditionary Force to push back Ottoman control of the Middle East once more. One of the first attacks was on Amman, which failed when Ottoman forces held the city against a relatively low number of British imperial forces. However the EEF pushed further north until they met one of the last remaining Ottoman field armies at Megiddo in September of 1918. The industrial scale of death throughout the war made many British soldiers conclude that the blood-drenched imagery in the Bible's Book of Revelations might be coming true. Part of the prophecy described a mighty battle at Armageddon; Megiddo is Armageddon in English, so they were uneasy about fighting there, fearing they might be witnessing the 'end of days'. The prophecy, as it turned out, was not true (at least, not in this instance), but it was Armageddon for the Ottomans, including Mustafa Kemal. For the 35,000 men on the Ottoman side, supported by over 400 artillery pieces, the battle was a disaster. General Allenby used a creeping barrage to cover the advance of his troops, including a very impressive cavalry charge. The Desert Mounted Corps managed to get behind Ottoman lines and attack from the rear as the main force charged in from the front. Of the 35,000 Ottoman soldiers at the battle, only 6,000 avoided being killed, wounded or captured. It was the biggest defeat the Ottomans suffered in the First World War, and on 30 October, a few weeks before the war ended in Europe, the Armistice of Mudros ended hostilities in the Middle East.

The last war the Ottoman Empire fought was against its mightiest foe. By the early twentieth century, the British Empire was at its absolute zenith, dwarfing the resources of the Safavids, Russia, the Habsburgs and Venice. Approximately 1.5 million British imperial troops, from at least half a dozen countries, fought in the Middle East from 1915 to 1918. Of course the British were more interested in victory in the West, but, even so, its resources allowed attacks on multiple fronts. Despite the fact that the Ottoman Empire was collapsing, itself facing attacks on multiple fronts, it acquitted itself well. The British suffered serious defeats at Gallipoli, Kut and Gaza (twice), but, in the end, borderline anarchy at government level combined with the seemingly never-ending resources of the British Empire meant there could be only one outcome.

By this time the Three Pashas had fled the capital, knowing that the disastrous war and capitulation had cost them their power and that the whole of the empire blamed them for allowing the Sublime Porte to be drawn into this destructive war. The Armenians got a taste of revenge when all three of the pashas had been assassinated by Armenians by 1922. They were mourned by no one.

18

The Sun Sets on the Eternal State

The Versailles Treaty is famous for setting out the terms of peace that ended the First World War, but it was not signed by the Ottoman powers. Mehmed V had died (of natural causes, aged seventy-three) in July 1918, and had been replaced by his brother, Mehmed VI. It was his representatives who were present at the signing of the Treaty of Sevres, which not only brought peace to the empire, but ended it too.

British troops were stationed in Istanbul; foreign soldiers on the streets of the capital represented a never-before-seen humiliation. But a far more urgent and important problem for the average person under Ottoman rule was that the entire empire was being dismantled. New countries that had never existed before – like Saudi Arabia and Kuwait – were being carved out of the corpse of the rotten empire. The people of the new Armenian state had reason to celebrate, but there was dismay in many other places that were now under either French or British 'spheres of influence'. In other words, these people simply swapped one empire for another, only the new rulers were even less interested in local cultures and politics than the old rulers had been.

When the terms of the treaty were revealed, the Turkish Grand National Assembly, led by Mustafa Kemal, rejected it, recognising it for what it was: the end of the empire and an ignoble capitulation after a hard fight. The story of Mustafa Kemal, Atatürk, and the birth of the republic is a very big book, which tells of a nation very different to the Ottoman Empire. What follows is the briefest of summaries outlining the messy end to the long, unbroken line of Ottoman sultans.

By 1920, none of the major world powers wanted an Ottoman Empire, and nobody within its borders had the means to resist. As such, Greece was expanded; many new countries in the Middle East were created, and Anatolia was to be carved up and divided among the European powers – except that in 1919, Greece declared war on the remains of the empire before the Treaty of Sevres could be implemented. The Greeks wanted to recreate the Byzantine Empire, to recapture Anatolia and Constantinople, to fashion a new Greek Empire. Western Europe, however, liked to frame the Greek endeavour in a more classical context: this was the twentieth-century version of the Greeks fighting Darius and Xerxes, and the Greeks were doing the West a favour by pushing out the 'barbarians'. The West lapped it up. British Prime Minister Lloyd George overtly promised the Greeks land at the expense of the Turks, and the Greeks were supplied with weapons on an industrial scale from multiple European countries (there were lots of leftovers from the recently concluded war).

Meanwhile, the rump of the Ottoman Empire lands that was starting to be called 'Turkey' had no allies and a lot of enemies. To be fair to Constantine I of Greece, this was the best opportunity to greatly expand Greek holdings since the Greek War of Independence nearly a century earlier. What had been the Ottoman army and was now known as the Turkish army was in complete disarray as many of the ethnically different troops and officers headed home to areas that were now outside Turkey's influence. The Greeks had more of everything: more men, more weapons, more support, even more artillery and aircraft. Hundreds of thousands of ethnic Greeks lived in Anatolia and along the Aegean coast, where Smyrna (Izmir), one of the great Greek cities, was still not under Greek control.

Mehmed VI was completely sidelined in the new setup, so it was down to Mustafa Kemal not only to form a new government and draft a new constitution but to fight a war he didn't want and didn't have the resources to wage. There was no one else; if he didn't provide the necessary leadership, the brand-new Republic of Turkey would be dead before it had begun. And so began the Turkish War of Independence. The Greeks quickly captured the Aegean coast and pushed inwards. By 1921, they had reached central Anatolia, an area that had not been ruled by the Byzantine emperors since the time of the crusades. Central Anatolia is arid, with sparse flora and fauna, and while Kemal didn't go as far as creating a scorched-earth policy, the natural environment did the job for him – and at this point the Greek army was at the end of a long, circuitous supply chain. The Turks met the Greeks at the Battle of Sakarya, where the fighting lasted for about three weeks, but the Turkish lines held. The Greeks had hit a brick wall, and they were a very long way from friendly territory. General Papoulas ordered a retreat; however, in order to hasten the march, much of the heavy equipment was abandoned. Now the Turks were being resupplied by their enemy. This was the turning point in the war and the Greek forces, from here onwards, did nothing other than retreat, losing skirmishes along the way until they reached the shores of the Aegean. The Greek plan snatched defeat from the jaws of victory, and Mustafa Kemal saved the country he had conceived. It's little wonder the man known as Atatürk is revered to the point of sainthood in Turkey today. No Atatürk, no Turkey. It's really that simple.

Meanwhile, Mehmed VI was a sultan without an empire. It came as no surprise to anyone that Atatürk remedied that in 1922, when he abolished the sultanate. The title of caliph lasted for a further year under Abdülmecid II (a son of Abdülaziz), after which the House of Osman was exiled from Turkey; there was no room for it in the new republic. Yet, when Mehmed VI boarded the train that would take him into exile, the Jewish director of the train company welcomed him with all the formalities befitting a sultan, an echo from the bygone past of a multicultural empire.

After fighting the fourth war of his military career, Atatürk never took up arms again, but he was now faced with the stark reality of creating a new country, quite literally, from nothing. There had never been a Turkey before. There was no basis for anything, so everything had to start from scratch. From this unprepossessing start, the Republic of Turkey was born in 1923. Like the sultans before him, Atatürk recognised that it was the Western nations that were strong and powerful and should be his model for the new republic, and he wanted his fellow countrymen to join him in looking to the West. The recent war of independence persuaded Atatürk to take a number of decisions. First of all, he moved the capital from the very edge of his new nation, where it had been an obvious target for attack, to central Anatolia, which was a more difficult place to reach. He chose Ankara, a small town that was vastly inferior to Istanbul, but in a strategic location that made it attractive as a capital city. It was also Atatürk who redefined the term 'Turk'. It was now about a shared language, culture and identity, personified by loyalty to a state whose role it was to unify its previously disparate groups. 'How happy is the one who says "I am a Turk"' is a motto of the republic. A Turkish citizen is a Turk, and a fiercely proud one, regardless of DNA ethnicity.

Turks generally didn't have surnames prior to the 1920s, but Atatürk declared that everyone had to have one; it became the law. Consequently almost every Turkish surname was made up and usually means something cool like lion or star, iron fist or standard-bearer. There is no equivalent to Shufflebottom in Turkey. The language was revamped and the alphabet was changed from Arabic to Latin letters. The modern Turkish alphabet is completely phonetic – if you can read it, you can say it; if you can say it, you can spell it. But the transition from the old to the new meant that a generation struggled to make the changes. As a young boy I remember passing Turkish government buildings where men with typewriters lined the pavements. Their services assisted not only those who were illiterate, but also those who found it difficult to read and write in the new alphabet (even though by then it had been around for fifty years). The men who provided this service have gone the way of the man (wearing a turban and baggy *şalvar* trousers) who came with his donkey to my grandparents' home every morning with a huge container of fresh (raw) milk. Time changes everything, and the need for such services has long since disappeared. But in keeping with his wish to be more like westerners, Atatürk did, literally, change Turkey's time when he exchanged the Islamic calendar for the western (Gregorian) one. This led to a bizarre and unanticipated situation where those born under the old calendar but buried under the new one appeared to have lived for about 700 years.

Atatürk had no time for religion; he believed it was a major factor in holding back the empire. The new republic copied the Western model of keeping state and religion separate; Turkey is a secular republic, not an Islamic state. The decision was not without controversy, and caused consternation among thousands of religious leaders who felt their power waning. Atatürk was very much the man in charge and had the rebelling imams and muftis rounded up and executed (it is difficult to get reliable figures for the number of executions, but they are believed to have been in the thousands). The great mosque of Hagia Sophia, once the largest church in the world, was turned into a secular museum.

As well as religion, Atatürk had no time for anything that smacked of the empire. The fez was banned as it was seen as a symbol of Ottoman decadence. The sentence for wearing one was death, which eradicated its use overnight; a hat is simply not worth dying for. The headscarf was not banned, but women were encouraged to dress in the style of Western women. More importantly, girls were now educated alongside boys, and primary school education became mandatory for all. There were sweeping changes to the legal system, and he abolished laws that denied freedom and equality to women. Further, and controversially, there was a mass exchange of populations: Greeks in Anatolia were encouraged to go to Greece, and people who identified themselves as Turks (mainly Muslim minorities) in Greece were encouraged to go to the new republic. There was far more traffic from Greeks leaving Turkey than the other way – and sometimes the Greeks left after ugly mob violence (Smyrna was set on fire by Turkish nationalist mobs, but this was never planned or sanctioned by Atatürk).

Dissenters to the new government were arrested and exiled. British politician Boris Johnson's great-grandfather Ali Kemal was forced to flee with his family and ended up in Britain. He returned to Turkey at a later date and even served briefly as a government minister before he was eventually executed for his liberal opposition views. If all of this sounds draconian, it needs to be put in the context of other revolutions. Compared to the French Revolution, the American Revolution and, especially, the contemporary Russian Revolution, the prodigious social changes in Turkey were implemented with minimal bloodshed. These seismic changes in the Ottoman way of life show that the Turkish republic was not a continuation of the Ottoman Empire. This republic was something different and went out of its way to eschew old customs and behaviours as a new society was forged. It became a beacon for Muslims in areas of the old empire where that traditional way of life was actively despised.

The parts of the Duducu family that had stayed on in Bulgaria after that country achieved its independence remained there until the Communist takeover in the 1930s. So both of my father's parents – both from families that had lived in Bulgaria for as long as anyone could remember, people who were pillars of the community in Shumen and who were the recent descendants of a man who had fought and died for Bulgaria – decided they were more Turks than Bulgarians and moved to the 'homeland', where they settled in Balıkesir, Turkey. Going right back to the first chapter of this book, Balıkesir was the very first city to be captured by the nascent Ottoman state in the mid-1300s – so, in a way, my family had come full circle, but they probably didn't know that.

Atatürk was a dictator. He carried out a coup to get power. However, he's one of the best examples there is of a benevolent dictator. He always wanted peaceful relations with his neighbours and was willing to forgive Greece's attack on Turkey as soon as the war was won. (Atatürk's place of birth is in Greece, where the house is now a museum with round-the-clock protection.) He put all his energies into dragging Anatolia into the twentieth century and nurturing Western ideals. It seems Atatürk's only vice was that he liked a drink. The nation gave him a yacht, but he had almost no personal wealth, choosing to live modestly in whatever government-owned houses were available as he moved around the country. He had a vision which consumed him and for which he worked tirelessly until the end of his life at the age of fifty-seven in 1938. It's no wonder bridges, airports, parks and buildings are named after him. Every town centre in Turkey has a statue of him, and for many years every home and business had his picture on the wall. He warned of the rise of Hitler, and as he lay dying he made his ministers promise that no matter how likely a German victory might seem in the looming war, they were never to take sides, but remain neutral. He feared another major war would destroy everything he had worked for. True to their word, the Turks remained neutral during the Second World War, despite being courted by both sides.

But what of the sultans? The Ottoman Empire had faced three major threats throughout its existence: the Habsburg emperors, the shahs of Persia and the tsars of Russia. The Habsburgs were deposed by Napoleon, so the Ottomans outlasted them by more than a century, and the subsequent Austro-Hungarian Empire, an Ottoman ally on a number of occasions, ended in 1918. The sultans survived when the Safavids had died out, and Persia was not a threat to the Ottomans throughout the nineteenth and early twentieth centuries. The biggest threat towards the end of the empire had been Russia, and yet the last tsar was deposed (and

The Sultans

later shot) during the Russian Revolution of 1917, which meant that there was still an Ottoman sultan when Russia overthrew its old system. The Ottoman Empire had the last laugh. It had survived all its rivals. The House of Osman still exists and is spread over a number of countries. After a ban of decades, some members of the family have been allowed to return to Turkey, where they live as private citizens.

The world has moved on, and there is no need for the sultans to rise up again, but the Ottoman Empire at its best was the glue that held together a myriad of cultures, ethnicities and religions in a way that kept the peace. That is worth remembering when violence from the Middle East makes the headline news. The Ottomans did a better job of keeping the peace in the past than we are able to do today.

List of Ottoman Rulers

1299–1324	Osman I
1324–1362	Orhan
1362–1389	Murad I
1389–1402	Bayezid I

(OTTOMAN CIVIL WAR)

1413–1421	Mehmed I
1421–1444	Murad II (first rule)
1444–1446	Mehmed II (first rule)
1446–1451	Murad II (second rule)
1451–1481	Mehmed II (the Conqueror; 2nd rule)
1481–1512	Bayezid II
1512–1520	Selim I
1520–1566	Suleiman I

1566–1574	Selim II
1574–1595	Murad III
1595–1603	Mehmed III
1603–1617	Ahmed I
1617–1618	Mustafa I (the Mad; first rule)
1618–1622	Osman II
1622–1623	Mustafa I (second rule)
1623–1640	Murad IV
1640–1648	Ibrahim
1648–1687	Mehmed IV
1687–1691	Suleiman II
1691–1695	Ahmed II
1695–1703	Mustafa II
1703–1730	Ahmed III
1730–1754	Mahmud I
1754–1757	Osman III
1757–1774	Mustafa III
1774–1789	Abdül Hamid I
1789–1807	Selim III
1807–1808	Mustafa IV

List of Ottoman Rulers

1808–1839	Mahmud II
1839–1861	Abdülmecid I
1861–1876	Abdülaziz I
May 1876–31 Aug. 1876	Murad V
1876–1909	Abdül Hamid II
1909–1918	Mehmed V
1918–1922	Mehmed VI

(REPUBLICAN CALIPHATE)

1922–1924	Abdülmecid II

Bibliography

While these are not always directly on this topic, they have helped to refresh my memory and confirm details:

A History of God by Karen Armstrong

International encyclopaedia of Islamic dynasties by Nagendra Kr Singh

The Crimean War: The Truth behind the Myth by Clive Ponting

Lords of the Horizons: A History of the Ottoman Empire by Jason Goodwin

The Sultan: The life of Abdul Hamid II by Joan Haslip

The War of Wars by Robert Harvey

Jerusalem: The Biography by Simon Sebag Montefore

Constantinople: The Last Great Siege, 1453 by Roger Crowley

City of Fortune: How Venice Won and Lost a Naval Empire by Roger Crowley

Islamic Gunpowder Empires: Ottomans, Safavids, and Mughals by Donald E Streusand

The Byzantine Empire by Robert Browning

The Imperial Harem: Women and Sovereignty in the Ottoman Empire. Leslie P. Peirce

The Great Siege: Malta 1565 by Ernle Bradford

Lightning over Yemen: Studies Volume: A History of the Ottoman Campaign in Yemen, 1569–71 by Qutb al-Din al-Nahrawali and Clive Smith

Ottoman Wars, 1700–1870: An Empire Besieged by Virginia H. Aksan

Paradise Lost: The Destruction of Islam's City of Tolerance: Smyrna, 1922 by Giles Milton

Mughal-Ottoman relations: a study of political & diplomatic relations between Mughal India and the Ottoman Empire, 1556–1748 by N. R. Farooqi

The National Army Museum Book of the Turkish Front 1914–18: The Campaigns at Gallipoli, in Mesopotamia and in Palestine by Field Marshal Lord Carver

Additionally, I have travelled to the old Ottoman capital of Istanbul and visited many of the sites and museums.

Index

About the Author

Jem Duducu attended UWCC and read Archaeology and Medieval History. He is the author of several titles in the '100 Facts' series for Amberley and of *Deus Vult: A Concise History of the Crusades*. Follow him on Twitter @HistoryGems.

Also available from Amberley Publishing

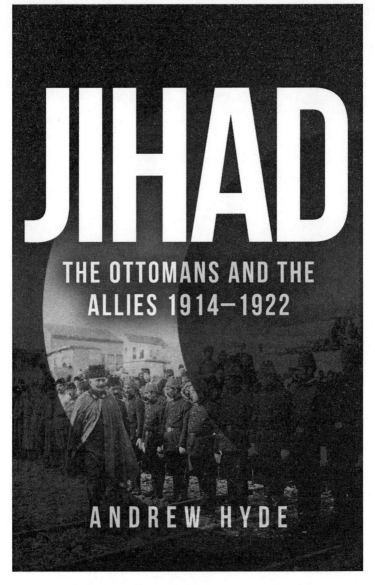